Liberating Intimacy

SUNY Series in Chinese Philosophy and Culture
David L. Hall and Roger T. Ames, editors

Liberating Intimacy

Enlightenment and Social Virtuosity in Ch'an Buddhism

Peter D. Hershock

State University of New York Press

Published by
State University of New York Press, Albany

© 1996 State University of New York

For information, address State University of New York
Press, State University Plaza, Albany, N.Y., 12246

Production by Diane Ganeles
Marketing by Dana Yanulavich

Library of Congress Cataloging-in-Publication Data
Hershock, Peter D.
    Liberating intimacy: enlightenment and social virtuosity in Ch'an
Buddhism/Peter D. Hershock.
        p. cm.—(SUNY series in Chinese philosophy and culture)
Includes bibliographical references and index.
    ISBN 0-7914-2981-4 (ch: alk. paper).—ISBN 0-7914-2982-2 (pb: alk.
paper)
    1. Zen Buddhism—Doctrines. 2. Spiritual life—Zen Buddhism.
I. Title. II. Series.
BQ9268.6.H47   1996
294.3'927'0951—dc20   95-38079
                                                              CIP

10 9 8 7 6 5 4 3 2 1

Contents

Acknowledgments

I would like to thank many people for the roles they played—often unwittingly—in the realization of this book as well as in the more personal transformations enveloping it. My son, Peter, through both example and opportunity has for fifteen years been initiating me into the bodhisattva life, always in the most immediate and uncompromised fashion possible. Jill Hershock likewise deserves much gratitude for her understanding and unwavering support over the last quarter century and for her willingness to constantly and caringly relinquish the horizons of our relationship. David Kalupahana was irreplaceable in his role of chairing my dissertation committee. The freedom he allowed me in terms of both research and exposition are deeply appreciated. Roger Ames was crucial in my coming to appreciate and respect the improvisational dimensions of the Confucian world. Along with Elizabeth Buck, he was also instrumental in my having the pleasure of remaining gainfully employed in Hawaii while working through the final drafts of the manuscript. To Yukali Ohno I am forever indebted for her unflinching and unforgettable lessons in both caring and impermanence. Perhaps more than anyone else, she has made me aware that we never know the meaning of our narration and that it is the nature of even the most perfect wave to break.

Finally, profound thanks are due to Son (Zen) Master Seung Sahn Dae Soen Sa Nim who first invited me into a truly personal connection with the practice of Buddhism and who encouraged my initial interest in pursuing a doctorate at the University of Hawaii. Most importantly, he introduced me to Ji Kwang Dae Poep Sa Nim, to whom I extend the deepest gratitude. Without her constant and often harsh support and her unerring demonstration of the sociality of Buddhist enlightenment, this work would never have reached satisfactory completion.

Preface

Having been asked to ascend the high seat in the dharma hall and speak about Buddhist enlightenment, the great Ch'an master Lin-chi begins by noting that according to the Ch'an lineage no sooner have you opened your mouth to declare anything about this great matter than you have made a mistake. And yet, he adds, if nothing at all is said, the assembled monks, nuns, and laypersons will have no place on which to gain a footing and will undoubtedly remain as stuck as they must have been to make their request in the first place.

Given this, he wonders out loud, "How, then, can I conceal the unifying thread, the social nexus (*kang* 網) of the lineage?" (T 1985.496b).[1] How, that is, can he not openly display what both binds all the buddhas, bodhisattvas, and patriarchs into a single family and what ultimately allows us to truly realize their understanding as our own? In immediate and energetic answer to his own question, Lin-chi poses a challenge: "Are there any capable persons to enter into contest (*chan* 戰), straightaway deploying their forces and unfurling their banners? If so, come before the assembly and give visible evidence of it!" (T 1985.496c).

Crucially for the nature of the conversation on which we are ourselves just embarking, instead of discoursing on the sutras, speaking about his own entry into the status of a master, or sitting down in meditative repose to manifest in turn the deepening phases of a revolution in awareness, Lin-chi asks for a worthy battle partner—someone to engage in the complete unpredictability of combat (*chan* 戰). What Lin-chi's challenge makes clear and what we shall spend the remainder of our time together here trying to adequately understand is that the key to Ch'an enlightenment—the 'place' from which it is possible to be fully realized and not merely talked or thought about—is direct, communicative crisis. That is, enlightenment has to do with relationship—not with any one individual's attainments—and in particular with the kinds of relationship in which everything is at stake and nothing is in principle excluded as impossible. In short, Ch'an enlightenment should not be seen as private and experiential in nature, but as irreducibly and intimately social.

This conclusion is bound to raise eyebrows. It has, in fact, become virtually canonical that Ch'an is an iconoclastic and contemplative (as opposed to scholarly) form of Buddhism which has from its earliest incarnations been a Janus-faced quest for an immediate and individual realization of our original nature or Buddhamind. According to the prevailing caricatures, in one of its visages can be traced a lineage branching off with Hui-neng and his "Southern School" and culminating in the almost militant dispositions of Rinzai Zen. In the other, a continuous line is seen running from Bodhidharma through the "Northern School" and on to the one-pointed quietism of Soto Zen.

As the standard account would have it, in the former lineage the practical emphasis in realizing our buddha-nature is on fathoming the public records (Ch *kung-an* 公案) of the tradition. Capsules of the enlightening encounter of master and student, these records could arguably be seen as a precedent for seeing liberation itself as public and social were it not for the fact that the behavior of all the relevant parties almost unilaterally seems to be antisocial where it is not simply incomprehensible. That is, the tradition's *kung-an* collections are rife with instances of shouting, kicking, striking, cursing and apparent abuses of logic—collectively referred to as "shock tactics"—which hardly seem consistent with the Buddhist ideal of compassionate nonattachment, and which certainly seem to be at odds with any claim that Ch'an enlightenment be deemed "irreducibly social." To the contrary, the public cases can often be seen as portraying Ch'an masters as apparently insensitive and intractably clever adversaries whose behavior may be intended as "grandmotherly" and in the student's best interest, but which it is nearly impossible to avoid seeing as anarchic and at times virtually sociopathic. Consider, for example, Nan-chuan's dismemberment of the temple cat, Chu-ti's severing of his attendant's finger, and Ma-tzu's propensity for delivering bone-cracking kicks and punches.

In the literally more sedate (Soto) tradition, the emphasis is on the much less flamboyant practice of silent meditation—an "inner work" which is said to directly express our enlightened nature and yet for all intents and purposes renders the presence of others entirely adventitious. Silent meditation is not antisocial like an unprovoked slap in the face or the dismemberment of the monastery cat, but it is difficult to not see it as an asocial undertaking. After all, meditation is carried out individually—whether alone or in the company of others who figure not as indispensable partners, but as independent and perhaps parallel travelers on the path to enlightenment.

On the one hand, then, there is a view of Ch'an as valorizing disturbingly confrontational behavior, and on the other hand as fostering a quietist withdrawal from worldly relationship. In neither is there any apparent precedent for claiming that either the enlightenment proper to Ch'an or the preferred practices by means of which it is realized or expressed are inherently social.[2] On the contrary, according to both views, Ch'an enlightenment appears to involve a kind a fierce independence which seems oddly out of keeping with the Mahayana commitment to the liberation of all beings.

Moreover, because of the typically unbroken bias of the Indo-European traditions for seeing knowledge, wisdom, and hence spiritual realization or liberation as the attainments of concrete individuals and not as in any significant sense fundamentally communal, the individuality of enlightenment is itself often taken to be a rational necessity. That is, because human action is seen as a function of conscious choices or intentions formulated on the basis of what we know or understand, and since knowledge and understanding are taken to be subjectively experienced and (at least ideally) objectively describable transformations of some 'one,' even if enlightenment were seen in terms of performance and not some exalted state of mind, it would still be the doing of a particular individual. [Note: Here and throughout this work, single quotations are used as a technical device to mark the difference between the emptiness of some focused aspect of our narration—(x); what we constitute by way of establishing horizons for relevance on that original boundlessness—('x'); and the linguistic designation we conventionally use in denoting the 'thing' thus constituted—("x"). For a discussion of the rationale for this device, see "An ontological digression: inverting the being-value distinction" in chapter one.]

And so, while knowledge, wisdom, and perhaps even enlightenment itself may well be thought of as transmissible from one individual to another, the very fact that we see this as a *transmission*—as the breaching of an original and ultimately un-mitigated disparity—only underscores our prejudice for seeing our selves under the rubric of a basic autonomy. Even we allow the possibility of simultaneous realization, the presumption is that something happens in two distinct places at once and not that it is this very disparity between 'here' and 'there' or 'me' and 'you' which has been nullified.[3] Given such a disposition, it is only natural that even if we encounter Buddhist texts denying the presence of any objective marks identifying the transformation referred to as "en-lightenment," we nevertheless presume it to have an indispensable subjective correlate: the experience of liberation.

Over the course of our conversation, it is hoped that both the bias toward an integrity-based concept of personhood and our pre-supposition of the foundational nature of experience will be so thoroughly undermined that our view of Ch'an will undergo a revo-lutionary shift in gestalt. In part, this will mean a movement away from the dislocating tension of subjective experience and objective behavior toward conduct itself as the locus of both personhood and enlightenment—that is, a shift toward seeing not individual exist-ence, but relationship or (better still) the movement of our narration as our true, original nature (*pen hsing* 本性).[4]

Not surprisingly, so embracing dramatic interdependence as our original nature will occasion a radical subversion of integrity and its customary role as the cardinal value directing our inquiries into and understanding of suffering, communication, personal au-thenticity, and, of course, enlightenment. Eventually, it should be-come evident that—at least as practiced in Ch'an—Buddhist salvation is not a liberation of any individual 'you' or 'me,' but rather of intimacy itself.[5]

Among other things, the characterization of conduct in terms of narration is meant to stress the ineradicably dramatic quality of our worlds—the impossibility of reducing them to complexes of objec-tive events which are meaningful only after the fact, as a result of what we think or say about them. Narration, in the sense in which it will be used here, is not at bottom relating as telling, but as bringing into connection, as healing or making whole. Thus, the suggestion that we see persons as narration is not of a piece with narrative models of the self like that recently proposed by Paul Ricoeur (1993) where what is essential is the definition—the identi-fication—of who speaks, who acts, who recounts about him or herself and who is the moral subject of imputation (p. 16). For Ricoeur, it is imperative that we move away from the philosophy of the subject—the exclusive constitution of the self in terms of what "I am"—but only to the extent that we realize that identifying our selves depends on the presence of and our interaction with others. To the contrary, from a Buddhist perspective what matters in realizing who we are as persons is removing the very presumption of ontological difference, of the distinction of 'self' and 'other'—in short, of relinquishing all of the horizons by means of which we identify our own 'selves' and those of 'others.' As will be argued below, as narration the ideal person is seen by Ch'an not as some 'one' acting *in* the world, but as that unprecedented conduct (narrative movement) by means of which entire worlds are healed: a bodhisattva, a buddha.

Far from having purely theoretical implications, this gestalt shift necessitates a drastic reevaluation of the claim that Ch'an is a tradition of practice, a "narration beyond words and cultural forms (*wen* 文)." In brief, it will no longer prove tenable to consider Ch'an practice as an individual activity reducible to or fully expressed in terms of moral training and meditative discipline—whether Rinzai or Soto style. Instead, it will be argued that Ch'an practice should be seen as an irreducibly interpersonal system for realizing virtuosic nonduality. That is, nurtured on the basis of what shall be termed the techniques of partnership and indirection, Ch'an arises as the continuously improvised relinquishing of our horizons for readiness, responsibility, and relevance—as the social realization of an incomparable and limitless buddha-land; the enlightening reorientation of our narration.

Now, it should perhaps be noted in advance that there is no attempt in what follows to critically evaluate the place of Ch'an in the historical development of Buddhism from its earliest times in India through its flowering in Japan and its transmission to the West. Among other things, this omission is liable to occasion the charge that while I often speak about "Buddhist enlightenment," my doing so without further qualification would seem to imply a failure to recognize that there are a variety of paradigms for Buddhist enlightenment as well as for Ch'an. The particular relevance of this charge, of course, is that some of these alternative paradigms are implicitly critical of seeing enlightenment in social rather than individual/experiential terms—one might mention Dogen's (later) Japanese Zen critique of the syncretic tendencies of Ch'an and the contrary centrality of psychology in the (earlier) Indian Nikaya tradition. And thus the question naturally arises and (in what follows at least) is simply left hanging as to whether Ch'an is simply an anomalous tangent. Perhaps more importantly for 'insiders' who have a personal stake in the matter, it may be wondered whether the apparent iconoclasm of the Ch'an perspective on enlightenment is supposed to place it at the zenith—or perhaps even the nadir—of Buddhist thought and practice.

There can be no doubt that an examination of contrasting paradigms for understanding enlightenment is crucial for any historical analysis of Buddhist thought. In fact, our impending conversation might be seen as a single step in developing the foundations for such an undertaking. But it is also the case that little doubt should exist regarding the dangers involved in engaging Buddhism from such a synoptic—and hence generally 'objective'—vantage. Briefly, it is all too easy to indulge the common prejudice of seeing late-appearing traditions as either degenerate or progressive forms of earlier ones and setting up some kind of evolutionary sequence among them. It may be that we then take a revolutionary perspective on Ch'an and judge it foremost or take a fundamentalist position and judge it retrograde. But in either case we will have done both Buddhism and Ch'an a great disservice by insisting on what the Buddha himself warned against—taking a stand on either 'is' or 'is-not.'

As Buddhism moved in turn from India to China, Korea, Japan, and on to the West, it has undergone what I feel is best seen as a largely discontinuous process of differentiation that resists hierarchic evaluation. In short, I would contend that in all of its forms and phases Buddhism is irreducibly *responsive*. Buddhism is not a body of doctrine or a central set of insights or even the enactment of a particular psychosomatic technology, but the ever-changing virtuosity of enlightening conduct. In a word, Buddhism is, in all its forms, an improvised expression of emptiness. Thus, it's not that Dogen's Zen view supersedes or even replaces the Ch'an view as I articulate it, any more than Ch'an superseded or replaced the Indian Nikaya. In fact, whenever the supposition of abiding forms/identities is truly absent, the analysis of history in progressive/regressive terms loses all justification.

And so, our conversation's lack of any explicit reference to alternative construals of enlightenment should not be seen as amounting to the dogmatic assertion of the superiority of early Ch'an, or even an absence of appreciation for the varieties of Buddhist theory and practice. To the contrary, it should be seen simply as a function of eschewing the synoptic vantage for the purpose of realizing an internal relationship with the unprecedented responsiveness that is uniquely Ch'an.

An interestingly related concern is that there is in the Buddhist canon very little direct precedent for the vocabulary being advanced here as uniquely suitable for understanding the meaning of the sociality of Ch'an enlightenment. It cannot be denied that terms like "narration," "sociality," "societality," "virtuosity," "intimacy," "indirection," and "partnership" are inextricably bound up with our present concerns and lives and reflect a sensibility in no way directly groundable in canonical Buddhism. Far from being a philosophical liability, however, this seems to me an altogether felicitous eventuality insofar as it forces us to drop the pretense of doing 'pure' or 'fundamental' Buddhist scholarship. That is, the use of such a vocabulary forces us to admit what is in any case unavoidable—that much of what we say about Buddhism does not and cannot have its sole and ultimate foundation in what is past, but arises as the world of the canon and ours are brought into lively integration or concourse. That is, the vocabulary is one that is improvised at the confluence of Ch'an and our contemporary world—indigenous to neither and yet curiously at home in both.

In this sense, very little of what we shall be doing is commentarial or exegetical in nature. Borrowing an analogy suggested by the novelist Robert Pirsig, our present conversation is not a philosophological (sic) exercise comparable to what a musicologist does to and with a piece of music. Rather, it should be entered into as original Buddhist philosophy—an unapologetically improvisational endeavor in which we are all along pushing the envelope of our theoretical and practical virtuosity.[6]

Part I

Theoretical Foundations of Ch'an Enlightenment

Chapter 1

Suffering: Divergent Conceptions of the Context of Enlightenment

There is no shortage of suffering. With greater or lesser intensity and profundity, each of us is at one time or another plunged into a world where things have gone awry, where a child is dying, where love goes unrequited, where pleasant illusions are being shattered, where sickness or old age causes our life to fall in on itself—a tortured parody of its customary radiance. While there may be an unfortunate few of us who pass our entire lives without ever experiencing love or success or consistently good health, none of us escapes the experience of disappointment, of sorrow or adversity or grief. Suffering, we are tempted to say, is a universal experience of mankind.

The Buddha would seem to agree. In the scriptures collected together in the canon, the Buddha is often found remarking that he teaches only suffering, its origin, its cessation, and the path to that end—the so-called Four Noble Truths. Indeed, one of the central tenets of the early Buddhist catechism was that suffering (*duhkha*)—along with selflessness (*anātman*) and impermanence (*anitya*)—is one of the three marks (*lakṣaṇa*) characterizing all existing things (*dharmas*). These facts notwithstanding, I believe that the temptation to regard suffering as a universal experience is one we have good reasons to resist. In fact, failing to do so not only paves the way to a misconstrual of the stated intention of the Buddha's teaching—bringing about the end of suffering—but to the idealization and eventual fossilization of enlightenment through a denial of its profound sociality.

In declining to accept the proposition that suffering is a universal experience, I am not, of course, denying that there is ever a point in talking about the most general characteristics of suffering. There

1

are many useful insights which depend in large part on such an abstraction from the uniqueness of my or your experience. Indeed, the Buddha's articulation of the eightfold path can be seen as depending on just such an abstractive analysis undertaken in the second and third of his noble truths. My contention is simply that the suffering which the Buddha sought to resolve was not this abstract or theoretical construct, but rather the actually lived suffering of people whose lives came in some way to be intimately interwoven with his own. If we are to understand Buddhist enlightenment and its relation to Buddhist practice, our first step must be one of strenuously resisting the inclination to regard suffering as essentially ahistorical—a phenomenon which has and will continue to recur in countless generations of sentient being. That, after all, is a suffering divested of its meaning-dimension, of all truly personal ramifications. While theoretical (which is to say universal) problems are necessarily resolved only by equally theoretical solutions, no theoretical solution can effectively answer to the always changing demands of actually lived suffering. And it is directly to these latter, irreducibly personal crises and their virtuosic resolution that Ch'an practice orients us. Ultimately, they provide our sole opportunity for realizing the sociality of Ch'an enlightenment.

Such claims stand in rather sharp opposition to the popular view according to which it is perfectly intelligible to assert that the problems we face as individuals are universal even though our very individuality insures that our solutions will necessarily differ, even if only very slightly. According to this way of thinking, cultural patterns can effectively be understood as serving orientational requirements that are essentially generic. That is, they can be seen as the concrete embodiment of diverse, ever-evolving, and yet relatively stable coping strategies developed by various communities in the face of commonly recurring problems or crises. What this amounts to saying, of course, is that the problems confronting us are not culture-specific, and that uniqueness (where it manifests at all) is evident only in our reactions or responses.

No doubt this is good news for the comparative anthropologist or sociologist who can then begin to develop a cultural taxonomy based, for example, on how various communities resolve the 'universal problems' of hunger or intergenerational aggression. But it also reflects a bias typical in post-animistic, explicitly 'scientific' societies like our own where it is adamantly held that creativity and will reside exclusively in individual, intelligent beings such as ourselves. Such a view belies, however, a merely presumptive belief that suffering has no intrinsically communicative dimension. We may learn from our problems, but not because they occur for the purpose of teaching us. Suffering is simply the unplanned and yet always law-conforming interruption of the smooth realization of our typically calculated, individual ends.

And so, while our responses to suffering may be individual and so characteristic, the same cannot be said for suffering itself. According to the popular view, our crises are not part of an inherently intimate history for which we are unavoidably and personally responsible, but are taken to be universally generated and impersonally constituted 'facts' to which we react or (awareness being on our side) respond, typically by either efforts to escape or control the conditions that give rise to suffering. That is, since the causes of suffering are objective or characterized with otherness, only its solutions can in the end be either significant or subjective—either yours or mine. Not surprisingly, perhaps, where such views prevail, there typically obtains a marked absence of tolerance for alternative solutions. After all, if the cause of our suffering is universal, how can *our* solutions fail to be equally so? While not a strictly valid inference, the history if its pervasiveness is both ample and bloody.

Especially for the Ch'an Buddhist, such a view of suffering must ultimately be seen as self-defeating. Granted that the intent behind all the Buddha's teachings and by implication all Buddhist practice is bringing an 'end to suffering,' investigating the reasons for this in some detail will prove crucial in establishing a legitimate context for understanding enlightenment.

Universality and Objectivity: The Dilemma of the Suffering Individual

Let's consider the case of hunger.

It seems to most of us quite self-evident that hunger is a universal problem. That is, hunger is a discomfort which all animals regularly experience and deal with, each in their own fashion and according to their individual predilections. Eagles seek out field mice, deer seek out tender shoots and leaves, New Yorkers seek out pizza. But hunger itself—the experience of a need for nourishment—is the same regardless of the species to which one belongs.

This line of reasoning seems so natural and flawless that we are inclined to regard it as simple common sense—certainly not as a highly metaphysical artifact. However, it is arguable that the grounds for such a claim actually amount to nothing more substantial than a disposition toward rendering experience in generic terms in order to facilitate our control of it while at the same time losing sight of what is sacrificed in the reduction. Phenomenologically, as lived suffering, the hunger of an eagle is not in any relevant sense equivalent to that of a resident of the Bronx heading downstairs for a pizza. The eagle's hunger is never simply the noting of a void capable of being filled generically. Were this the case, the eagle could as well swoop down to eat corn or wheat as it could some small game.

An eagle hungers for a mouse—a furtive, watchful creature given to hiding among clumps of grass and termite-ridden tangles of fallen scrub oak branches. Flying so as to keep its shadow from crossing the path of its prey, with any luck the eagle will plummet from several hundred feet in the air and snare it unsuspecting on hunt-sharpened talons. The entire complex of organic desires, physical skills, environmental set, and interspecific conduct and coordination which describes the hunger of an eagle is at every point dissimilar to those constellated when an insurance adjuster descends two flights of stairs and orders pepperoni pizza to go. At bottom, hunger is an experienced quality of relationship obtaining among two or more species, a relationship which is universal or generic only to the precise extent that we enter it in a spirit of ignorance or *avidya*. While there may well be a universal problem of 'hunger,' its solution must be equally universal—'eating,' the consumption of 'food'—and this has virtually nothing to do with the intensely personal act by means of which a mother eagle snares the youngest male of a new litter of field mice.

At this point, the advocate of the received opinion is likely to throw his or her hands up in despair and complain—surely you are not going to deny that we all eat? Not at all. We all eat, and each in our own way. But what our eating solves is never the universal problem of hunger. To the contrary, what is satisfied is your or my actual hungering, our specific needs to literally incorporate this or that living being, digesting the energy bound up in their organization and turning it to uses which are uniquely our own. And at the level of lived and not merely theoretically resolved suffering, the feeding of an eagle, a deer, a New Yorker, or a Chinese from Taiwan are neither ultimately the same nor different. No actual act of eating is ever replicated exactly, nor (as the Buddhists would say) does eating itself have any abiding self-nature. The mere fact that it is possible to lump a great many acts together under the rubric of a single concept or word does not warrant the belief that they can in anything but an arbitrary sense be assimilated to or identified with one another—not, at least, in the absence of setting definite horizons for what we are willing to take as relevant. Failing to realize this fosters a tendency to justify our disregard of the entire, unimaginably extensive and intensive network of interdependencies which are decisively focused in every act of determining that and what something 'is.' And so we find ourselves, for example, trying desperately to alleviate world hunger in ways so fantastically impractical that 40,000 children are dying each day of malnutrition.

Importantly, from a Buddhist perspective, this should not be assumed to force us into asserting that suffering is necessarily individual—a matter of so-called subjective experience. To the contrary, the Buddhist commitment to realizing the interdependence of all things requires us to resist seeing hunger as a particular feeling which can be legitimately isolated from the rest of a living being's unique manners of perceiving and desiring, its ways of moving and keeping still, of revealing and concealing, of being born, procreating, and dying. By analogy, if a living being is like a piece of improvised music, hunger may be likened to a single chord or phrase within it, a chord 'composed' characteristically of several, relatively distinct notes. But while this chord has a special meaning in the context of the entire piece, taken in isolation, abstracted from the harmonic structure of the piece as a whole, it has neither unique precedents nor consequents. It is an abstraction empty of any truly musical import. The same is true of 'hunger' taken as a universal—that is, abstractly marked—phenomenon. What the word "hunger" refers to is not any actual living being's concrete realization of a need for sustenance with all the attendant considerations of how it moves and perceives and communicates. To the contrary, it refers if at all to a constellation of marks (*lakṣaṇa*) which bears no more intimate connection to the always uniquely articulated, interspecific relationship felt as hunger than the group of notes referred to as a "C#min7" does to the chorus of Dave Brubeck's "Take Five." And yet, if pushed to it, we typically are not only comfortable with but adamant in asserting that pieces of music like "Take Five" are 'composed' of chords like C#min7ths, and that the crisis in Somalia reflects material conditions that are of a piece with those in Bangladesh or any other impoverished nation where 'hunger' is killing thousands every day.

An Ontological Digression: Inverting the Being-Value Distinction

At this juncture, it is highly instructive to pause and consider in an anticipatory fashion what underlies this comfort and intellectual ardor and whether it may serve us well or ill in the attempt to understand what the various buddhas (and not necessarily *we*) mean by suffering and its resolution. At bottom, the *belief* that music is composed of and with notes, chords, and distinct rhythmic patterns or that hunger amounts to a condition universally identifiable in terms of felt distress in the abdominal cavity, of irritability, decreased concentration, low blood sugar, and so on itself depends on the presupposition of independent or identifiable entities. In sharp contrast with that of the Buddha and his Ch'an compatriots—and certain strains of contemporary physics notwithstanding—the worldview in which such a belief seems plausible is fundamentally atomistic. That is, entitative existence is at some level presumed to be basic—even if the entities considered are recurrent 'processes' or even 'experiences.' In consequence, wholeness is seen under the rubric of accumulation, of composition or construction. It is something brought about or caused, not that from which all 'things' are abstracted.

And yet this latter view more accurately describes the direction of Buddhist metaphysics in which there is an explicit refusal to assert the self-existence (*svabhāva*) or independence of any 'thing.' The doctrine of *anātman* or nonself, is not nihilism—the counterpart and hence intimate complement of thingism—but a celebration of unsundered and nonabstract wholeness. It is a realization of the fact that music is *only analyzed into* 'notes' and 'chords,' that living is only abstractly parceled into 'organic molecules,' 'cells,' 'drives' and their 'satisfactions,' that suffering is only intentionally construed as a universal problem admitting a myriad unique solutions. These analyses may be helpful. They are surely a convenience. But they should not be presumed to mirror the structure of the world prior to its articulation through our karma or intentional activity.

In other words, the universality of 'hunger'—its being liable to recurrent identification—must be seen as a function of the characterization of experience. It stands as evidence only of the abstraction of abiding features or marks based on the prior projection of consistently (or habitually) adopted perceptual values. Likewise for any opening up of objectivity by way of positing a 'real' difference between 'us' and what we repeatedly identify as 'the same.'

Now, especially in the Mahayana tradition of which Ch'an is ostensibly an exemplar, all marks or characteristics are understood as *dispositional* in nature. They do not reveal or even denote some absolute essences or world-features originally independent of our consciousnesses and their doings. To the contrary, what all characteristics reveal are our own lived inclinations and aversions—patterns of liking and disliking rooted in an aboriginal schism of the experienced and the experiencer. These various segregations, so crucial to the definition of our egoic identities no less than the objects of our liking and disliking, are by all Buddhists decried as artificial and ultimately conducive only to further suffering. Neither Being nor beings precede envaluation—the introjection/projection of values—but arise only as a function thereof. If, as the Mahayanist insists, all things are originally empty (*śūnya*), their very definition as things cannot but be our doing, our karma.

The salient point here is of a piece with the metaphysical pivot of the *Diamond Sutra*, one expression of which is that no bodhisattva is a 'bodhisattva,' we only designate him or her as "bodhisattva." Applied at various points in the sutra to beings, buddhas, truths, and indeed to all things (*dharmas*), this formula radically undermines the segregation-enhancing architecture of existence or self-identity. The first term in the formula (dharma, for example) evokes an irreducible wholeness or ambiguity with which we are presently and attentively responding. The second appearance of the term ('dharma') refers us to what is constituted as a result of our disambiguating projection of limits to relevance, our convenience-motivated decision of 'what is' and 'what is-not'—a decision establishing relatively fixed horizons for the emptiness of the dharma in question. The term's final appearance ("dharma") denotes the particular linguistic designation we conventionally associate with our projected value or 'dharma.' Most generally, then, nothing should merely be seen as what we value or consider relevant, and certainly not as some ontologically independent entity to which some word in our lexicon refers. That is, no [dharma] is a '[dharma]', it is only designated as "[dharma]". Our utterances, no matter how carefully sophisticated, never refer to what precedes thinking, but only to our projected value horizons—some preferred 'this' or repulsive 'that.'

Now, regardless of the unsalutary consequences of writing under the dictates of a grammar based on the distinction of subjects
and predicates, it should not be supposed on the basis of the above
that *some determinate [dharma] exists* prior to our (either individual or cultural) projection of '[dharma].' Whatever is 'prior' to
thinking and our variously biased acts of envaluation has no name,
no location, no worth or lack of it. It is not one or many, material or
ideal. We may be content with saying it is empty or better yet
ambiguous, but even this may still and untruthfully imply some
substance or thing which has the characteristic of being
indeterminate.

In the world of the bodhisattva as described in the *Diamond
Sutra* and as evidenced in the recorded sayings of the masters of
Ch'an, all 'individuals' or 'entities' are best viewed as distillations of
lived experience—distillations on which we may become intoxi-
cated if proper caution is not taken in making use of them. Indeed,
the more abstract and ideal, the more concentrated the spirit we
distill, the more likely we are to lose contact with the world of
mutuality. According to Ch'an, that world is one in which 'reality'
connotes not some special quality or substance or transcendental
well-spring, but simply living in such a fashion that when crises
arise—challenges to us physically, mentally, emotionally, or spir-
itually—we are able to carefully respond with them. In reality so
defined—as an operational context and not an object as such—truth
cannot be seen as a standard (logical), or an ideal (conceptual), or a
mirror of nature. Truth ceases to be what is correct, but is instead
understood simply as correcting—just as reality has ceased to be
taken to be something objective and is realized instead as neither
subject nor object, but as precisely that relation in which the two
dissolve in creatively apt conduct.[1]

Granted the objective existences of things and/or features,
when things go awry it makes perfect sense to attempt either
putting them directly back in place—the strategy of control—or
removing ourselves from proximity with those things which can be
identified as the cause of disruption—the strategy of escape. But the
ideal of escape is what the Mahayana has derided as the Hinayana
solution—the solution of separating from the wheel of birth and
death and thus inculcating a practical dualism. And as we shall see
in part II, especially for the Ch'an Buddhist, control must be seen as
highly suspect, appealing as it does to an explicitly constructive
model of harmony, embroiling us in direct effort and intention, and
hence binding us with more and yet ever more karma. Thus dis-

posed, the very acts by means of which we hope to alleviate suffering depend on and deepen the principal conditions without which suffering itself cannot arise.

Objectivity and the Decision of 'Self' and 'Other'

In sum, for the Buddhist, suffering cannot have an abiding self-nature and so should not be identified with any particular or set constellation of marks, no matter how convenient this identification may initially appear. What such abstractive identification fosters is not concursive harmony, but the discourse or flowing apart of a central, decision-making, action-generating, and hence karma-producing 'self' and those experiences which come about as a result of its interaction with an inferred and often resistant periphery of things (*dharmas*)—both objects and other supposed subjects.

As stated earlier, none of this is intended to deny that there is a level of generality where we can speak and reason intelligibly about suffering or hunger. What is being denied is that whatever is so discussed has ever been actually experienced by any living creature and that such discussions have any real bearing on resolving the always unique sufferings and hungers by which sentient beings are so often bound. Bluntly put, it is neither necessary nor without exception beneficial to *discuss* hunger in order to alleviate it since the objectivity occasioned by discussion distances us from any solution to lived hunger just as surely as it does from intimacy with that hunger itself.

The importance of all this for our present conversation is that as long as we naively accept the viability of seeing suffering as a universal problem or concern supposedly addressed and rectified by the Buddha's teachings and (in our case) the practice of Ch'an, we will systematically read into those teachings and that practice a universality in light of which they will appear either damagingly inconsistent or as peculiar reformulations of philosophical, psychological, and practical truisms with which we have long been familiar. In other words, we will understand Buddhism in general and Ch'an in particular as alternative takes on the same world and hence the same problems that our own religious, philosophical, and eschatological traditions have been investigating or articulating for several millennia. Nothing could be more infelicitous. What Ch'an Buddhism offers is not ultimately a new view or theory about *the* world and how it has come to be, but an entirely new world—an unprecedented narration in which value precedes and engenders all existence.

What we are embarking on, then, is a line of reasoning which is radically empirical in the sense that it refuses to buy into the fallacy of objective sameness and difference—the fallacy that because we can *speak* objectively about things being the same or different, that they were so prior to and independently of our saying so. As suggested above, if we take the Buddhist doctrine of *anātman* seriously—especially in its later expression through the *Prajñāpāramitā* conception of emptiness—neither 'what is' nor 'what is not' can be seen as ultimately independent of us. Rather, they must be recognized as projections of value—an orienting or biasing of our awareness toward or away. Without such an orientation, there is quite literally nothing to say, no 'thing' to point out or designate.

Emptiness should not, however, be understood as something we can assert, a kind of underlying ground on which our projections are directed. We are in fact warned explicitly of the dangers of such a move by—among others—the great Buddhist philosopher Nagarjuna who informs us that while "(t)he Victorious Ones have announced that emptiness is the relinquishing of all views, (t)hose who are possessed of the view of emptiness are said to be incorrigible (MK 13.8)." Emptiness is not a kind of Buddhist surrogate for Being or Substance. Indeed, as the relinquishing of *all* views, it is perhaps best understood as the practice of embracing ambiguity. As long as we are concerned about 'things,' as long as we introject a knowing subject and project known objects, emptiness fails to obtain. Emptiness obtains only as awareness exquisitely poised, unbiased by any habitual disambiguations. In this sense, emptiness is not exemplified by the ideal of an absolute ground, but by the fluidly graceful virtuosity of a master of *t'ai ch'i chuan* who is able to move in any direction at any time, precisely as needed.

Sameness and difference both imply resistance—a selection (or more radically a projection) of horizons for relevance, boundaries for conduct without which no self-identical thing can be said to exist. In this sense difference and identity mark the curtailment of emptiness, and speaking objectively thus entails (for the Buddhist) the adoption of a stance with respect to our awareness by means of which a bound viewer/observer comes into being. We *make* our 'selves' different from what is observed and then discover justification for our inability to directly and infallibly control the flow of time/events. This, we assume, amounts to a proof of real difference between us and what happens to and about us. The circularity is vicious.

But if instead we refrain from marking our 'selves' off as different from experience and if we accept the Buddhist thesis that experience always (even if often only inevitably) conforms with intention—the doctrine of karma—we find it impossible to perceive any nonarbitrary distinctions between who we are and how things have come to be. In short, speaking objectively indicates our willing or unconscious/conditional projection and acceptance of a dualistic world. Once the schism between an introjected 'self' and a projected, experienced 'other' is accepted and naturalized, it will never be convincingly closed by logical or conceptual means. Suffering will seem intractable.

An important corollary of the realization that identity and difference are artifacts is accepting that no experience corroborates or validates any other. Experiencing is always and irreducibly unique. As the Buddha's doctrine of impermanence (*anitya*) makes clear, there are no abiding things or states, and it is only in talking about experiencing from a sufficient, often logical, distance that the appearance of sameness emerges and with it the possibility that one 'event' or 'experience' can validate and not merely enhance another. In fact, the language of classical empiricism wherein it makes sense to say that experiences of certain types "come to us" is highly problematic in that it lays an obscuring, objective gloss over the act by means of which 'experiences' are constituted—the act of setting horizons (temporal, spatial, conceptual, emotional, etc.) for relevance; what Ch'an refers to as ignoring the emptiness of all things. Experiences don't come our way, but are created—excised from the whole narration of which 'you' and 'I' are also mere abstractions. In the immediacy of the actual, the problems confronted by any living creature are always part of the fabric of experiencing, and experiencing is never generic, even if our thinking about it is.

Curiously, we already know this from an early age. In stark contrast with the received view, when we find ourselves in the midst of confronting our life's problems, we will hear nothing of their being generic. As every one of us knows who has not come out of adolescence unscathed by love, there is nothing more self-evident than the fact that the suffering we endure when we are abandoned by our lover is unlike that undergone by anyone else at any other point in the history of the species. Family and friends may try to console us by confessing that they have had the very same feeling themselves, endured precisely the same wretched hollowness that to us seems so absolutely unique, but we will not, perhaps cannot, believe them. If we say as much, the typical rejoinder is that given sufficient time and distance we will be able to see the truth of their claims—the fact that nearly everyone at one point or another goes through the experience in whose thrall we are unfortunately imprisoned.

Reasonable as many of us think it sounds, this reiteration of the received view should, rather than setting our minds at ease, raise a host of troubling questions. First and foremost of these is, why is the recognition of the universality of our experience of suffering dependent upon placing the latter at a sufficient (temporal or logical) remove? The usual response to this invariably involves some mention of the fact that only in this way are we able to rationally reflect on our experience—to view it objectively. This is a deceptively simple move. We are easily persuaded by the mention of "facts". It is a 'fact' that when we are too deeply involved with someone or something we cannot see the whole picture. We judge on the basis of the biases determined by our perspective, by our intimacy with the persons or experiences in question. Underlying this 'fact' is the conception of true knowledge as not depending on perspective. We can see what something really is only when we can attain proper closure with respect to it, when we can (*as it were*) see it from all sides at once—a feat necessarily involving our acting as ahistorical agents, attaining what Thomas Nagel (1987) has referred to as "the view from nowhere."[2]

While we shall turn in subsequent chapters to the critical examination of the relationship between a bias toward objectivity and our conceptions of sociality, existence, knowledge, truth, and meaning, it is imperative to stress that a normative insistence on objectifying the experience of suffering cannot but prejudice our understanding of enlightenment—forcing us into assuming it will be at once *common*—that is, identifiable—and private or subjective: an event experienced and yet liable to corroboration. As stated above, the rationale for viewing our experience objectively is ostensibly that it allows us to assert the existence of significant identities spanning what are apparently isolated or private streams of consciousness. In short, objectivity is sought after as a means of avoiding a lapse into (or remaining stuck within) an intractably solipsistic particularism. The *possibility* of objectivity is not, of course, given *a priori*, but is admitted on the basis of our evident ability to speak intelligibly to others using words that do *not* amount to mere names. Our ability to speak of love, grief, hunger, and the like, and to apparently be understood, is taken to suggest that there is something common to all our experiences that these words either refer to or in some still unclear sense represent. As something experienced in common even if individually, the end of suffering (enlightenment) must be taken to be something other than us—a goal we can seek. Yet this is flatly denied by the Buddha on numerous occasions when he remarks that in attaining enlightenment he attained nothing at all and when he insists that there are, in actuality, no marks by which the enlightened can be distinguished from those who are not.

For just this reason it is also crucial to stress that the idealization of objectivity and the *presupposition* of the unassailable privacy of personal experience—a presupposition rooted with equal tenacity in both the Cartesian and traditional Indian belief that consciousness is in some sense concealed or bound up within matter—are mutually entailing. Hence, the Buddha's insistence that consciousness be seen as an emergent system arising with the contact of a sense-organ and sense-object. Consciousness is not located *in* the organism (either as a constituent element, identifying feature or transformation), but is understood as the peculiar quality of the relatedness of that organism and its environment.[3] Consciousness is, in this sense, fundamentally public, not private. If this is so, changes in consciousness must be seen as changes in conduct and the attempt to objectify experience by setting it at a great enough distance that we are no longer moved by it is only to detach ourselves from the social context in which the creative transformation of consciousness is paradigmatically located. Thus, while it is the case that (as will be argued later) the Ch'an resolution of suffering entails a dissolution of the horizons we typically establish for ourselves as 'individuals,' this is not to be seen in terms of an abstraction (escape) from social interaction—an orientation to seeing others as 'like me'—but in terms of preserving the uniqueness of our own place in the world while systematically relinquishing the horizons we have hitherto projected in marking off what is 'me' and 'mine' from what is 'other.' That is, we relinquish those features of our experience which lead to the assertion of either identity or difference.[4] In Buddhist terms, this is referred to as realizing emptiness—the practice of relinquishing our hitherto prevailing horizons for relevance/meaning.

Similar charges can be leveled against defending the objectification and universalization of experience by situating the process of objectification in the larger project of rationalizing experience—of rendering it analytically intelligible in the hope of being better able to control and direct it. If we allow that consciousness arises in a social context, in relationship, suffering must be seen as in some quite real and irreducible sense interpersonal and any attempts to control our own experience or its conditions must be seen as manipulative of the experience of others. Insofar as what we take to be essential in experience is an abstraction, such manipulation necessarily disregards the living uniqueness of those with whom we are interacting. In so ignoring their uniqueness, we commit an act of violence which robs them of their character, which forbids them a creative presence not only in our own lives, but theirs as well.[5] In terms to be more completely elucidated below, the strategy of ending suffering through control commits both us and those among whom we live to a life where sociality is maximally attenuated, where the unprecedented or improvised is radically subjugated to regularity.

Narration and Personal Conduct:
The Communality of Suffering and Its End

As a means of illustrating the direction in which I think it appropriate to move in coming to a contextually valid, Buddhist understanding of suffering, I would like to take a look at an extremely rich story present in the *Therigatta* (vv. 213–23). Once, there was a young woman named Kisagotami, the wife of a wealthy man, who had apparently lost her mind because of the death of her child. Carrying her dead child, she wandered from house to house in her village, begging her neighbors to give her some medicine that could revive the baby. Finally, someone referred her to the Buddha who was staying at Jevatana.

She approached the Buddha and, throwing herself at his feet, begged his assistance. He told her that to heal the child, he would have to have four or five mustard seeds from a house where no son, father, mother, daughter, or slave had died. Thanking the Buddha, Kisagotami set out, going from door to door in search of a house where death had never entered. Finally, she reached the very outskirts of town without having found a family that had not been visited by death. She returned to the Buddha and in his quiet presence her mind cleared. From that day on, she was one of his devoted followers.

According to our usual set of presuppositions, the point of this story is that suffering is universal. Kisagotami learns that grief is an experience common to all of us, one that is perhaps inevitable given the nature of sentient being. Among these presuppositions, however, is a more or less well-articulated belief in the objectivity of identity and hence in the reality of essences or universals—a belief which finds no purchase in the scheme of early Buddhism or the Ch'an tradition to which we shall later turn in some detail.[6] In fact, for reasons which will hopefully become increasingly apparent, I would maintain that a consistently Buddhist interpretation of the story suggests that there are two alternative and profoundly practical implications of Kisagotami's trip through her village. First, she is made to realize that there is no free zone where impermanence and suffering do not reach. This is not to say that impermanence or suffering are everywhere the same, but only that there is no place in the world where one can go to avoid being confronted with changes and crises. Superficially, this means that no happiness can last indefinitely, that no good situation can be maintained forever. But more importantly for the Buddhist practitioner, the ubiquity of impermanence guarantees that no gridlock is intractable—that no matter how hopelessly stuck or stricken we feel, this bondage is also something arisen only in passing. All situations are negotiable.

Secondly, and for us most crucially, she learns that suffering always occurs in the context of a communally- articulated life-story. The Buddha does not simply tell her that everyone experiences such grief, but asks her to go from house to house inquiring of the inhabitants of each whether death has occurred there. It might be supposed that this is only a pedagogical device, a way of forcing a "hands-on" realization. But that hardly suffices. We have to recall that Kisagotami is not just "a woman," a faceless player in a generic tale, but someone known with greater or lesser intimacy by everyone in her village. When she knocks on a door and asks if a death has occurred in the home, rather than being answered with a brusque yes or no, her own pain will call forth that of the person she meets.

In all likelihood, she is invited into the house and haltingly told or reminded how the eldest son—a boy named Sanjaya—was to have been married just a year ago. On a routine hunting trip, he had slipped down into a ravine and broken his back against a boulder lodged in the limbs of a fallen tree. He had died a month later in the very room in which they are speaking. She would be told about the son's bride-to-be—a teenage girl who is perhaps Kisagotami's own younger cousin or niece. She would hear about the effect the death has had on Sanjaya's brothers and sisters, about how his father still could not smile even though laughter had returned to the house among the youngest children, the ones with the shortest memories. All of these people would have names and birth dates, distinctive traits and dreams. They are friends and relatives whose life-stories include and are included in her own.

Hearing these stories and being drawn ineluctably back into the fabric of her neighbors' lives, their hopes and fears, their sorrows and joys, Kisagotami must have begun already to feel herself being healed. But it is only upon returning to the Buddha and reporting her failure to secure the mustard seeds that Kisagotami is said to have truly awakened. Relating the stories of her neighbors, Kisagotami actively understands that suffering is never merely objective or subjective, but profoundly and irreducibly interpersonal, shared. By entering the homes of her neighbors and asking about the intimate fortunes of their families, Kisagotami dissolves the barrier of grief-induced madness thrown up between herself and her life-companions. By relating those fortunes, including them now as part of her own, she opens herself to the unlimited reciprocity of true community. It is in that moment of profoundest narration that 'one' and 'many' dissolve. That is her awakening.

One of the implications of the personal nature of suffering is that its power is not a function of its being an *event*, but of its meaning-generating role in a person's life. *What* happens is decidedly less important than *how* it ramifies among all those whose stories are in even some very small way included in and inclusive of our own. The case studies of clinical psychologists amply testify to the truth of this—what proves traumatic for me and severely distorts the development of my character was for you an occurrence of no lasting effect or importance. Being empty, events have no essential nature or significance but are like all things and at all times in open transformation.[7]

In actuality, whenever we speak of "my suffering" we are not merely making an assertion about a generic transformation of consciousness which we are at this point accidentally enduring. Rather, we are speaking the names of all our friends, relatives, and enemies and the relations established with them through the particular intentions we have formed, the karma we have created. In this sense, while suffering is irreducibly personal, unlike the pains which af-

flict us all from time to time, no suffering is in reality 'mine'—
something I can possess or dispossess. And so, while suffering is
always uniquely embedded in a history in which I am a principal
player, it is never mine alone but always *ours*. The true locus of
suffering is not the objective, so-called "natural" world of individual
'people' and 'things,' but the fathomless intimacy of *narration*.
Thus, it is never merely my experience which is marked with
distress and gone awry, but the entire drama—the world as a
whole—from which both 'you' and 'I' are only artificially (even if
relevantly) abstracted.

As persons, and consistent with the Buddha's denial of the
existence of any beginning to the cycle of birth and death, we did not
come to be at such and such a time and place, but rather are
continually *coming about*. Rather than being seen as individuals,
the truth of suffering leads to seeing each of us as the unfolding of a
complex of relations not only between the members of a sometimes
gradually and sometimes wildly articulating cast of characters—the
primary of which is a nominally singular narrator—but between
various times, places, actions, and levels of meaning as well. Contrary to the experience-biased intuitions of any centrist construction of both the person and of sociality, such a life-story is not the
product of the narrator—the 'I' or ego referred to in Buddhism as
"the self" (*ātman*)—who eventfully *asserts* him/herself as the most
important character in each of our tales and expends most of his/her
efforts in commenting on and plotting the course of the narrative's
unfolding. The subject to whose experiences we seem to be uniquely
privileged is, in fact, but a single aspect of who we are as narration.

Just as a movie cannot be identified with or reduced to the
musings of a voice-over narrator, but necessarily includes all the
other characters developing in it as well as a unique group of settings and locales, a soundtrack, and so on, a person cannot be
reduced to a thinking and acting individual. Instead, a person should
be seen as an ambiguity-celebrating narration irreducible to even
the sum of all its parts. The 'one' we usually refer to as "me" and the
subnarratives he/she constructs in justification of a purported existence among but essentially apart from or independent of others are,
in actuality, no more central (or for that matter, periphcral) than
the neurotically self-reflective individualists that Woody Allen so
frequently and brilliantly caricatured in films like *Annie Hall*.

There is necessarily, then, a tension involved in speaking about
narration and our 'selves' in a single breath. In part, this is a function
of the recursiveness of narration itself, and in part a consequence of

our 'realistically' informed belief that stories are intentionally constructed out of logically and temporally prior facts or happenings. As
a world, narration folds back on itself at many points, each typically
identifying itself as an 'I' or 'me' apparently situated directly in the
midst of things. Indeed, the very languages we speak are dialects of
the 'self'—dialects wherein subject differs from object, where qualities adhere or inhere, where stories are told and listened to by
storytellers and their audiences. We must, however, try bearing in
mind that this tension between on the one hand the stories we tell
about and in construction of our 'selves'—our identities as 'persons'—and on the other hand the narration or world/person of
which 'you' and 'I' are simply abstract parts, is itself a function of
the hubris and confusion that underlie existential objectification
and the belief that we are self-identical individuals. And so, while
there may be times when grammar and stylistic considerations
insist that we speak of narration as if it were something 'we' do and
not that out of which 'we' arise, in actuality the very distinction
of whole and part, of creator and created, is—for the Buddhist—
entirely spurious. Once again, all differences are made.

As indicated in the preface, narration should not, therefore, be
understood primarily as telling, but as realizing intimate connection, as healing, making whole. Far from being a function of the
storytelling ego who at times habitually and at times obsessively
identifies him or herself as the *axis mundi* or center of the world
through a juxtaposition with 'others' positioned at one or another
level of circumference, narration is best seen as a dissolution of the
selfish geometry of control and escape.

In the context of a metaphysics in which value is seen as the
origination of any 'being' and in which ambiguity is understood as,
if not basic then at least pervasive, unlike the divisive telling
practiced by the egoic 'self,' narration announces a healing creativity. While the stories 'we' tell settle or fix what is otherwise unset-
tling, they do so only through an original denial of our reciprocity
with what is being told. That is, certainty is purchased at the price
of ontological and so axiological isolation. And yet, even these tales
must be recognized as features unavoidably derivative of the ever-
burgeoning narration out of which 'you' and 'I' have been carefully,
if not always consciously, abstracted. Thus, while our selfish telling
may function as a primordial means of ascertaining or comprehend-
ing the world through its fixation in the 'self'-articulated forms of
concretely told narrative, the narrative movement or conduct out of
which we have chosen to identify our 'selves' as more or less dis-

crete beings is by no means prohibited from blossoming in unabated creativity. The constant reference in the Mahayana texts favored by Chinese Buddhism to the interpenetration of myriad buddha-lands is in this sense a means of denying an ontological status for the difference among various places and articulating instead the realization that our 'world' is a single and limiting construal of the 'same' narration which a buddha constitutes as a realm in which everything without exception is continuously accomplishing the buddha-work of enlightenment. As such, conduct is the irrepressible unfolding of new worlds which our self-spoken and 'self'-articulating stories only imperfectly and obscurely mirror.

And so, while as selfish individuals we tell stories about who we are, selecting these or those events as useful and rejecting others as out of character for the constitution of our 'persons,' there is another level at which there is no 'one' telling the story, at which we are truly persons and not merely 'self'-articulating 'persons.' As a useful analogy, think of storytellers ('persons' or 'selves') as being like dots strung out along one side of a strip of paper and their narratives as wavy, often overlapping lines on the opposite side. A person—narration or a world in the fullest sense—is the folding of this paper into a mobius strip, a process by virtue of which the opposition of 'teller' and 'tale' is completely nullified—rendered a function of point of view. As the analogy suggests, whether we are the same or different from our narration is a matter of orientation.

As 'selves' we differ not only from each other, but from the lives we lead, the actions we undertake, the decisions we make. In the terminology of Ch'an, as 'selves' or 'persons,' we live *yu-wei*. Conversely, as persons we enjoy a liberating absence of all such horizons, living spontaneously, wholly without precedent or *wu-wei* 無為. Thus, as terms of art, narrative—a thing told and hence which decides—will be associated with the doings of the self; and narration—what we will later and more fully describe as a mode of envaluation—will be allied with the harmony-realizing and yet suffering-occasioned improvisation of Buddhist personhood. Narratives distinguish 'selves' while narration fosters the timely—that is, dramatic—interpenetration (*t'ung* 通) of all things, the realization of what the Ch'an master Huang-po refers to as *i-hsin* 一心, or "one-mind."

If this is so, if suffering occurs in the dramatic context of a narration in which there can be no substitutions, in which no characters are generic, then the *experience* of suffering must have some relation to our expectations about how our narrative can and should flow. That is, unlike the biologically explicable experience of pain, experienced suffering depends partially on who we take ourselves to be and partially on what we feel we have reason to expect of our life-experience. As such, suffering can be seen as a function of the collision of actuality and a set of ideals and expectations which inform our particular way of telling the story of our life—an undesired interruption, blockage, or diversion of the narrative out of which our 'selves' are born and nurtured. The extent to which this is a negative experience depends less on what happens than on how well we are able to meaningfully work this interruption into the flow of our narrative. Once again, suffering is not a thing or event with specifiable and abiding characteristics, but a lacuna, the appearance of a diverting interstice or void. In the language of Buddhist metaphysics, suffering must be seen as having no marks (*lakṣaṇa*). That is, its nature is irreducibly axial, not ontic—a function of orientational stress and impedance.

Granted all of the above, the end of suffering is best construed neither as an escape nor as the attainment of unbreached control, but as the creative incorporation of what originally arises in our experience as a disruption of the order or timing of our life-narrative. A talented jazz musician will take an accidental or mistaken chord or note and improvise with and around it, creating in the process an entirely novel passage within the context of a perhaps quite familiarly ordered piece of music. And, in much the same way, the interruptions of suffering afford us the opportunity of conducting ourselves in an unprecedented and manifestly liberating fashion. It is through suffering that we first become aware of the karmic constraints both binding and continually bifurcating our narration. It is, however, and as numerous Ch'an masters have insisted, only by improvising with our karma that the dualisms and divisiveness it reinforces can be healed.[8]

All this not withstanding, it remains the case that while actuality contributes a radically unique component to our suffering, the ideals and anticipations we entertain are in large part a function of the societal and cultural milieu into which we find ourselves born. This milieu does not only provide the original, raw conceptual material out of which we will fashion our sense of self, the experienced texture of our karma. It supplies us as well with a horizon of possibility within which we can expect our will to be more or less effective and beyond which we are led to believe our energies would be spent in vain.

As implied by much of the recent research into the manner in which 'persons' are conceived in different cultures, we are not born of biological parents alone, but emerge as well from within a cultural matrix of which each of us is a uniquely creative articulation. Among the primary dimensions of this matrix are the linguistic, the mythic, the religious, and the technological orientations of the community under consideration. That is, what we take a person to be depends on how we speak, on the stories we have heard and tell about the archetypes of our communal experience, on the kinds of questions we pose for nature to answer, on the concrete mode of our listening, and on the tools we use in insuring our continued existence. Seen in this way, persons are neither natural nor inevitable. Rather, they are narrative creations emerging in conversation—literally "turning together"—at the highly charged, karmic nexus where the vector of individuality supplied by the genetic and psychodynamic uniqueness of one's parents and the vector of commonality supplied by the matrix of cultural dimensions intersect and interdepend.[9]

Playing off the ideas forwarded by systems theorists like Ilya Prigogine (1980), we might suggest that suffering is a fundamentally personal form of chaos out of which it is possible for new narrative orders to evolve. In this sense, the ending of suffering is not a transcendence of the embodied, feeling self, but a transformation thereof. And since the 'self' or 'person' arises only in a cultural matrix, enlightenment must itself be seen as a process of both personal and cultural transformation.

Perhaps the single most significant ramification of seeing persons as narration—worlds presented in and as conduct—and of (at the same time) admitting the irreducibly personal nature of suffering is that the end of suffering cannot be understood as fundamentally experiential. The end of suffering is not realized as an achieved state of consciousness if by that is meant an internal, psychological state, but in responding with others—in conduct itself. Kisagotami's release from her debilitating grief does not occur, then, as an insight but with her welcoming her community back into herself and her inclusion of and inclusion by the Buddha in the intimacy of that healing narration.

Stripped of our egoic glosses, it becomes clear that even the narrative through which our 'selves' are engendered is not private. That is, our life-story does not have the form of an autobiography composed entirely after the fact from behind the closed doors of remembered perception. Rather, it reveals itself only in an always ongoing conversation in which there are many partners—some of them human, some not—all of whom are capable of making wholly unexpected contributions with which we must in one way or another respond.

One of the purposes of this work as a whole is to tell a convincing story in which a seminal and profoundly practical realization of the sociality of enlightenment occurred in T'ang-dynasty China. According to this story, one of the crucial conditions for this realization was the presence in China of radically different conceptions of both the nature of personhood and suffering than had traditionally obtained in India—differences in light of which the Buddha's teachings disclosed previously unsuspected ranges of meaning. As a means of establishing a context for regarding this story as plausible, I would like to contrast the broadly Indian and Chinese conceptions of suffering and personality through an examination of the implications of their disparate approaches, both ritually and philosophically, to the practice of ancestor worship. It is to that narrative-supporting task that we shall turn in the following chapter.

Chapter 2

Culture and the Limits of Personhood:
Common Rituals and Uncommon Tales

All of us were born. All of us will die. With luck, we shall all become mature adults and contribute to the birth of a new generation. Insofar as we are merely biological organisms, these are events seemingly open to objective description—facts which can be precisely located in the world of calculable space-time coordinates. And while it may be true that no two individuals experience these events in exactly the same place at exactly the same time—to the extent that birth, puberty, procreation, and death are considered universal and objective organic phenomena—such differences can easily be seen as amounting to no difference at all.

But insofar as we are persons, such objectivity and universality are chimerical. To the extent that experiencing is personal, it is rooted not in the scientific world of reversible time and objective measurement, but in the narration of irreducibly unique figures on a common cultural ground. Being born, being initiated into adulthood (arriving at puberty), being married (which is traditionally equivalent to procreating), and dying are processes which are undeniably personal in just this sense, and the study of these turning points reveals a great deal about the way 'persons' arise in different cultures, about what they suffer, and what is meant by liberating endeavor.

That, at least, is the approach that will be taken here in setting up a context for claiming that the Ch'an tradition's recognition and practical realization of the sociality of enlightenment is in large part a function of Buddhism's having taken root in Chinese cultural soil. However, for reasons which include but are not restricted to considerations of space, only a very limited form of such an inquiry will be undertaken. While all four of the turning points mentioned above are traditionally seen as figuring in the completion of any personal narrative, and while all are typically surrounded by a more or less complex set of culturally prescribed rites and rituals, birth and death stand out as singularly important background elements in the narrative construction of suffering. The remainder of this chapter falls into two parts, then: first, a somewhat theoretical discussion of the narrative function of birth and death; and secondly, a practically informed examination of the personal implications attendant to a contrasting emphasis on ancestor worship (China) and on re-incarnation (India). But before directly involving ourselves in these discussions, a fairly extensive caveat is in order.

Stated in the language of description,[1] every culture prescribes a set of ritual contexts within which the seminal events in a life-narrative ought to occur, within which certain narrative threads are supplied or allowed for and others are not. In effect, these rituals serve to nurture and encourage the public embodiment of particular type(s) of selves. For example, a bar-mitzvah taking place in a Jewish family in New York and a vision quest entered upon by a young man in a Plains Indian tribe are similar in marking the transition from childhood to being an adult, but they differ quite decidedly in the narrative structures they engender and with which they are compatible. Thus, while cultures cannot ultimately determine what kinds of 'persons' arise within them, they do regulate the process whereby such 'persons' are articulated; not through the direct, external control of any given individual, but through internally deployed constraints on the structure of personal narrative and the kinds of selves foregrounded therein.

As suggested above, if suffering is not universal, but personal in nature, it is best seen as a break in our ongoing narration—that is, a disruption of our persons. Yet, it might be alleged that suffering is "part of the material" out of which we create our narratives and not their interruption. To be sure, at the level of consciously constructed narrative—the level where 'you' and 'I' exist as relatively 'self'-made 'persons'—discomforts, challenges, and tragedies often form crucial pivots on which our tales are made to turn. In this sense, they are certainly appropriated elements. But that the 'events' which we refer to as "challenging" or "tragic" are so qualified indicates that they initially acted as catalysts in a transformation or reorientation of our narrative that is itself constitutive of who 'we' are—the storytellers who consciously decide to remember and make use of them. Alternatively, these events may have been repressed or simply forgotten—lost along the way—and hence in no way serve as material for our present narrative of 'self.' In this latter case, however, their nonmateriality cannot be seen as equivalent to meaninglessness or evidence of the fact that they were even unimportant for us as persons. What is 'tragic' or 'painful' or 'useful' varies from 'person' to 'person' and from time to time and is, like all 'things,' a function of setting horizons for relevance, of ignoring/obscuring the unbroken emptiness of all things.

As material for our self-authored narratives, instances of suffering are indeed 'things' or 'events.' But the entitativeness that marks them as 'instances'—as a material or substance on which we may or may not draw in defining who 'we' are—is a result not only of objectifying them by separating ourselves out as 'sufferers,' but of our taking the relevant, segregating horizons to be real limits. And this cannot happen without our intention, without our both making and being embroiled in the catchments of our karma.[2]

However, simply because there are, from a Buddhist perspective, no things and because any 'event' or 'material' is seen as the constitution of 'something' through a projected sundering of emptiness (śūnyatā), we might be led to wonder whether all 'events' should be seen as suffering. In an extreme, metaphysical sense, perhaps that would be justifiable. But suffering then becomes abstract, a general undergoing, and loses its dramatic force, its narrative importance. I would be inclined, therefore, to suggest a polarization of interruption and augmentation. Both imply a change in our narrative, but augmentations are found agreeable—they fit. Interruptions confound us as discomforting, disagreeable, indicating that something is not fitting or working properly. This carries the sense of the Buddhist duḥkha—a sense of being awry, productive of discontinuity.

As such, and at the level of self-narrative, suffering is a challenge that either forces us to consciously reformulate the manner in which we are inclined to respond to others—to redirect our story— or to creatively incorporate the energy of that challenge by using it to maintain or accelerate the development to which we are currently committed.[3] Alternatively, where narration is not broken up into a 'teller' and a 'tale'—the realization of Buddhist personhood— suffering opens up the possibility of the spontaneous reconfiguration/reorientation of our world as a whole. Given the basic ambiguity of reality as understood in properly Buddhist terms, these are not, of course, meant as mutually exclusive. It is for this reason that while the Buddha was entirely correct in remarking upon enlightenment that there was nothing further needing to be done, for sentient beings living in the midst of their horizon-making distinctions, there seem to be an infinity of tasks to be undertaken and completed prior to realizing the transformation of their world into a pure buddhaland. And this in spite of their walking beside the Buddha himself. Thus, while the bodhisattvas from the buddha-field of the Tathagata Suganandhakata originally experienced our world—the realm of Sakyamuni Buddha—as noxious and impoverished, they came to realize that in fact this was completely erroneous, a function of their own unmet expectations, their own doing (VS, ch. 11). And so, it must be recognized that when a culture ritualizes transitions like those marked by weaning, initiation, marriage, or becoming an apprentice or a grandparent, it in effect creates channels through which narration can flow continuously and relatively unobstructed. To break out of this pattern is to risk a break in narrative continuity. In a word, it is to suffer. In this sense, the assertion of a radically unique personality is a counter-cultural act, a rebellion which is difficult not because of the external restrictions placed on us, but because of our unwillingness or inability to face the suffering which necessarily results from that break with norms, a suffering which will be assuaged only by way of creative improvisation.

The opportunities, however, for such improvisation can never be curtailed in any significant degree by such ritually maintained contexts for the telling of our life stories. The reason for this is quite simply that precisely insofar as rituals nurture the growth of *persons*, they establish the grounds for interpersonality, for the mutual and necessarily unpredictable interaction of a more or less large group of persons. In this sense, they differ markedly from the societal orientation toward institutional interaction—that is, interactions between generic agents or "mere people." Thus, the Jewish boy and the Plains Indian youth are both given new names at their initiation and are spoken to and questioned not as "an adult," but as this irreplaceably unique person. In short, by being social in nature, the constraints of culture on personal development cannot preclude innovation, but necessarily and most concretely bring about its possibility.[4]

Hence, while it may be analytically useful to note that all cultures ritualize birth, initiation, marriage, and death and to then develop, for instance, a classification of personal types based on the similarities of various forms of ritual guidance in the telling of life-narratives, it is possible to lose sight of the vibrantly improvisational nature of personal narration. The objectivity gained by such an analysis and classification does allow us to get a handle on things, to compress and make manageable the virtually infinite variation in the ways people tell their coming to adulthood or their coping with the imminence of death, but it is nevertheless the perpetration of a violence which reduces a story to mere plot structure, a life to a series of events. The great danger in this is, of course, the tendency for us to merely talk *about* such persons, not *with* them. Description is useful, but it is only conversation that holds the promise of being truly creative.

Birth and Death: The Primordial Horizons of Narrativity

If persons are narrations, birth and death cannot be essentially biological events, but are instead the always unique horizons within which it is possible for us to direct our own narratives. Like the rising and setting of the sun, far from being unaffected by the manner in which we come to know them, birth and death are functions of (both personal and cultural) perspective. Thus, whether we conceive of dying as a final end to life, as a transition to a place of judgment, or as the prelude to a new incarnation radically alters the way in which it will both figure in and reconfigure our narratives.

In keeping with their irreducibly horizonal character, birth and death differ from any of the other most decisive moments of our lives by resisting our presence. Unlike, for example, initiation or marriage which can occur only if we enter into them first hand, birth and death transpire only in the exclusion of our direct attendance. Whether boldly or tentatively, we may approach these places—these topics—in the stories we tell of ourselves, but we can never fully arrive.

In the case of birth, this claim seems relatively uncontroversial. While there is some evidence that it is possible to retrospectively experience the penumbra our own births, such experiences at age 30 or 40 are narratively incommensurable with those that presumably occurred at our actual delivery from the womb. The case of death is more complicated. At least in the context of religious or cultural traditions where some form of conscious survival is alleged to occur following the demise of the physical body, it is effectively claimed that a person is not limited to only asymptotically approaching death, but is capable of actually crossing over that point to experience what lies beyond. However, where the self or person is viewed narratively and where relata are *not* held to exist prior to their relations, such a continuation of consciousness after our physical demise simply represents a more or less attenuated extension of personal existence—an extension of our narration—rather than life after "death." Where persons are seen as intrinsically narrative realizations, death can only be the forgetfulness whereby a given narrative is broken.[5]

It might be objected that this holds true as long as we adopt an intrinsic perspective on ourselves as narratives, but that it is surely possible to avoid doing so and to be able to precisely locate the point at which birth and death occur. There are, in fact, many ethical dilemmas—what to do about abortion and the fate of comatose patients, for example—that beg us to definitively answer the question of exactly when someone comes alive and when they die. But even if one takes up an extrinsic perspective and descriptively views either their own or someone else's life, neither birth nor death will ever be found. As long as we eschew the projection of a set of horizons for relevance within which it is possible for something to be *identified*, all we can see are birthing and dying, processes which—like everything else—have no nonarbitrary limits.[6] In fact, birthing and dying are constantly interpenetrating one another, and it is just their balanced interplay which we call living. In this sense, birth and death are simply expedient abstractions, the result of a radical polarization whereby the middle, the actual, is excluded in favor of substantiating or fixing what are in reality constantly flowing horizons.

For our present concerns, what is significant about this is that it is not we who originally set the parameters of this polarization and who decide what belongs inside the horizons of birth and death and what does not. We first come to know about our birth and death only through the stories of others—only through the mediation of our families and our culture. We realize the importance of including our birth and death in the recursively structured narratives which are our selves only because these 'events' are intrinsically intimate parts of the (not necessarily fully encompassing) narratives of our families, our friends and the more extended communities in which our own storytelling has and will be played out.[7] Birth and death are quite literally public lore. They are processes whose nature involves being witnessed, and much of the texture of our own mature narratives depends on precisely what our culture tells us about them.

For this reason, it is in being born and in dying that we are most like others—not because the relevant circumstances are 'essentially the same' or because the meaning these events have in our life-stories are in any way necessarily alike, but rather because our birth and death are the places to which we can trace the emergence and resolution of our personal narrative in its fully recursive form. They mark the cardinal points at which we are witnessed emerging from and inevitably flowing back into what is a fundamentally communal story. And thus, even in societies as individualistic as our own, birth and dying are not private affairs, but are invariably announced, mattering profoundly for the story through the shared telling of which we come most intimately together.[8]

Birth and death represent, then, particularly effective focuses for identifying the disparate manners in which various cultural matrices directly contribute to the realization of both persons and the suffering they endure. Death is particularly significant in this regard because while we never anticipate our own birth[9]—taking it instead as that always unreachable place from which we have emerged as recursively structured, improvised tales—our anticipatory awareness of death serves to fold our narrative back on itself. We are repulsed by death, by its unimaginability, and that folding back (or being thrown back) on ourselves leads to full recursiveness. Our narrative begins playing explicitly into itself and realizes its fundamental incompleteness—realizes that completion is equivalent to cessation. Death reveals itself narratively as the impossibility of continuing to move forward. We can only dwell on that stasis or return to where we are dynamically present. And so, death lies paradoxically in a future which we will never experience and which at the same time profoundly situates us in the present.

In this respect, birth and death are in marked contrast. When we first become aware of our birth sometime in late infancy or in the toddler stage, we are already moving forward with no possibility of reversal. And yet while it is as true of birth as it is of death that it is a place we can neither reach nor go beyond, this is not in itself a cause of suffering. Although our birth lies in a past we can never retrieve, it is revealed to us as the occasion of our continual burgeoning into the future. In virtually all of the world's cultures, this is seen in a wholly positive light. To be born is almost without exception a cause for unmitigated, ritually intensified celebration. Among the world's major cultures it is only in Hindu culture that a "normal" birth is seen, at least indirectly, as suffering.[10] According to the metaphysics of the Vedas and Upanishads, birth is evidence of impropriety—evidence, that is, of a person's having formed intentions and acted in such a way as to make him/herself incapable (if not unworthy) of returning to Brahman, to universal consciousness. Embodiment is in this sense an opportunity to rectify one's mistakes, but it is also an indication of a failure to have already done so.

Interestingly, it is only in the context of being able—by way of accepting a metaphysics of re-incarnation—to anticipate our own birth that it is seen as suffering. Birth brings about a process of gradual unweaving or emergence from the communal narrative in the normal course of which we will eventually be able to recursively structure a unique narrative. It is this very burgeoning of our own narrative, however, which establishes a relation between suffering and birth—a fact of which Indian civilization seemed acutely aware. In distinguishing our selves from the cultural matrix framing our birth and our ongoing interactions with others, we leave behind the comfort and security of the narrative ligatures by means of which a culture regulates the growth of persons. While this individuation is understood, especially in less traditional cultures, as a crucial part of our realizing who we are, it necessarily leads to greater vulnerability, to what systems-theorists refer to as increased improbability. As we move away from the culturally prescribed equilibrium, we render our selves increasingly open to interruptive crisis, to suffering.

While it is true that initiation and marriage are also anticipated and contribute profoundly to our sense of self, they typically come later in life than our first grapplings with death and, perhaps more importantly, they take on their full meaning only in the context of intensifying the structure of anticipation/recursion already brought about by narratively—that is, personally—confronting our eventual demise. Initiation accomplishes this by forcing us to address our self explicitly as a project, as the identity-forming coalescence of new goals and responsibilities. Marriage serves much the same purpose through binding us to an other who not only mirrors us but who along with us gives birth to children that literally incorporate not only our genetic endowments, but our problems and our strategies for their solution. Initiation and marriage are anticipated, then, but essentially as bridges. They convey us from one phase of personal development to another, and while our culture may provide a guiding context for our efforts to make these transitions, our eventual success is nevertheless something only we can achieve. In this sense, they are concrete modes of continuity through intentional self-transformation, connecting us to others in such a way that we are vulnerable—open to growth-inducing challenges—and yet greatly expanded.

Death, on the other hand, not only severs connections, it is in no sense our own achievement. To the contrary, it is the horizon of our ability to improvise new paths, to either circumvent or creatively transform and incorporate what disrupts our tale. Thus, although we say that we confront our death, this is not actually the case. What we confront is our culture's story about death and so the topology of our recursion is set not by elements unique to us but held in common with our entire community. In folding back on ourselves through the anticipation of death, we are enfolding our culture and its notion of what it is to be a person. Thus, to the extent that we are fully recursive narratives, the study of death and the rituals surrounding it tell us a great deal about what persons suffer throughout their lives.

The Narrative Meaning of Death:
The Disparity of the Indian and Chinese 'Person'

At the time when Buddhism was being transmitted from India to China (somewhere between the first century BCE and the third century CE), there were already long-standing traditions of ancestor worship prevalent in both cultures, and, at least at a superficial level, the primary motives and rites involved seem to have been quite similar. In both China and India we find the offering of ritually prescribed food and drink on the day of each new moon and on other significant dates in the yearly calendar, and in each case the primary motive seems to have been keeping the departed spirits happy so as to insure general prosperity in the family and in particular the birth of sufficient male progeny.

Given these similarities, one might be tempted to conclude that the function of ancestor worship in establishing and maintaining the relevant cultural matrices is practically invariant across the two cultures and that the nature of the 'person' nurtured by those matrices is likewise quite similar. As we shall see, however, the centrality of the family as a structure of deferential relationships in Chinese culture and of rebirth in that of India renders any apparent similarity at the level of either the rites themselves or the intent behind their timely performance purely adventitious. As narratives, the Indian and the Chinese 'person' are not only dissimilar, they are in many respects very nearly incommensurable.

This disparity becomes evident as soon as we ask *who* the ancestors are; that is, what place they occupy in the narration of each culture's worldview. At least by the time of the *Upanishads* and the *Purāṇas*, the story about what happens to an Indian person who dies went something like this. Following a ritual cleansing, an offering of rice balls is made and the body cremated. At this point, the family circumambulates the funeral pyre and, being instructed to neither look back nor indulge in any open show of grief, proceeds to a river or brook where they immerse themselves and wash before heading home. There, a feast is prepared and the death is celebrated. Again, lamentation may arise spontaneously, but it is ritually pro-scribed. On one of the following two days, the skull of the dead is shattered and placed along with the bones of the deceased in an earthenware jar which is then either thrown in a holy river or buried in consecrated ground.

According to the *Purāṇas*, with the cremation of the physical body, the deceased person acquires a subtle body (the *ātivāhika*) which is supported by daily offerings. On the tenth day, the eldest son goes to the cremation ground and offers a ball of rice (*piṇḍa*) in order to insure that the deceased can shed the *ātivāhika* body and gain that of a *preta* or ghost.

Offerings are made on each new moon for a year to sustain the *preta* body, after which time another ceremony (*ekoddiṣṭa*) is held in order to assist the discarding of the *preta* body and the transition of the dead person into the world of the ancestors or *pitṛs*. At this point, four vessels of water, sesame seeds, and scents are prepared and offered. One is for the *preta*, and one each for his father, grand-father, and great-grandfather. The contents of the first pot is poured into the other three while mantras are recited and from this point on the deceased counts as the first of the *pitṛs* and the great-grandfather is dropped from the ranks of ritually attended ancestors. This marks the completion of the full set of *saṃskāras* which—spanning the time from pregnancy through assumption into the ranks of the ancestors—define full membership in the Hindu socioreligious community.[11]

While this marks the completion of a person's ritually ordered life, it is by no means the end of the cultural story told about the fate of the dead. In fact, there is a larger narrative framework within which the above story is embedded and without which the exact nature of the ancestors remains quite obscure. Typical of the various formulations of this larger narrative is the following excerpt from the *Bṛhadāraṇyaka Upaniṣad*:

> Those who meditate on the truth in the forest with faith, pass into the light, from the light into the day, from the day into the half-moon of the waxing moon, from the half-month of the waxing moon into the six months which the sun travels northward, from these months into the world of the *devas*, from the world of the *devas* into the sun, from the sun into the lightning. Then one of the mind-born goes to the sphere of lightning and leads them to the *brahma-loka*.
>
> In the *brahma-loka* they live for a long time. For these there is no return. Those who, through *yajñas* (rites), gifts and austerities, conquer the worlds, pass into the smoke, from the smoke into the night, from the night into the half-month of the waning moon, from the half-month of the waning moon into the six months during which the sun travels southward, from these months into the world of the fathers (*pitṛs*), from the world of the fathers into the moon. Reaching the moon they become food. There the *devas*, as they say to King Soma, increase, decrease even to feed upon them there.
>
> When that is over, they pass into space, from space into wind, from wind into rain, from rain into the earth. Reaching the earth they become food. Again they are offered in the fire of man. Thence they are born in the fire of a woman with a view to going to other worlds [of animals, men, etc.]. Thus do they go around. But those who do not know these two ways, become insects, moths and whatever there is here that bites. (VI.2.15)

From passages like this,[12] it is clear that not everyone becomes an ancestor and that those who attain this status do not keep it.[13] In general, the Upanishads suggest that there are four possibilities at death: {1} the person who dies has already realized his or her true nature and returns immediately back to Brahman; {2} the person becomes a *deva* and gradually attains entry to the *brahma-loka*; {3} the person becomes a *pitṛ* who, upon the exhaustion of his/her merit becomes food for the gods (*devas*) and eventually condenses and falls back to an earthly incarnation; or {4} the person, due to having led an evil life, immediately incarnates as one of the lower forms of earthly life.

What is significant about this account is that being an ancestor or *pitṛ is* only a way-station on the path to rebirth on earth. That is, an ancestor is not ultimately freed from the travails of earthly existence, but is granted a relatively brief respite in the world of the *pitṛs* on the basis of merit acquired in this life. In this sense, becoming an ancestor is simply the adoption of a new form of existence and the connection with any particular family is by no means necessary or unbreakable. Just as one can incarnate as an animal and have no further direct relationship with one's descendants, becoming an ancestor does not automatically entail maintaining a familial bond with your offspring. Moreover, insofar as the ultimate goal is to separate entirely from the finite and mortal world of action and suffering—to return to the unconditioned by realizing that the self (*ātman*) is the absolute (*brahman*)—becoming an ancestor is evidence of a failure. In this sense, it is a perversion, a turning away from the ordained path of realizing identity with the universe as a whole and toward continued relationship with (what delusively appear to be) others. To become an ancestor is to remain in bondage. The person who attains liberation is one who vaults beyond the duality of subject and object, beyond any relations whatsoever.

From the above, it should be clear that achieving ideal personhood in the context of Hindu culture is a matter of freeing oneself from all human relationships. Thus:

> when one reflects properly, one comes to know that the things of this world are as valueless as straw . . . all creatures—the superior, the middling, and the inferior—in consequence of their respective acts, are entangled in grief! . . . As two pieces of wood floating on the ocean come together at one time and are again separated, even such is the union of creatures in this world. Sons, grandsons, kinsmen, relatives are all of this kind. One should never feel affection for them, for separation with them is certain. (*Mahābhārata*, Śāntiparva 174.4–17)

In this context, the dutiful performance of the rites of ancestor worship, like the execution of the tasks proper to one's caste, are not meant primarily to foster human relatedness, but to prepare the person for their separation from all relations. The individuals to whom one is now related are important only insofar as they help you to realize your true nature, to separate from them entirely, and to return to union with Brahman.[14] In his study of ancestor worship in India, Dakshinaranjan Shastri remarks that the motive of ancestral rites in India is "the enlargement of one's individual self." By performing the five great sacrifices, one aims to realize that the *pitṛs*, the *devas*, animals, and indeed Brahman are inseparable from us in the sense that we already contain them. Such a one "absorbs the entire universe within him. He is at once identified with the entire universe" (Shastri 1963, 110). In a word, the aim of personhood is the total transcendence of place, role, and relationship.

As shall become apparent, from a Chinese perspective, this is equivalent to a loss of reciprocity that is itself tantamount to a loss of personhood. To contain the universe is to be cut off from relationships with others, to live in an intrapersonal, not an interpersonal world. In a word, it is not (as for the Indian) to be liberated, but deprived.[15] The ritual process of ancestor worship illustrates this quite dramatically.

While the first step in disposing of and honoring the dead is, just as in India, a ritual cleansing of the body, the Chinese custom is not to cremate but entomb the dead, usually three days after the death occurs. Where the means are available, the burial is done in a vault in which models of servants are placed along with other useful objects, food, and drink. As is made clear by the traditional belief that those bereaved by a death are incapable of communicating with the ancestors, the dead are not immediately considered to be ancestors. On the day of the death, the family is to openly express their grief, to wail and lament, and visibly alter their appearance. The children, especially, are supposed to be too upset to eat until the burial—usually three days after the death—and are to occupy themselves only with preparations for the entombment. Mourners eat a restricted diet, sleep on hard pallets, and are not to engage in their usual routines of work or study. During this period, the corpse is offered regular meals and those who come to console the family are required to also address the dead. Once the burial has occurred, a symbol of the dead is incorporated into the altar of the ancestors and they are gradually taken up into that company. Ritual offerings are made for the newly departed at various points for two years and those in deepest mourning are expected to restrict their activities through the third anniversary of the death (Ebrey 1991, 16, 23).

From the foregoing, it should be apparent that whereas the Indian sees death as a potentially permanent break from the bondage *inherent* to human embodiment and so accentuates the cleavage by destroying the body completely, the Chinese views death as a transition which one tries to mitigate or soften by treating the body of the dead as a focus of the same patterns of deference that were previously accorded to the no longer living relative. The inclusion of impersonators of the dead who actually received and consumed the offerings at ancestral rites in (especially Chou dynasty) China was not, then, mere histrionics but rather the ritual maintenance of the reciprocity enjoyed by father and son, by husband and wife.

Interestingly, while the Chinese see the relationship between the living and the dead as being one of ritually defined interdependence, they do not have anything like an explicit account of the type of existence proper to ancestors. In sharp contrast with the overarching narrative of rebirth in which there is a succession of ever more subtle bodies and, barring the attainment of final liberation, eventual re-incarnation, the Chinese do not continue to see the dead person in terms of any particular *form*, but rather solely in terms of his or her *relations*. The person is not—as is true in India— an essence or universal self which is gradually disentangled from even the most subtle forms of bodily existence and relatedness, but is instead a contributing factor in the ongoing saga of their family. Thus, ancestors are kept well-informed about important family events—into of passage, marriages, deaths, and so on—and are not excluded from the day-to-day affairs of their descendants. For example, each of the many steps in arranging a marriage was traditionally to have been reported to the ancestors and three months after the wedding the new bride was to be personally and formally introduced to her husband's ancestors in their shrine (Ebrey 1991, 22).

As the quite elaborate ghost tales told and recorded throughout China illustrate, the continued ministrations of the living for the dead are understood as essential to the smooth functioning of the community. Whereas in classical India, ancestral rites were arguably carried out almost entirely for the benefit of the survivors—the exception being the injunction *against* lamentation as a way of helping the departed to let go of their human attachments—the popular Chinese belief was that the rites served to maintain an appropriate relationship between the living and the dead by means of which *both* benefited. Neglecting to perform the rites was thought to lead not only to ill for the survivors, but to eventuate the fall of the departed spirit (*shen* 神) from role of ancestor to that of a wandering and often malevolent ghost (*kuei* 鬼). In short, the destiny of the departed spirit is seen as a function of their always ongoing relationships with others.

This stands in very marked contrast to the cultural narrative of the *Upanishads* wherein the destiny of an individual is entirely a matter of their own karma—their own actions and intentions. Whereas the Indian person is judged by universal law (*ṛta*) and migrates through the worlds accordingly—now incarnating as an insect, now as an animal, now as a god or human—the Chinese person is neither judged nor conceived of as being able to shed their humanity. That is, specifically human relationships remain both constant and crucial to the constitution of the personhood of the dead. Thus, whether embodied or not, the Chinese person or self is irreducibly human.

In his collection of essays entitled *Confucian Thought: Selfhood as Creative Transformation*, Tu Wei-ming points out that "to be fully human requires the courage and wisdom of constantly harmonizing oneself with an ever-enlarging network of relationships" (1985, 21), a learning process which is seen within the Confucian tradition as carried by means of the performance of ritual (*li* 禮). Far from being a fixed standard of outward behavior or doing what is objectively right (*yi* 義)—that is, people obeying the ruler— ritual is considered to be a means of cultivating attitudes whereby true harmony arises and not mere agreement—that is, revering the ruler (Graham 1989, 11). Learning to properly perform a ritual is thus a means of self-transformation. As with learning (*hsueh* 學) generally in the Confucian tradition, this does not mean the acquisition of empirically established facts, the accumulation of new information or beliefs. Rather, learning is "a process of training the self to be responsive to the world and culture at large" (Tu 1985, 68). As Chad Hansen has persuasively argued, knowledge in the Chinese tradition is best seen not—as is common in both the Indian and Western philosophical traditions—as a matter of true propositions, but rather as a "species of skill," an activity and not a state (1981, 322 ff.). Thus, while the ideal of the Upanishadic tradition is for the person to realize, to know, that their self (*ātman*) is no other than Brahman and to thereby be released from any binding relationships and hence any obligation, the ideal of the Confucian tradition[16] is to open up the self toward others, to become ever more responsive and responsible.[17]

Seeing persons in terms of the concrete and constantly deepening realization of human relationships suggests not only that self-cultivation is essentially social in nature, but that personhood is not an ontological given but an achievement. Learning who we are involves the acquisition of skills affecting not only our outward conduct, but the conduct of our inner attitudes or dispositions. It is not, as was the case in India, a process of *divesting* ourselves of what were taken to be the obscuring tendencies of human interconnectedness, but one of achieving the kind of creative flexibility that allows us to appropriately relate to anyone at any time whatsoever. That is, self-discovery is gaining skill in relational improvisation.

If the relational nature of personhood is granted, the Chinese practice of ancestor worship can be seen as having the consequence of insuring that everyone shows deference to someone else. What we discover in carrying out the rituals of worship is that none of us are independent agents or knowers. Instead, we are obliged to experience the fact that no living person can rise above the need to practice deferential conduct. Thus, a person should be seen as an unmitigated between-ness, a spontaneous interplay.[18] Moreover, if a person is understood as a focus of relations, and if suffering is irreducibly personal, it must be concluded either that the end of suffering is equivalent to a loss of personhood or that both suffering and its end are themselves essentially social.

While it is not possible to state categorically that the former is the disposition of Indian culture—both because the Indian view of the person is not fundamentally relational and because it is arguable that the loss of personhood (*pudgala*) in India ought to be seen as the attainment of our true selves (*ātman*)—the conclusion that ending suffering signals freedom from relation-limited personhood seems at least to be consistent with the presuppositions undergirding the narrative of self set forth in the *Upanishads* and the *Purāṇas*. For the Indian, the fall into narrative interplay which occurs with birth is a misfortune, a galling limitation of the self from which all suffering derives. The end of suffering is logically—if not factually, as in the case of traditional ascetics—a withdrawal or detachment from sociality. The overwhelmingly most important technology of self-transformation and liberation indigenous to India was the practice of yoga—an internalization of attention resulting eventually in an eruption out of the finite and relationally bound into mergence with Brahman. Far from being a technology applied in the midst of communal life, yoga was traditionally the province only of those who had left the home life; those who were no longer father or son, mother or daughter, husband or wife. While the philosophical significance of "leaving the home life" may have been the resolute transcendence of all egoism, the spiritual promise was that of realizing who I really am, and so the ultimate realization of personhood and of freedom from suffering entails nothing short of discounting and distancing one's self from the contingency of human relatedness.[19]

Contrary to the Indian ascetic, the Chinese sage is someone who (even in the radical Taoism of Chuang Tzu) not only does not forfeit his or her particular place in the web of human relationships, he or she takes the task of correcting—rendering true or straight— all these relations with others as his or her primary concern. Thus, in China birth is not seen as a loss of freedom, a binding in a negative sense, but as the establishing of one's originating relationships. Birth is entering into an intimate and enabling embrace with others, and it is only within this embrace that one's true person arises. Suffering is not—as it arguably is in Hindu India— relationship itself, but rather a certain quality, a disruption or perversion of relationship. Ending suffering is not an escape from or transcendence of relationships, but the process of rendering them always appropriate. In this sense, freedom is akin to virtuosic musicianship—skill in responding to potentially or actually disruptive contingencies in a creative and harmonious way.

Chapter 3

Dramatic Interdependence and Improvisation: Sociality as Orientation

According to the Buddha, none of us has a self. Regardless of how things seem, there are no abiding, independently existing entities we can identify as 'me' and 'you.' To the contrary, it is claimed that we are impermanent (*anitya*) and dependently arisen (*pratītya samutpāda*). Like a bundle of reeds—the five *skandhas* of form (*rūpa*), feeling (*vedanā*), perception (*samjñā*), impulses (*saṃskāra*), and consciousness (*vijñāna*)—each one of which stands upright only as long as all of them lean together, a person is not an isolatable integer or simple whole, but a community. With the removal of even a single reed, the entire structure collapses.

This analogy—like that of the chariot used by Nagasena in explaining the doctrine of selflessness (*anātman*) to King Milinda (*Milindapanha* II.1)—suggests that we should view persons as whole and yet inherently open systems which arise as a function of a set of subsystems for which they act in turn as environment. That is, a person is not a "thing," but should be seen as an organizing or structuring process which has qualities or characteristics which can be predicated of none of its parts, whether considered singly or as a group.[1] To be a person is not to be a substantial entity, but rather a complex of relationships.

While this representation of the relational structure of personhood stands as a pointed correction to the predispositions of the Buddha's Indian audiences, we might anticipate its potentially psychological flavor to be less than fully satisfying in the context of a culture where the relationality of personhood is understood in more explicitly communal terms. That is, while the Indian Buddhist might be willing to see persons as systems, the systems in question are most liable to be taken as psychophysical in nature. Moreover, the relevant subsystems—the five *skandhas*—would be understood in such a fashion that inquiry into them directs us toward individual experience and action. This is in fact exactly what we find in the locus classicus of early Buddhist meditative technique, the *Satipaṭṭhāna Sutta*. With this in mind, neither the so-called Hinayana concentration on individual enlightenment nor the eventual demise in India of the Mahayana and its almost militant emphasis on the liberation of all sentient beings are particularly surprising.

By contrast, it would seem that a Chinese Buddhist would be culturally conditioned toward seeing such systems in overtly sociophysical terms. That is, not only persons, but the systems they comprise—the *skandhas* of body, feeling, impulses, perception, and consciousness—would be liable to being understood as irreducibly communal. As evidenced in the salvation or liberation narratives prevalent in the cultural traditions of Indo-European descent, the tendency there has been to consider the limit of personhood as roughly coincident with the horizon segregating the public and the private. In some cases (as with the resurrection mythology of medieval Christianity) the body is clearly included within this horizon, in other cases not. But in general what most crucially defines 'me' or 'you' is in not altogether metaphorical terms what lies most deeply within. For the Chinese, however, this has never been either explicitly or predominantly the case. To the contrary—and as is made quite clear by the starkly divergent narratives articulating on the one hand the almost magical potency of a true ruler and the other hand the purpose and effects of banishment—what most manifestly defines 'me' or 'you' is for the Chinese not something we carry within us, but the relative health and movement of the body politic.

And so, if our attempt at warranting the sociality of Ch'an enlightenment is to succeed with any measure of legitimacy, we must first take special care to avoid appealing to the psychophysical individual in expressing the nature of sociality. At the very least, a radical shift must be made away from our typical and experience-conditioned bias for presupposing as ontologically valid the discursive individuation of 'self' and 'other.' Instead, and consistent with the dispositions of Chinese culture in general, not only sociality, but persons must be understood primarily as functions of envaluation—that is, as specific orientations of conduct.

Nonlocal Subsistence: The Ontological Mode of Relational Personhood

One of the more challenging implications for sociality entailed by a relational view of personhood is that, strictly speaking, we are not located anywhere at all. At the very least, the impermanence of all things insures that, as persons, we are temporally ambiguous or indeterminate—that is, we are neither momentary (the annihilationist error) nor absolutely enduring (the eternalist error).[2] More importantly, however, if we arise interdependently, and if all causes are projective (identified as a function of selecting horizons for relevance and hence inquiry) and not substantial in nature, we are also spatially indeterminate.

From a general systems-theoretical point of view, this amounts to saying that as a *system* of relations we are not independent of either our environment or the subsystems without which we could never have come about. For the systems-theorist, the standard appeal to the continuity of either our psychological or bodily states as being definitive of a strictly localizable personal identity does nothing to undermine this fact.[3] As Gregory Bateson points out in discussing a systems-theoretical model of the self: "The total self-corrective unit which . . . 'thinks', 'acts' and 'decides,' is a *system* whose boundaries do not at all coincide with the boundaries either of the body or of what is popularly called the 'self' or 'consciousness'" (1972, 317–18). To the contrary, it would appear that, "In the web of relationships which form what we call the self there are *no clear lines of demarcation* whereby it can be asserted, 'This is I'" (Macy 1991, 110–11, emphasis added).

Accepting this, and contrary to most of the prevailing views in philosophical and sociological circles, it no longer makes sense to think of sociality as something which arises only after the fact of our individuation as more or less 'selves.' In short, a consistently Buddhist conception of sociality will depend on our negotiating a middle path between asserting or even assuming the priority of either the individual (for instance, Locke, Rousseau and Vedanta) or of the collective (for example, Durkheim, Mauss, and some versions of Marx). From a Buddhist perspective, appealing to individuality as the ontological ground for sociality errs in identifying persons with either states of their body (materialism) or with their—ostensibly private—states of consciousness (subjectivism). On the other hand, appealing to the collective errs in identifying cultural/social institutions as the ontologically prior ground out of which concrete individuals emerge. In each case, we implicate ourselves in foundationalist projects that deny the irreducible interdependence of all things. The doctrine that all things are *anātman* or absent of an identifiable and enduring self applies equally to both the 'individual' and the 'collective.' These may be conventionally useful abstractions, but in actuality, nothing like either of them obtains.

As powerful and well-suited as it is to the task of theoretically modeling the Buddhist view of persons, however, systems-theory is not an entirely neutral frame of reference. While it goes a long way toward dissolving the usual dichotomy of the individual and society, and hence toward stressing the spatial indeterminacy of personhood, it is not altogether clear that systems-theory breaks completely with the root premise of the logic of identity and difference—the supposition that each 'thing' is self-evidently different from what it is not. Yet it is just this supposition which undergirds all foundational ontologies and which the Buddha clearly seeks to eschew in his refusal to make assertions based on either 'is' or 'is-not' (SN II.7).[4]

At the very least, the language of systems-theory happily allows for the objective differentiation and identification of systems and mere aggregates. While the boundaries between systems nested together in a working hierarchy are held to be fundamentally open and hence arguably nominal in nature, the difference between what counts as a system and what does not is taken to be unquestionably real. That is, certain boundaries are taken to be something other than horizonal projections of value/relevance. Likewise, all systems—whether those referred to as individuals or societies—are self-maintaining, relatively invariant patternings that emerge out of the ubiquitous continuum of the space-time matrix. In particular, social systems are held to be relatively autonomous entities that emerge from the association of an indeterminate number of generically conceived human beings or subsystems to which they are finally irreducible and from which they are functionally distinct.

Thus, from a systems perspective any disparity in the way various cultures conceive persons might well be admitted to influence the exact texture of the societies to which they give rise, but not the nature of sociality itself. Sociality would in this sense amount to a kind of universal, a patterning which can be objectively described apart from any particular subsystems it comprises.

As tempting as it is to affirm this claim, doing so would inevitably involve us in perpetuating the same kind of violence that we have already argued occurs with indulging the tendency to classify personal types on the basis of similarities or differences in the manner in which various cultures ritually guide the telling of our life-narratives. Just as such a taxonomic endeavor eventuates the reduction of a life-story to a mere sequence of events by disregarding the inherently improvisational, recursive, and tirelessly ongoing nature of personal narration, viewing sociality as given in the generically conceived interaction of concrete individuals reduces sociality to a fact—something like an observed state of affairs. And with this objectifying reduction of sociality comes our own exclusive elevation as autonomous, observing subjects. Simply put, it amounts to an instance of committing that most common of intellectual sins described by Pierre Bourdieu as unjustifiably introducing into what we study the principles of our own relationship to it (Bourdieu 1977, 2). As was remarked in regard to the problem of classifying personality types, this amounts to nothing less than fostering and legitimizing the tendency to talk *about* persons rather than *with* them. A more radical break is necessary.

In their proposal of a focus-field model for representing personhood in the Confucian tradition, David L. Hall and Roger T. Ames provide a significant alternative to the prioritization of the interior and psychological dimension of human being in our conception of persons, and one we would thus expect to have particular relevance in unfolding the Chinese Buddhist understanding of persons. To begin with, it ostensibly allows relationality and not individuality to be seen as ontologically basic. It is not that various systems—say individual sentient beings—enter into relations and so give birth to families and other social or societal systems, but that such individuals are abstracted from the same field of relations out of which these "higher order systems" have also been abstractly identified. A marked advantage of such a model is that is enables us to see relationality in fully reciprocal or horizontal terms rather than hierarchically vertical ones, and to avoid some of the implications of localized importance attendant to the systems model. For Hall and Ames, persons do not enter *into* relationship, but are in fact constituted by them.

And yet, the focus-field metaphor itself unfortunately replicates much of the objective and binary feel of all centrist conceptions of personhood. On the one hand, it implies the possibility of determining by observation that a person is *this* focusing of the field while I the observer am yet another. In effect, the language of focus and field requires the admission of a metaperspective from which it can be determined what is being focused—the field of relationships. Something acts as an 'outside-stander.' Moreover, the metaphor continues to represent the person as a part of the world, as a limited phenomenon on the perhaps infinite ranges of the field. In short, persons are still seen extrinsically, as objectifiable 'things' arising on or out of a surrounding field of relations. Such a model thus shares some of the guiding presuppositions of J. Mohanty's discussion of persons in terms of layers of selfhood according to which some relations—like those with family members—are closer to the core of who we are, while others—like those with other individuals sharing our birthday—are significantly less so. A person is still taken to be a relatively coherent center in the midst of an encircling world, and the discrimination of near and far is still understood as crucial to who and what we are. Persons are not entire worlds, but aspects or focuses within them.

From a Buddhist perspective, what is apparently missing from such models is a realization that the world is neither an objective context for our personal existence, nor a merely subjective or ideal construct. That is, the systems and focus-field models fail on the one hand to explicitly and unmitigatedly embrace the priority of orientation rather than being or existence—an embrace crucial to at least Mahayana Buddhist metaphysics—and, on the other, to fully appreciate the indispensable role of karma or dramatic interplay in any adequate depiction of (at least Buddhist) personhood. And so, while it is widely admitted that a Buddhist model of personhood must reflect in some measure the processive nature of all things, none of the prevailing models address with sufficient care the irreducibly dramatic quality of sentient impermanence.

Karma, Conduct, and the Narrativity of
Chinese Buddhist Personhood

Taken seriously, Hui-neng's claim that "it is precisely Buddhist conduct that is the Buddha" (PS 42) makes evident the necessity of seeing the ideal Buddhist person in terms of conduct—that is, his or her lived relations with others—and not according to any set of individually possessed marks or states of consciousness. But strictly speaking, it does not require us to admit that the original nature (*pen hsing* 本性) of such persons must be seen as irreducibly dramatic narration. The necessary linkage between the relational nature of personhood and the dramatic nature of narration may, at least in East Asian Buddhism, be brought into useful focus by the doctrine of karma.

In very brief, the function of karma in the conceptual scheme of Buddhism is to undermine the belief that each of us exists as individuals in a world which is both objectively real and disparate in its origins from our own intentions and knowing. According to the doctrine, the circumstances in which we find ourselves cannot be divorced from our intentions and actions, but are understood instead as an intimate function thereof. That is, the world is not a realm into which we are accidentally born or thrown in a Heideggerian sense. Rather, it should be seen as an unerring expression of who we are and have been. And so, not only the other people with whom we are in relationship, but the historical and cultural settings for those relationships and the particular quality of their unfolding are all our doing (*karma*), our responsibility.

The Buddha was clear in denying that this responsibility should be construed in an absolute or megalomaniacal sense. He claimed, for example, that Brahma was not the creator of the universe, but had simply been deluded into thinking so because he was the first being to appear in this world cycle. Nevertheless, who we are and the world we live in should be seen as functionally inseparable. If we had different karma, we would be living in different circumstances, in a world otherwise configured. And so, if we did not share intentions conducive to the realization of a world in which there occurs a crisis in Somalia, an ongoing tragedy in Sarajevo, and a string of apparently senseless murders of foreign tourists on Florida's highways, we would simply have been born in 'other' worlds. These may be thought of in terms of parallel universes, birth in other solar systems, or what have you. That is not particularly important. The karmic point is simply that our intentions are constitutive of what-has-come-to-be and how, and that there is no nonarbitrary line demarcating what we are responsible for and what we are not.

I would submit that for the Buddhist, this means that our world is irreducibly dramatic. The English word "drama" derives from the Greek *draein* ("to act" or "to do") and has since come to be associated not only with deeds generally but with performances displaying the manner in which our choices determine the meaning of our jointly articulating lives. Likewise, the Sanskrit *karma* not only implies purposive action but also the inescapable meaningfulness of our purposes for how things have already and will yet come about. In short, recognizing our karma ultimately means seeing not only that whatever is occurring depends on some initial conditions and the working on them of objective laws (whether fixed and absolute or merely statistical), but on the quality of the relationships being realized, the problems and blockages being worked out here. Hence the Buddha's remark that of deeds done and accumulated with deliberate intent, there is no arbitrary wiping out. That wiping out has to come to pass either in this very life, or in some other life, but only at its proper occasion. "Without experiencing the result of deeds so done, I declare there is no making an end of *dukkha* (crisis)" (*Aṅguttara-nikāya* V.292).

It is not, however, that karma amounts to a system of individual retribution or pay-back (L *re + tribuere*)—a sort of "eye for an eye, tooth for a tooth" balancing of behavioral credits and debits. Such conception may not be wholly inaccurate when applied to the Hindu tradition as exemplified, for example, by the *Bhagavad-gītā*, but it profoundly distorts the preferred uses of the term in a Buddhist context. To begin with, the Buddha's insistence on the selflessness and impermanence of all things prohibits our seeing any individual agent as the maker and undergoer of karma. When, for example, Sati suggests that consciousness is the "feeler who experiences the fruit of deeds," the Buddha declares him woefully misguided since consciousness—the locus of experience—is itself empty or dependently arisen (MN I.259–60). At the same time, the Buddha steadfastly denied that any deeds are without experienced consequences. In other words, karma should be understood as a nonlinear conditioning of the topology of experience as such.

The Buddhist concept of karma is thus explicitly conditional rather than deterministic. It involves not merely volitional action but the occurrence or flowing together of complexes of intentional acts, their consequences, and the specific characters or natures of the various participants in their occurrence (see, for instance, the *Aṅguttara-nikāya* 1.249 and the *Mahā-kammavibhaṅga-sutta* [MN III.207ff.]). Granted as well that any consistently Buddhist ontology places value prior to being, the importance of volition (*cetana*) should not be construed as due to its power or mechanical influence as such, but because it marks a decision among relative values—the projection of what is liked and desired, disliked and avoided, or left quite out of consideration. That is, since non-volitional actions or behavior do not mark the incursion or expression of new values and hence the reorientation of our conduct, they will not further condition the unfolding/enfolding of our relationships. In a word, they do not precipitate a diversion or reconfiguration of the *meaning* of what is coming about. Intentional acts, on the other hand, mark the investment of new values, the creation of new relational pathways or the further intensification of old ones. Intention may or may not alter the facts of our lives, but it works ineluctable changes on the direction of our narration. At the risk of oversimplifying, we might say that intention works directly on the plot of our interdependence, the pattern of its dynamism.

In light of all the above, karmic fruit—the result of volitional activity—is arguably best viewed less as individually determined retribution than as the conditional arising of dramatic resolution in conduct. In short, karma guarantees the opportunity for resolving discursive or deharmonizing relationship, a process which allows us to be once again freed or loosened (L *re + solvere*) from a binding connection. Far from amounting to a retributive fate, the operation of karma brings about the possibility of truly relinquishing our ignorance.

To pick an example from our own tradition, Hamlet's dilemma should be seen as quintessentially karmic—that is, it involves not only his own character with its strengths and weaknesses, but those of his family members and the various other nobles with whom he is implicated in the political upheaval of the times, the history of the Danish people, the climate of their land, and the unique architecture of their self-preservation. Especially in light of the Confucian virtues informing the Chinese Buddhist's sense of rulership, what Hamlet is confronted with is not merely a question of either avenging his father's death or not, but of finding out who he truly is and what it means to be an authentically human heir to his father's throne—a person capable of setting the entire kingdom in order or disarray simply by adjusting his own bearing or orientation (see, for example, *Analects* XV.5).

Karma supplies a failsafe context for learning how the manner in which things have come to be configured is intimately a function of our own motives, our hopes and dreams, our longings and fears, and the profoundly tragic, comedic, and at times even poetic relations these nurture or retard. It is for this reason that the juxtaposition of "is" and "seeing as" is particularly felicitous, implying as it does the divergence of a world of mute fact and a world which is explicitly understood as thoroughly heuristic.

Now, since the doctrine of karma decisively rules out accepting the premise that some things just happen—are a matter of chance or luck—rather than occurring as a function of choices made by *everyone* implicated therein, it entails accepting that our fortunes are always intimately common. There is, in fact, no such thing as a lonely fate—a destiny pertinent to one and only one. It is particularly apt, then, that in choosing a term to translate the Sanskrit "karma," the Chinese did not select (for instance) *tso* 作—which has the connotation of making or doing and implies individual activity—but *yeh* 業, which refers at once to both our estate and all that contributes to its acquisition and maintenance.

For the Chinese, this places under the umbrella of karma not only the physical/geographical context in which we grow up, but a cultural and social one as well. As focused by the concept of *yeh*, karma explicitly involves our occupation, business, or profession, and so implies what kinds of people we meet and work with and in what capacities. It implies the kinds of status we enjoy or are barred from, the kinds of risks and challenges we encounter, the tools we use, the education to which we and our relatives are entitled, the range of possible partners we have in marriage, and so on. What karma signified for the Chinese was not, then, the just desserts of an individual's behavior, but rather *the prosperity and way of life of an entire family*—quite literally, the qualitative integrity of its entire world. Quite explicitly for the Chinese Buddhist, it is never just 'your' or 'my' experience that is marked by suffering or harmony, but our entire world which is gone awry or faring well.

Ultimately, there is no center to identify as an objective locus of personal subsistence. Who we are is not answerable in terms of some specific focus, but in terms of the movement of our world—our narration—as a whole. Thus, when the Buddha denies taking a stand or adopting any fixed locus, it is the propensity of the Chinese Buddhist to understand this not simply as entailing the relinquishing of habitual perspectives, but as pointing out that persons in the truest sense have no location at all. In this light, it is hardly surprising that Pai-chang says that "if one is liberated, a thousand follow; if one is confused, ten thousand are deluded" (HTC 119.425a). Our fortunes are irreducibly communal. What occurs for any 'one' of us necessarily affects us all.

In a similar vein and echoing the Buddha's own words, Huang-po makes it quite clear that "It is precisely the Tao (path) that has no location which is called Mahayana mind. This mind is not present inside, outside or in-between. In actuality, there are no 'locations'" (T 2012.382c). Later, in speaking of "supreme enlightenment"—the province of a truly Buddhist person or buddha—Huang-po says that it means having no place to anchor. It is "conducting yourself as all the buddhas have . . . responding without any fixed perspective" (T 2012.383b).

We shall return to these claims in a more practical context later, but on a philosophical level what the wording of these claims suggests is at the very least that conduct cannot be taken to be synonymous with behavior. As mentioned in the introduction, in the service of at least verbally marking the incommensurability of conduct and behavior, it may be noted that the former derives from the Latin *conducere* (*com*/together + *ducere*/to lead) as its past participle and so can be understood as "having been led together," suggesting the further Buddhist gloss of "evident karmic connection." In this sense, conduct arises conditionally as mutual articulation or personal expression. Since "conduct" is also cognate with "conduce" and "conducive," we also can include within its connotational field helpfulness or contribution. Conduct is thus best seen as a *contributory or furthering relationship*. By contrast, "behavior" derives from the Middle English *be*/thoroughly + *have*/ to hold oneself and thus implies individuality rather than communality, possession rather than contribution, and a reflexive rather than radiating and appreciative concern—a concern which gathers and holds value rather than offering it.

All of this is implied by *hsing* 行, the Chinese term that has been rendered throughout our conversation as "conduct." Originally, *hsing* had the primary senses of walking or walkways and doing in the sense of working. Indeed, of the twenty or so most common terms incorporating the *hsing* radical, fully half have the meaning of a road, marketplace, or thoroughfare. In a largely nonvehicular society, walking connects us, establishing and maintaining in the most concrete and daily fashion our ongoing interrelation. No path or thoroughfare proceeds from wilderness or desert to more of the same, but only from family to family, from village to village. Our roads and the markets lining them are evidence of the diverse manners in which we are continually being led together, the unique ways in which we benefit and share with and in one another's labor.

Likewise, in its connotation of doing/working, *hsing* directs our attention toward endeavors in which simple materials are skillfully combined to bring about some new or qualitatively superior benefit. In working, we make use of things. But far from exhausting them, we increase their value, give them a new life, a new dimension of relationship and so meaning. At the same time, truly successful work requires that we maintain a focused and innovation-ready attention. And so while our labor augments the things we take up in working, the feedback loop established therein raises in turn not only the quality of our consciousness, but that of our communal narration, the lives we lead with and among others. Working is thus originally not a simple means to some material end, but a form of practice—an act of creative self-transformation.

In sum, we may say that *hsing* denotes the primordial expression of our mutual contribution or furthering. Not surprisingly, the secondary meanings of *hsing* include business or trade—meanings, it will be recalled, that are held in common with *yeh* or karma. Moreover, since *hsing* was also used as a translation of both *saṃskāra* (habitual dispositions) and *bhāvanā* (Buddhist practice), conduct in a Chinese Buddhist context does not refer to one particular type of being led together or karmic connection. Like the English "length," which entails both shortness and longness, the Chinese *hsing* entails the whole spectrum obtaining between binding relationships and those that are liberating. That is, the specific qualities of conduct are a function of orientation.

Thus understood, and contrary to the expectations of an Indian (or for that matter a typical European) listener, it is not some interior essence or spirit substance but conduct itself to which Hui-neng directs us in his insistence that we look into our own original nature (*pen hsing*) and become buddhas (PS 2). At times, conduct spawns 'sentient beings' with all their selfish conflicts and humanitarian attempts at agreement, all their fervently held conventions and their covert transgressions of them, their search for certainty and their forceful attempts at creating an abiding, unifying order. At other times, conduct reveals the flowering of incomparable buddha-lands, the furthering of the bodhisattva life, the virtuosic improvisation of horizonless intimacy. In the former, we find ourselves considered by and considering others to be essentially disparate 'individuals,' each immersed in the deeply private and differentiating 'worlds' of our concern. In the latter, we open to participation in the field-like generosity of authentic personhood, in the true suchness (*chen ju* 真如) of unhindered and unhesitating enlightenment.

In keeping with the vocabulary being developed over the course of our conversation, conduct is best seen simply as narrative movement—as the always ongoing, nonlocalized reorganization of an entire world as such. Conduct thus neither refers to nor ultimately depends on what is psychological or subjective—our likes and dislikes, experiences, intentions, and so on. Indeed, experience should not be seen as the necessary prelude to conduct, but rather as what is culled from it by the discriminating functions of the six senses. At the same time, conduct is not something purely objective—the states of our bodies, our environment, and their interaction—from which we as independent observers can deduce the nature of reality. Instead, conduct should be seen as what remains when the discriminating standpoints from which subject and object may determined have been entirely eschewed—in short, as the realized meaning of karma.

Now, it is not easy to accept—even as an intellectual premise—that what we truly are, our original nature (*pen hsing*—literally, "root disposition"), is narrative movement, the ramifying of stories. Because we can and typically do identify and describe ourselves as bodies, as intending subjects, as egos, or as members of various communities, we assume that there *is* something about which all these identities are centered that makes them 'mine' or 'me.' Whether this 'something' is conceived of as substantial or not in no way alters fact that as soon as we take the problem of who we are to be synonymous with the problem of personal identity, we are committed to the differentiation of a central ego and a periphery of one or more others. My states of consciousness, my desires and emotions, my bodily states, and my relationships with family and friends are all constitutive of who *I am* only because they are in some way gathered together as *mine*. The ultimate basis of this gathering may perhaps remain a mystery, just like the gathering of the stars and planets in the night sky, but that all of what I identify as me or mine revolves around some center is manifestly evident. Or so our day-to-day experience tells us. As long as we remain sane, we do not become scattered into a plurality or suddenly identify ourselves as or even with our friends or neighbors. Accepting the possibility that we are at root the orientation of a story or narration is for most of us—given our cultural, religious, scientific and experiential biases—tantamount to entering a kind of acidic cloud of unknowing in which our hard-won sense of self would be relentlessly dissolved.

As an experienced 'fact,' the difference of self and other is as manifestly incontestable as the difference between sunrise and sunset or the 'fact' that the sun moves around the earth. For better or worse, and for all its naturalness, it is also just as much a function of point of view. As long as we are confined to the surface of the earth, we cannot but see the sun as rising and setting. We cannot but view dawn and dusk as temporally and spatially discrete events. And yet, once we attain a sufficiently high perspective (though by no means a Nagelian view from nowhere), it is possible to see–all our ordinary experience to the contrary–that sunrise and sunset form a single golden ring wedding the dark and light sides of the planet. Dawn and dusk are inseparable.[5]

Likewise for 'self' and 'other.' The assumption that a person should be identified as a central gathering of—to use J. Mohanty's felicitous phrase—various "layers of selfhood" is, at bottom, no more justified than the long-held belief that the earth is at the center of the universe. To extend the analogy, the Buddhist claim that persons are both temporally and spatially indeterminate, amounts to a Copernican revolution of the self whereby it is seen that not only is the experienced centrality of our place in the world without any ultimate ontological basis, the gathering with which we identify our selves is actually a learned process of simply divorcing that over which 'I' cannot exercise *direct* control. Thus, just as Copernicus exploded the determinate centrality of the earth in the heavens and helped eventuate the realization that there is in fact *no center* of the universe, a consistently Buddhist view of personhood exhorts us to relinquish our hold on our selves as the focus of all that we experience.[6] As will be argued later, this amounts to nothing other than undertaking the practice of emptiness, a practice which eventuates an evolution away from conceiving of enlightenment as a change of the status of a given individual by means of which the "world" is left behind to seeing it as personal transformation—the realization of the Pure Land, the birth of an entirely unprecedented buddha-realm.

Improvisation and Regulation: The Paradigmatic Modes of Narrative Movement

Values establish meaning. That is, in a karmically ordered universe, it is our intentions, the vectors of our desire that disambiguate, that determine the intensity and orientation of our narration. For the purpose of our conversation, this biasing of conduct is most usefully seen in terms of a polarization on the one hand toward security, control, and closure, and on the other toward vulnerability, spontaneity, and openness—what we have been referring to as the "societal" and the "social." Biased societally, conduct establishes, maintains, or undermines universally adhered-to structures of regulated behavior with the aim of realizing agreement. Institutions— whether formal ones like marriage or informal ones like the conventions regulating business negotiation—originate in societality. Likewise for appeals to the necessity of law and obedience, the adoption of fixed principles of behavior, and the celebration of absolute or eternal order.

In sharp contrast, conduct which is biased socially establishes, maintains, or undermines the joint improvisation of our narration with an aim toward continuously realized harmony. Here, there is a marked absence of the preordained and an effort to insure the continued viability of our uniqueness. Instead of the at once individuating and homogenizing disposition of societality, sociality accentuates our interpenetration while at the same time disallowing our reduction to some universalizing sameness or identity. If the societal marks a bias toward institution, sociality marks our inclination toward adventuring—whether in the reaches of uncharted mountains or seas, or in the infinitely rich worlds of erotic involvement.

Oriented societally, our relations with others appear to be extrinsic in nature and communication is almost invariably understood as a successful transfer of information in the context of discourse—literally, the "flowing-apart" of those present, their identity-fixing articulation as distinct individuals or 'selves'. Socially oriented, our relations are understood as profoundly intrinsic, a dancing interpenetration, and communication as a resonance in the context of realized concourse—not, that is, as a process of exchange or influence, but one of "flowing-together" in creative integration.

Embracing the dramatic indeterminacy of personal subsistence and hence the primacy of conduct necessarily and radically transforms our understanding of what it means to live in community and so what is involved in working toward resolving society's ills—the most obviously shared level of our suffering. For example, when our conduct is oriented societally and persons are taken to be autonomously embodied individuals, each with their own private feelings, impulses, perceptions, desires, and conceptual perspectives, the vast majority of social problems are easily and with heavy intellectual warrant traced to one or another conflict of individual and collective interests. At the crudest level of description, these ills are naturally taken as correctable only through the imposition of some behavior-modifying structure to which all members of a society are equally and continuously subject. Being social in this sense often entails a sense of conforming, of sacrificing one's personal inclinations for the realization of aims more generally held valid. The so-called "socialization" which occurs over the course of our development from infancy through childhood, adolescence, and adulthood is thus typically described as a gradual supplanting of our originally selfish values or goods with those better suited to the smooth realization of aims held by all members of our society, albeit often in only the most generic sense. That is, we learn to regulate our feelings and impulses, eventually the very nature of our awareness, in order to "fit in"—insuring thereby the agreement or congruence of our behavior with more or less universally maintained standards.

Under such an evaluative aegis, when societys ills are consciously confronted, solutions are often imagined as resulting from their subjection to some calculus weighing individual versus collective goods or values. But because the "voices" of the individual and the collective are so different, because the grammars of their desires or goods are so disparate, negotiations seldom conclude for long, and for the most part the debates swing restlessly between the anarchic and totalitarian, the utterly natural and the thoroughly contrived, from spontaneous creativity to the necessity of measured unfreedom. In general, the belief is that the grafting of individual and collective interests will remain viable only in the presence of law and the strict definition of rights to which each and all are entitled. The underlying metaphor is thus almost always that of possession—who gets what when? what do we have the right to enjoy? what individual ends must be forfeited for the good of all?

Such a calculative understanding of "being social" is deeply at odds with the direction suggested by our articulation of Chinese Buddhist personhood. To reiterate, if persons are the ceaselessly dynamic interrelation of all of a story's characters and actions into a recursively structured and constantly evolving whole, they cannot be held to be located at or identified with any particular form, place or time. Persons are not located *in* narratives. They are not *a* character, but rather all the characters, all the actions, all the places and events which occur as what we refer to as "the world." Insofar as our karma sets the overall topology of our ongoing experience, there is nothing that we are not responsible for, nothing which we can point to and say—"that is not me."[7] As narration, our distinction of 'inside' and 'outside' is purely dramatic. In actuality, there is *no* outside, and the only complete answer to the question "who am I?" does not entail our being opposed to or separated from others, but is simply everything that has and is coming about.[8]

Asking about the relative value or merit of our individual and collective needs and desires is already evidence that we are living as if none of this were so. In short, weighing the individual versus the collective by way of some altruistic calculus is possible only when the self is construed as essentially autonomous and communality held to emerge only as the fruit of our submission to some form of regulation and institution. If we accept such a view of personhood, it follows that the metaphor of possession is workable, perhaps inevitable. Living in community is then always and unavoidably a forfeiture of some individual possibilities or freedoms, some curtailment of our essential and expressive being. But if not, if we live instead as if the narrative model of personhood were indeed the most true, the question of having or not-having proves profoundly inappropriate for negotiating solutions to conflict. It is perhaps not merely a felicitous irony that the Chinese translation of the Buddha's declared refusal to take a stand on either 'is' (*sat*) or 'is-not' (*asat*) literally means not indulging in either 'having' (*yu* 有) or 'not-having' (*wu* 無).

As long as persons are seen as narration, there are no basic social units according to which we can define (or set limits to) sociality. Granted the impossibility of standing outside of our narration to objectify it or its contents, it is not even clear in what sense it is legitimate to even ask what sociality *is*. If we are asking, "What sort of a thing is sociality? what objective state of affairs does it correspond to?," we apparently commit the very error Bourdieu warned against—in identifying ourselves as a narrator objectively studying/describing the social sphere, we project into it the principles of our (wholly artificial) relationship to it. If we refrain from removing ourselves to the position of outside-standers, it would seem that sociality cannot be defined in terms of its being 'this' or 'that' since it ceases to be a destination or state of affairs we arrive at and achieve closure with respect to in the course of our inquiry. If anything, it should be seen simply as a liberating and yet profoundly intimating direction taken by our mutual articulation or concourse. In terms that we shall later endeavor rendering as clear as possible, sociality is in a very real sense conduct that is unprecedented or *wu-wei*.

The Disparity of Suffering: Interrupting the Social and the Societal

For the Chinese and especially the Ch'an Buddhist, what is actually given are not others arrayed about a real and central self, but—if anything—interpersonality. Given, then, is the interpenetration and continual reorienting of narratives which (being recursively articulated) are incomplete and thus not purely or intrinsically subjective, and which (because they emerge only between the twin horizons of birth and death) we can never stand outside of in order to wholly objectify as 'things' (*dharmas*).[9] In other words, what is given is the normally excluded and inherently dynamic middle between the individual and collective—what we have been referring to as *conduct* or the movement of our narration as a whole.[10]

Whereas sociality consists of being open to the challenges of other narratives and involves a commitment to responding to those challenges in a spontaneous—that is, nonhabitual—fashion, societality consists of the attempt to forestall such challenges and to appeal to regular and essentially reactive forms of behavior, the efficacy of which is a function of their ideal independence from the unique concerns of any given person's life-story. Thus, the societal is concerned with enduring institutions in the context of which both ourselves and others are seen as abstract or generic individuals. Insofar as the political institutions of the United States are concerned, we are each citizens not because I am Peter and you are Kathy, but because—like some 200 million other citizens—we were born in one of the fifty states. Our relations with others are thus extrinsic in the sense that who we are is not a direct function of the presence or absence of particular persons with complete and unique life-histories, but rather of wholly interchangeable others. What is paramount is not the persons we encounter, but how people are placed with respect to us in the institutions guiding our behavior.

In this sense, the societal has much in common with both Bourdieu's habitus and Durkheim's collective, being an orientation toward customs or traditions which disregard the uniqueness of each of us as persons and tend to bring about an awareness of our being "a people".[11] Insofar as the social is concerned with direct and unrepeatable encounters with other persons as irreplaceable characters in open-ended improvisation, it tends to eventuate a transgression of all predetermined roles and to encourage a steady irruption of the unexpected.[12]

Recalling that we defined suffering above as the unexpected interruption of a given narrative, it follows that the precise nature of any instance of suffering depends on whether it arises in the context of conduct (narrative movement) that is social or societal. For example, by virtue of its valorization of the unprecedented, sociality involves an openness to or cultivation of vulnerability.[13] It is arguable, then, that conduct oriented socially is prone to the occurrence of the unprecedented and so to interruption or suffering. However, since the concrete form of this openness is an orientation toward improvised conduct, sociality includes within itself the means of ending suffering, of creatively integrating the disruption into the ongoing flow of our narration. That is, while sociality indeed increases the likelihood of the unexpected coursing through our narration, it also raises the probability that this will augment rather than obstruct its movement.

But, insofar as the social and societal have both been defined in terms of orientations toward establishing, maintaining, or undermining various forms of conduct, it is clear that sociality alone is no guarantee of the ending of any given crisis or incidence of suffering. Conducting oneself socially can, that is, as well undermine as cultivate improvised responses to others. And to the extent that this is the case it should be seen as performing a regulative function, of acting as a brake on uncontrolled innovation. If such conduct is persisted in, our overall orientation undergoes a kind of inversion, swinging around to a more and more markedly societal heading, and we find ourselves bringing about increasingly habitual forms of conduct, viewing both self and other in an increasingly universal or generic light. Eventually, we will exit the interpersonal as such and leave ourselves closed to challenge. Where this closure is particularly strong, as in catatonics and certain forms of paranoid or schizophrenic encapsulization, there is neither the possibility of new crises arising nor the means for resolving those already embodied in the world of our narration. Thus, while societality tends to decrease the likelihood of suffering by decreasing our vulnerability, it at the same time decreases our ability to resolve crises or end suffering by encouraging increased inflexibility—fostering the often obsessive preservation of dispositions and material conditions which we have found to be productive of experienced equilibrium.[14]

To summarize, societality marks an orientation toward the regulated agreement or coexistence of our self and others, while sociality marks an orientation toward the improvised interpenetration or integration of persons or life-narratives. In more concrete terms, what this means is that in the societal, others are experienced largely if not entirely through the roles they play—admittedly with greater or lesser aplomb. The typical office party is in this sense predominantly a societal and not a social gathering. In fact, our interactions with grocery clerks, banktellers, lawyers, doctors, teachers, and (sadly enough) even our friends and family are often entirely mediate or societal in nature. When roles are dropped or (as is more often the case) shattered, we generally experience others in an entirely novel light. They come alive, have unanticipated histories, dreams, interests, or depths which can either entrance or threaten us, but which cannot leave us unmoved, unchanged. Even when societality is aimed at undermining a given society's institutions—as, for example, in a Marxist revolution, a feminist rejection of patriarchal practices, or an adolescent's ubiquitous attempt to challenge authority—others are seen as *people*, not as persons in the full narrative sense. Others are capitalists or workers, women or men, teenagers or adults, us or them. Our path and theirs may run parallel or intersect—often violently—but they are never the same.

The contrary is true of sociality. In that the social implies a radical openness to others as "co-authors" of our story—of ourselves as persons—our path and theirs are related intrinsically in the sense that we are characters in a shared narration. In its most intensely realized form, this involves the recognition that 'you' and 'I' are in actuality aspects or expressions of the same person.[15]

In any typical span of time our conduct can be seen as either shifting from the societal to the social and back again—often with such speed and fluidity that we are unaware of the reorientations until long after the fact—or as an ultimately amorphous alloy of the two. Because of this, we are in a very real sense often living in more than a single world. But since establishing or maintaining sociality requires more of us, more attention and energy, we as often as not tend to dwell in the societal, relying on habitual and hence efficient forms of behavior and resting content with institutionally defined relations with others. Resisting this, we at least initially experience an increase of uncertainty, an instability resulting from the stream of our narration flowing into and being entered by that of another. In this confluence, a great increase of energy manifests. What had seemed impossible or unimaginable no longer is so. What seemed fixed and settled dissolves. To extend the metaphor, the stream emerging from this confluence may be much wider or cut a much deeper channel than its predecessors. It may throw itself over previously unseen precipices or wend an entirely new path across familiar terrain. Either way, we are profoundly and irreversibly transformed.

Chapter 4

Communicative Conduct:
The Paradigmatic Locus of Ch'an Enlightenment

We are now at a point where it is possible to say in a preliminary fashion what it means to see Ch'an enlightenment as fundamentally social. Very briefly, an enlightenment which is social cannot be reduced to a privately realized state of consciousness, but should be seen as a qualitatively unique *way of conducting ourselves* in the narrative space of interpersonality. Insofar as sociality is an orientation of conduct toward the improvised interpenetration or integration of previously disparate life-narratives, the arising or awakening of Ch'an enlightenment can be seen as the meaning of continuously relinquishing those horizons by means of which we identify and differentiate ourselves from others: the always ongoing realization of unprecedented harmony with others.

Enlightening Communication:
The Socialization of Buddhist Pedagogy

Granted this, it is not surprising that among the most notorious features of Ch'an Buddhism and its later Korean and Japanese progeny are their virtual canonization of recorded encounters between master and student. Indeed, of the enlightenment stories collected together in the various anthologies of Ch'an biographies, the majority of them pivot on a crucial, crisis-resolving communicative encounter. That is, enlightenment most frequently manifests not while sitting alone in the forest or meditation hall, but while conversing—in the interview room, in front of the assembly in the dharma hall, in the kitchen, on the dirt path leading to the monastery's fields—anywhere that master and student enter unpredictable and lively relation with one another. In short, Ch'an enlightenment is characteristically realized in the unprecedented conduct—the spontaneous leading together—of student and master. Not coincidentally, this conduct often involves such a dramatic release of tension that master and student find themselves bursting out in stomach-knotting fits of laughter and skeins of earthy, spring-like verse.

This differs markedly from the traditional narrative surrounding the Buddha's enlightenment—a narrative which accords rather well with the Indian disposition for seeing spiritual attainments as a concomitant (if not a result in part) of withdrawing from social interaction. Having forfeited his family life, his royal inheritance, his teachers, and finally even his fellow seekers of a solution to the riddle of life and suffering, the Buddha is said to have awakened in solitude, seemingly in perfect consonance with the Vedic and Upanishadic theme of an ascetically abstracted individual realizing the universal truth of Brahman. Also consistent with conventions dominant in India at the time of its compilation, the early canon represents the typical pedagogical situation as an essentially monologic dharma talk wherein the Buddha speaks to an assembly en masse. Where an individual does figure, he or she does so less as a partner in true conversation than as a foil for the Buddha's instruction-oriented questions and answers. Following the talk, students were ideally supposed to retreat into the forest much as the Buddha had done—for meditation and hopefully realization. When some insight does occur in the context of the talk, what is foregrounded is not a dynamic and mutually engaging conversive relationship, but some dawning realization that occurs as a result of listening.

Indeed, the standard opening for Indian Buddhist sutras—"Thus have I heard . . ."—should not be seen as a purely innocuous phrase appropriate within an originally oral tradition. To the contrary, it reflects as well the historically prevalent Indian belief that one of the primary and most reliable sources of knowledge is hearing—in particular, hearing the disquisitions of an authority. That is, such an opening announces an implicit affiliation with an epistemology founded both on the possibility of objectivity, of absolute and not merely conditional truths, and the conviction that such truths can be conveyed from the interiority of one being to that of another by way of some intervening medium. That is, knowledge is construed in terms that emerge from and subsequently reinforce a prioritization of individual subjectivity or experience. By contrast, the traditional Chinese construal of knowledge focuses not on linguistically conveyable epistemic states (knowing-that) but on epistemic activities (knowing-to). Knowledge is not something *gained*, but *done*—the realization of appropriate conduct in the manifestly public space of interpersonality.[1]

What the *form* of the sutras collected as the early canon suggests is, then, a bias characteristic of the Indian context in which it developed—a bias toward seeing knowledge as something that can be possessed and transmitted and not as a relation which obtains only as mutual enactment.[2] The advent of the Ch'an anecdote marks a refusal to continue fostering the boundary logic of identity and difference—a logic implicit in any hierarchic pedagogy of transmission, any model of communication founded on the discriminating schism of those who speak and those who merely hear, those who assert and dispense and those who can only assent or negate, receive or reject. In place of such a literally discursive model of enlightening communication, Ch'an orients us toward what might be described as a choreo-poetic pedagogy of joint improvisation. Here, the "vertical" separation of master and student is seen strictly as the result of a projection of horizons, a making of boundaries where in fact none originally obtain. It is in the spirit of such a realization that Lin-chi—while valorizing the "true man of no rank"—insists that whenever we meet 'buddhas' or 'patriarchs' we should kill them. In short, the pedagogical process in Ch'an cannot legitimately be conceived in terms of the conveyance of some lasting and objective insight across boundaries and distances assumed to be equally objective. Instead, it must be seen as consisting precisely of our mutually relinquishing all such horizons—what we shall refer to henceforth as enlightening concourse.

This, it would seem, should be seen as the underlying significance of Hui-neng's refusal to hand down his robe and bowl to some chosen disciple. To be sure, the ritual inculcates a belief in the substantial difference between the enlightened and the unenlightened and wrongly implies that enlightenment means getting something, acquiring some status, some insight. Hui-neng's refusal is in part, then, consistent with the central iconoclasm of the *Heart Sutra*: there is no attainment and nothing to attain. But it also marks a watershed in how Buddhism articulates the relationship between communication and enlightenment. In effect, Hui-neng is indicating that we must resist both the metaphor of transmission and the subjectivity in which it necessarily shrouds awakening. In a sense that we will be exploring below, enlightening communication ceases to be understood as a process of dissemination, and becomes instead one of crisis-resolving harmonization.

And so, while the dharma talk remained a feature of the life of the Chinese Buddhist, a transition gradually took place from it being a paradigm of the enlightening communication of master and student to being a mere context for it. That is, while the one-many distinction remained as a frequent context—one master and many students in a public forum—the focus shifted away from the talk as such to the intimate, disparity-dissolving encounter of the master and a single student. When this communicative encounter is wholly successful, even the "one-on-one" focus dissolves. Then, it no longer makes sense to think of the master's role as involving a kind of spiritual largesse and the student's as entailing mere receptivity. To the contrary, the intentions underlying such a discourse—or "flowing apart"—are precisely what must be forfeited if our readiness to awaken (*tun wu* 頓悟, or what is typically translated "sudden enlightenment") can manifest fully, without either precedent or reservation.

In terms of the distinction made earlier between the social and societal as orientations of conduct, this shift is one away from the insight-bestowing and behavior-modifying model of the lecture and its implied societality to the improvisation-encouraging embrace of the nondifferentiation of the student and all the buddhas and patriarchs. Thus, when Lin-chi leaps down from the dais and stands glaring into the eyes of a student bold enough to engage in dharma combat, demanding that the latter Speak! Speak!, any hesitation on the student's behalf signals a loss—of both the battle with Lin-chi and any chance for realizing enlightenment. Firmly entrenched in his or her role as 'student,' and so forcing the relationship in the direction of discourse, the student is shoved away with distaste—not because of any inherent lack, but because of his or her hesitation and its implied consideration of precedents for behavior. In short, the failure to engage Lin-chi in unrestrained sociality or improvised conduct forces each of them apart into an imprisoning regularity fraught with all the liabilities for suffering that arise whenever our narration is subordinated to the decision of what is 'self' and what is 'other.'

Disentangling Language and the Meaning of the Buddha Dharma

One of the ramifications of this reorientation of the pedagogical situation is that it cannot be presumed unproblematic for us to analyze the communicative encounter of master and student as if the words they exchange either contain or convey some key for disclosing the meaning of their relationship. Doing so actually imports an entirely foreign set of concerns and values based on a view of communication as implying a successful transference (of information, intention, insight, and so on). To the contrary, in much the same way that the Buddha is said to have taught the dharma for the relinquishing of *all* views and not merely some (presumably false, flawed or simply useless) views, Ch'an insists with great vehemence and at great length that it is a narration (*chuan* 轉—often mistranslated as "transmission") beyond words and cultural forms. That is, Ch'an does not bracket off its own linguistic expressions as in some way privileged. It functions not only beyond *some* linguistic and cultural forms, but beyond all speaking and listening, all exchange of gestures and conveyance.

But if this is so, if it is not the master's and student's words that are ultimately relevant, where does the meaning of their involvement with one another lie? Where do we—or the contemporary student of Ch'an (Zen) for that matter—appeal in an effort to open up the meaning of enlightening communication? The short answer to both questions is conduct. The long answer is phrased as succinctly as possible by Pai-chang Huai-hai in his response to a student asking him the meaning of a difficult passage in the sutras. "Take up words in order to manifest meaning and you'll obtain 'meaning.' Cut off words and meaning is emptiness. Emptiness is the Tao. The Tao is cutting off words and speech" (HTC 119.423c).

In interpreting this passage, it is first of all essential that we appreciate the rich polysemy of the term "tao." In general, the term functions both as a noun—in the sense of a path, a way, a manner, a method, and as a verb—in the sense of blazing a trail, proceeding in a certain way. In Chinese Buddhism, Tao is also used to denote both the Buddhist Path or Way (Skrt *mārga*) and the fruit resulting from its practice. That is, Tao connotes both the Noble Eightfold Path and the enlightenment which it allows to be realized.

In saying that meaning is emptiness and that emptiness is itself the Tao, Pai-chang is effectively defining meaning as practice. It is not something obtained. Nor is it something contained—inherent to some verbal formulation or pattern of thought. Rather, meaning must be seen as a virtuosic *response*, something given in conduct. In order to begin fully appreciating the subtlety of this definition, it is crucial that we come to an at least rudimentary understanding of the role of emptiness (*śūnyatā*) in the Buddhist tradition. Insofar as Pai-chang's suggestion that emptiness is the Tao is an allusion to one of the key phrases in Nagarjuna's *Mūlamadhyamakakārikā*, it is to that work that we must temporarily divert.

Nagarjuna defines emptiness as the relinquishing of all views (*dṛṣti*) (MK 13.8), in the context of which there are no horizons for relevance and, hence, for inquiry and integration (MK 24.14).[3] Emptiness, he claims, is not a substance, the transcendental ground of being, a void out of which all things come. Rather it is dependent origination itself. It is the Middle Path—the way between declarations of 'is' and 'is-not' to the resolution of all crisis, the end of suffering (*duḥkha*).

In the Buddhist tradition, the term "views" is variously used in a manner equivalent to our own "standpoints," "theories," "interpretations," or "opinions," and in general denotes a conceptual or verbal expression of and/or perspective on the way things are or have come to be. Views are conceptually mediated, mental constructs about the perceived—constructs which inevitably distort not so much the way things are (since in Buddhism the ontological status of being is denied) but rather our ways of conducting ourselves toward and among them. Thus, the *Aṭṭakavagga*—one of the oldest Buddhist texts—states that, "The wise one . . . has got rid of the three poisons (ignorance, hatred, and greed) and he does not enter the mud of conceptual thinking" (Sn 535). So thorough is the Buddhist critique of the structure (and not merely the content) of having views that even the Buddha's teachings (*samma-dṛṣti*) are likened to a raft which must be discarded once it has served its purpose.

According to the early tradition, views are seen as deriving from a commitment to opposite-thinking, the tendency to see things in terms of basic dichotomies of which is/is-not is the most virulent. Confusion and ignorance arise on the basis of the sedimentation of these distinctions/identifications—what in early Buddhism are referred to as *samskāras*, habituating impulses or dispositions (with respect to speaking, thinking, and acting).

It is hardly surprising, then, that Nagarjuna claims that, "When ignorance ceases, there is no occurrence of dispositions." What is of paramount importance for understanding the operation of a consistently Buddhist hermeneutical system is that Nagarjuna immediately goes on to remark that "the cessation of that ignorance takes place as a result of the practice (*bhāvanā*) of that [nonoccurrence] through wisdom" (MK 26.11). This *practice* of the nonoccurrence of dispositions is nothing other than the ongoing process of relinquishing of all discriminating boundaries as they arise—in short, the practice of emptiness. To view things discriminatively—that is, under the rubric of discourse and not concourse—is to set limits or horizons for relevance, to disregard some level of the interdependence of all things and therefore to circumscribe a range of possible and acceptable responses to what has been discriminated. In the context of Buddhist metaphysics, the only consistent notion of being—the determination of 'what is'—amounts to such a projection of horizons for relevance, a setting of limits to inquiry or horizons for explication. When such limits become fixed, action (*karma*) is said to be defiled or productive of ill; a situation correctable only through practice (MK 17.15).

As Pai-chang's association of emptiness and cutting off words and speech makes clear, the root cause of this fixation is to be found in discourse—in that "flowing apart" by means of which 'this' and 'that,' 'self' and 'other' are abstracted from the living flux of interdependence and frozen into self-identical, enduring entities. With the invention of such entities (*dharmas*), we experience a transformation (and often a narrowing) of the scope of our improvisations—on the one hand a reduction of understanding to what can be (monothetically) grasped, and on the other hand a channeling of our conduct along lines dictated by the divisions we have made. And just as the transition from hand tools to power tools marked a general shift away from finished character as the primary criterion for excellence in the building trades to quantity or speed of production, the invention of a new vocabulary—of a new or more highly refined set of distinctions—always brings about a new way of communal life, the establishment of a new set of conventions.[4]

That language is conventional in nature and that no word or words have an intrinsic correspondence with an independent reality is crucial to the complexion of Buddhist hermeneutics. In fact, there is not one, but three terms repeatedly used in canonical discussions of language that are typically translated by the English "convention": *saṃvṛtti, prajñapti,* and *vyavahāra.* All three words refer specifically to forms of conduct (including in Buddhism mental and verbal activity) which originate in the concrete ways in which members of a given community come to interact in a coordinated fashion. In this sense, conventions do not necessarily and certainly do not primarily depend on any sort of conscious, conceptually mediated agreement. Rather, they are "institutionalized" or public strategies for coping with forces (both internal and external) tending toward the disruption of the community. Language can be seen, then, as embodying what might be referred to as cultural *saṃskāra*—dispositions to act habitually or impulsively—and the injunction to "cut off words" understood as a call to move beyond merely reacting on the basis of our dispositions and instead to fully and sensitively respond to the situation in which we find ourselves. In the Ch'an tradition, this is encapsulated in the phrase, *sui shih, ying yung* 遂事應用: "according with the situation, responding as needed." True understanding—the practice of wisdom (*prajñā*)—far from involving the grasp of abiding standards or justified beliefs, therefore entails stepping outside of the circle of the linguistic in order to once again participate fully and immediately in the world-creating vitality of concursive improvisation.

It is only in light of such an understanding of the role of language that it is possible to appreciate the Ch'an master Ma-tzu's insistence that his students neither record nor remember any of his talks:

> Even if I were to explain as many principles of the attainment of the Tao as there are grains of sand in a river, your minds would still not be augmented in the least. . . . Even if you talk about the Tathagata's expedient teachings for as many eons as there are grains of sand in the Ganges, you'd still never complete your explanations and they would be like unsevered barbs and chains. (TTC 45.406c)

The meaning of the teachings is not a function of language, but of one's own conduct. Hence the adamant assertion in Ch'an that a master has nothing to transmit to his/her students. The point of their teachings was not to inculcate a form of thinking or point out a direction for thought, but to bring about a resonance or coordination of conduct between master (the enlightened person) and student. In short, meaning is not—as it is in the western hermeneutical tradition—a "direction of thought," but rather a change in the vector of our conduct. It is the creative and yet skillfully appropriate response to a partner in concourse.[5]

If knowledge and meaning are construed along such lines, the aim of hermeneutics is best seen as the cultivation of an ever-increasing sensitivity and flexibility in our responses to others—whether human or not—and the challenges they present for our narration. Far from marking the closure of the hermeneutic circle, understanding cannot amount to an act of appropriation or taking possession, but rather consists in the enactment of integration through letting go—the practice of relinquishing.

But we naturally ask—if all this is so, what rationale is there for collecting verbal accounts of the master-student encounter? If, as Ma-tzu insists, recollecting words is actually a hindrance, what is the point of canonizing the banter of Ch'an master and student?

Nonduality as Enlightening Concourse

Of the many teachings of the Mahayana which were imported into China from the later Han dynasty onward, none came to enjoy either a wider or more profound currency than that of nonduality. Especially as appropriated by Ch'an, what nonduality means is not merely refraining from ontological commitment—from making determinate statements about the nature of things existing or not existing—but the virtuosic responsiveness of a bodhisattva who has realized the lack of any difference between samsara and nirvana, between his or her mind and that of the Buddha and all the patriarchs. The achievement of Ch'an nonduality, far from representing a mere eschewal of intellectual commitment to any identifiable 'this' or 'that'—the abstract apprehension of some universal sameness—signifies the lively birth of a buddha-world in which distances both spatial and temporal have become so relativized that they no longer act as barriers or even segregating horizons (*ching* 境). In short, it may be understood as the achievement of unlimited skill in means (*upāya*), unlimited virtuosity in improvising the liberation of all 'beings'. If the encounter of Ch'an master and student is of canonic importance, it is not because of *what* they say, but *how* they relate—because their conduct serves as a unique exemplification of realized nonduality.

Interestingly, the literature of the Hua-yen school—the theoretical counterpart of Ch'an—is luxuriant with descriptions of what we must refer to as instantaneous travel or influence, of macrocosms fitting comfortably in microcosms, of lands where even Mara—the nearest Buddhist equivalent to Satan—is found doing the buddha-work. Such 'miracles' indicate not only the incredibly fluid, expectation-defying nature or disposition (*hsing* 性) of the Mahayana Buddhist cosmos, but the remarkable extent to which the importance of location or perspective is maximally attenuated therein. On the one hand, this is only natural in a context where persons are not seen as individuals, but as narration. On the other hand, the deemphasis on location—on being advantageously or disadvantageously *placed*—is also a way of valorizing improvisation and hence sociality.

Crucially, Hua-yen's alliance of the impermanence and interpenetration of all things also very strongly orients us toward seeing the world as both originally ambiguous and profoundly surprising. That is, insofar as there are at no level any simple, autonomous existents and since any thing 'involves and is involved by' all things, no matter how stable or full of momentum the present worldconfiguration appears, this is merely a function of identifying with some point of view—of establishing perceptual and hence responsive horizons. Just as the relationships obtaining among all the events previously related in a story can be completely inverted or transformed with a particularly radical twist of plot, the Mahayana cosmos and the meaning of its occurrences can shift direction instantly and in ways that are entirely unanticipated. Change need not be serial—a matter of spreading influence—or cumulative, but can be realized immediately, throughout an entire world-configuration. Much as a shift in perceptual gestalt transforms the 'vase' into 'two women in conversation' without any line being redrawn or individually interpreted, in the Mahayana cosmos it is possible to 'move' instantly from samsara to nirvana, from the world of 'selves' and 'others' to a horizonless buddha-land.

It is not, then, that ambiguity is a function of our imperfect sensory or cognitive faculties. To the contrary, it is all certainty and definition that must ultimately be seen as contingent, as conventional or chosen. In this light, it is not coincidental that the initial awakening of the sixth patriarch, Hui-neng, occurred with his listening to a recitation of the *Diamond Sutra*, the philosophical crux of which we have already discussed in chapter 1. Liberation is not an escape from the world, but a relaxation of the boundary conditions projected for our supposed, individual existence—a relaxation which returns the world to its originally surprising fluidity, which makes it possible for an illiterate and fatherless peasant child to realize the absence of any difference between his mind and that of the buddhas and patriarchs.

It is arguable, in fact, that the unexpected has a curiously central role in the Chinese conception of order as an anarchic (literally principle-less) harmony. At least according to the *I Ching*—one of the Five Classics that informed the cultural persona of the Chinese for over two thousand years—it is precisely the unexpected that insures the interrelation of *all* world configurations. Thus, while the Indo-European tendency has been to associate order and precedent, predictability and universality, for the Chinese the opposite has generally been maintained. The creative integrity of the whole depends on and grows by virtue of changes which lack any linear, causal genealogy.[6] Seen in such a light, the fact that many of the most famous Ch'an anecdotes pivot on apparent non-sequiturs, on violations of both logic and etiquette, and even on such unprecedented acts as dismembering cats and severing fingers, may be understood as reflective of a thorough alliance of order and the unexpected, of harmony and improvisation. In a word, true harmony cannot occur in the absence of spontaneity.

Moreover, it must be appreciated that for the accomplished Chinese Buddhist, nonduality connoted a refusal to stand anywhere along the entire spectrum running from having (*yu*) to not-having (*wu*), from possessing to lacking, from holding-on or back to grasping-for. Rather than just refraining from making categorical statements about the nature of things and the world they constitute—the Indian dichotomy of *sat* (is) and *asat* (is-not), for example—nonduality entails opening in complete dissolution of the horizons segregating what is preferred and what is not, what is 'mine' and what is 'yours.' Only in this way is it at all possible to remove all hindrances to our readiness for awakening (*tun wu* 頓悟).

Granted this, Pai-chang's suggestion (HTC 119.442a) that enlightenment is nothing other than perfecting the path of offering or *dānapāramitā* is not merely a way of valorizing generosity or charity for solely moral purposes. To the contrary, it is a metaphysically cogent way of insisting that enlightenment means actively eschewing the demarcation of what is 'within' and what is 'without,' what is 'self' and what is 'other,' without falling into the trap of seeing this emptiness as a blank and insentient void.

It is not the case, then, that Pai-chang's declaration that the path of enlightenment is one of not making or selecting anything— of conduct that is *wu-wei* (HTC 119.425a)—implies a quietist restraint from all involvement with others and activity in the world. To the contrary, the indicated realization of nonduality must be understood as an orientation of conduct away from the restrictions

imposed by precedent and regulation and toward the improvisational virtuosity of unmitigated responsiveness. In such a light, Lin-
chi's insistence that we must kill 'the Buddha' if we meet 'him' on
the road is not witless iconoclasm, but a profoundly metaphysical
caution that any ostensibly objective difference signals a shattering
of nonduality, the projection of difference-making horizons and the
concomitant appearance of a virtual self—that central locus about
which all such horizons are manifestly arrayed.

Indeed, it is just such a reorientation which is expressed in both
Huang-po's teaching of *i-hsin* (one-mind) and Lin-chi's declaration
that realizing our buddha-nature is conducting ourselves as true
persons without any position or rank (*wei* 位). Most importantly for
our own conversation, it is only by fully appreciating the profoundly
metaphysical implications of this reorientation that Hui-neng's remark that "it is precisely Buddhist conduct/practice (*hsing* 行) that
is the Buddha" (PS 42) can be properly understood as requiring us to
see enlightenment as social in nature—the realization of a uniquely
variegated and unprecedented buddha-world—and not as a fundamentally private experience or state of consciousness. In this sense,
i-hsin does not refer to a realm of abstracted unity like that ostensibly proposed by the Upanishadic articulation of Brahman, but rather
a dramatically evolving world whose unity is not a function of
exclusive self-identity, but rather of harmoniously articulated concourse or flowing-together. *I-hsin* should not be seen, then, as a
practical reduction into the brilliant anonymity of universal existence, but as virtuosic communication—the centerlessly creative
narration of all things.

In summary, realized nonduality shifts communication away
from being seen as a function of the referential and typifying use of
language—a kind of transmission, toward playful coordination or
mutual realization. Taken seriously, *i-hsin* means at the very least
eschewing all hierarchy in communication. For this reason, the
model of verbal discourse seems ill-suited for understanding the
enlightening encounter of master and student, the culmination of
Ch'an practice. Discourse entails the separation of speaker and
listener, of teller and told. It may be that in conversation we exchange positions time and again, but at any given instant the ideal
is that one of us speaks and the other(s) listen. Communication is
seen as a serial process, a process that occurs over time through
transference or exchange. This promotes seeing what is communi-
cated as a kind of commodity, as something passed on or at least
back and forth. Applying such a prejudice to enlightenment forces

us to see it as a thing, an experience, an event, something limited enough to hand over or down. Even when the language used is the language of the body, the assumption is that the same canons hold true—communication is based on giving and receiving, on having and not-having.

But this is precisely what the Buddhist metaphysics of ambiguity denies. Communication in a truly interdependent world, a world of uninterrupted narration, cannot be reduced to discourse since the viability of the latter rests on the legitimacy of an appeal to some "bottom line" serving as a ground for our agreement or mutual assent. In the absence of such a ground, and under the assumption that 'self' and 'other' are actually and not merely projectively separate, all discursive attempts at communication would necessarily fail.

Discourse entails the maintenance of our difference as individuals involved in a process of exchange through the regulating institutions of a shared/common language and amounts to an always completeable project of making or getting a point. In sharp contrast, concourse not only tends to elide such differences, it eludes definition even where it playfully incorporates the prevailing conventions by means of which we typically regulate one another. Unlike discursive communication, concourse does not depend on the existence of a typifying medium. Instead, it should be seen as arising only with the relinquishing of all media. The Mahayanic emphasis on *upāya* or skillful means, far from being a recognition of the ultimate and independent value of the certitude provided by our conventions, actually celebrates their employment as a pivot—not as the point of conversation, but as relatively fixed opportunities for us to turn together in unhesitating improvisation.

Improvisation as Communicative Paradigm

In sharp contrast with a group of people subject to the segregating constraints of discourse, the participants in frcc improvisation—the members, say, of the Grateful Dead or Ornette Coleman's Double Quartet—are all simultaneously composing and listening.[7] Regardless of whether the musicians involved all start playing at once or if one of them offers an initial note, chord, or rhythmic figure, it is never the case that any of them are trying to make a statement, to exteriorize something they want to "get across" to all the others. Nor are they simply playing or producing variations on a preordained theme. Instead, it is always the communally realized temperament of the music—its "feel"—that both evokes their performance and embodies the meaning of what they play.

A communally improvised piece of music like the Double Quartet's "Free Jazz" does not propose anything about the world or even about the states of the musicians' minds. Playing together, the eight musicians create a new world, a jointly performed tale in which each of them is continually becoming someone else, someone who is neither identical to nor different from all the other characters in play. Drummers and bass players do not play off of one another as individual sources of raw musical material so much as they hear themselves and are heard as a throbbing musical heart that both drives and is driven by all the horn and piano players. Whenever a solo appears, it is not conceived and then executed in seriality, but courses through the musician and his instrument, flowing from that unlocated, unlocateable source of the unexpected lying outside of every horizon, every name and form.

This flow comes about when the musician stops checking, when he stops figuring out what to play and abandons the projection of the known, the hunger for closure, for sense. Then a 'miracle' occurs—the flying sinuosity of a completely unpremeditated and yet beautifully dovetailing saxophone or trumpet solo. At such moments, we are not making music, but are being continuously remade, reborn by it. Losing our boundaries, slipping into the incandescent concourse which is the essence of musical improvisation, we no longer anticipate or follow our fellow musicians but are released into an unmitigated oneness in which anything can occur even though absolutely nothing is lacking. There is no deliberation, no calculation—only the singing we have become in the total absence of any 'song.'

The aim of improvisation is not to negotiate or regulate an agreement about how things are, but rather the creation of a novel harmony through jointly articulating a new world—be it musical, poetic, choreographic, or erotic. The words, notes, gestures, or play of sensations that we use in improvising are, in fact, of no *lasting*, individual importance. Nor is it the case that we improvise in order to get somewhere, to arrive at some predetermined end by whatever means possible. Falling prey to such a disposition is in Buddhist terms to turn into a hell the very 'other shore' toward which we move with the help of the raft of the Buddha's teachings. Improvisation is concerned with opening up, here and now, no matter what the circumstances. In Buddhist terms this means making use of our karma rather than indulging our entanglement in the often beguiling trap of destiny.

Where the concourse of musical improvisation is taken as paradigmatic, the aim of communication cannot—as it is in verbal discourse—be taken to be reaching final agreement, but is seen instead as the unceasing realization of harmony. Whereas agreements are mediated by universally assented to and propositionally structured concepts and amount to the end result obtained by means of a more or less complex process of calculation, harmony in the sense used here is to be seen as an immediate quality of our ongoing responses or conduct—the vibrantly unpredictable tenor of improvisationally realized interpersonality. In short, while the meaning of discursive communication amounts to *what we agree on* and can indeed be articulated in advance as a goal, meaning in concursive communication is seen as *how we harmonize*, in the absence of any predetermined destination or itinerary.

In the former, our focus is on some typified expression of individual concerns—something each of us has or possesses. Meaning in this sense is grasped and participates in the maintenance of our difference as independent subjects engaged in the discussion of some object. What discussion accomplishes is the translation of some unique aspect of our world into a typified object which then flows apart and (in the ideal case) perfectly equally into each of our ostensibly separate streams of consciousness. What we discuss becomes something each of us manages to possess through a kind of cloning or virtualization that allows it to be divided among a potentially infinite number of knowers, each of whom can claim it as their own. And so, while calculatively disposed partners in communication may aim at agreeing with one another, this can only be accomplished by agreeing on or about some thing which serves not only to link them, but hold them inexorably apart.

By contrast, concursive meaning reveals itself in the manner in which our world grows. In this sense, meaning is never something transmitted from some definite 'here' to an equally defined 'there,' but should be seen as the quality of that recursion by means of which our narration extends and deepens its wholeness. Arising in the unmitigated flux of interdependence, concursive meaning is directly given in conduct—as *ours* and never as merely *mine* and/or *yours*. The participants in concursive communication are oriented not toward some mediating thing/idea/event or even toward one another.[8] Instead, and in language that is dissatisfying in its appeal to prepositionality, 'they' are taken up into their relationship in such a way that each 'one' ceases to exist. What remains can be referred to as "concourse," but in actuality it has—like enlightenment—no identifying marks. We may characterize it as "harmony" as opposed to "agreement," but that is just skillful means—a distinction which may be useful but is by no means absolute. That is, since existence is a function of envaluation, concourse cannot be a thing (*dharma*) or state arrived at and then maintained or lost, but should be seen as creative orientation, where creativity implies not making or inventing, but the realization of what we shall later refer to as intimacy, or boundless interpenetration (*t'ung* 通).[9]

Envision, for example, two strangers who meet on a dance floor. Where the orientation of their conduct is effectively discursive, each of them is essentially bound up in and by their thinking, their considerations of the other as 'dance partner,' 'potential lover,' 'fellow networker,' and so on. When their thinking is in agreement, these distinctions act as a kind of cement, binding them in a common definition of 'reality' even as they provide a useful and yet finally insurmountable interface. Such strangers are bound both in the sense of maintaining their contact as 'dancers' or 'lovers' or 'professional acquaintances' and of being thereby limited in the range and depth of their relationship and creativity. To the extent, however, that their conduct is concursive, there is no thinking and hence no impediment to the realization of an entirely new, untypified, and untypifiable relationship. In Ch'an terms, the realization of no-thinking (*wu-nien* 無念) is the entry into the bodhisattva life—the life of unhindered responsiveness, of unexcelled skill in means. Paraphrasing the *Heart Sutra*, in concourse there are no 'dancers,' no 'dance,' no 'dance-floor' or 'band.' Irrepressibly fluid, the dancing is at once unique and mythic or archetypal. No moves are anticipated even if they repeat, *mudra*-like, and yet none precipitate a break in the flow in the musical waving of which each 'dancer' is a part and each of whom are manifestly inconceivable apart form this swinging openness, this enjoyment of what will forever elude placement in any of the three times. Afterward, there may come doubts about where this is all heading and what to *do* next, but in the fullness of concursion there is neither from nor to, only an us depending on neither 'you' nor 'me,' 'her' or 'him.' And this is so even if the dancing is with 'death' and the partners are father and son in a hospital room.

None of this should, however, be taken as necessarily allying concourse and exclusively 'positive' moods, emotions, situations, or outcomes. Indeed, as the Ch'an indictment of monks who seek only peace and quietude strongly suggests, the exclusive imagination of enlightened life and communication in entirely 'positive' terms is hardly better than indulging in so-called negativity. Bias is a problem—perhaps *the core* problem—regardless of the content or quality it foregrounds. Thus, while the ideal of universal agreement—so prevalent in the Indo-European philosophical traditions—tends to involve our seeing discord as a sign of pathology, a difference to be eradicated, the ideal of harmony involves our respecting discord, seeing it as a sign of continued vitality. Since there is in fact no harmony as such where there is only a single tone, the harmony achieved through improvised concourse must be seen as a relation of interdependence. That is, the presence of 'discord' should be seen as nothing other than an opportunity to relinquish one or another impeding horizon and evolve new and ever more flexible ways of responding—a new character, something to be prized and not lamented.

And yet, it would be improper to understand the meaning of harmony in a Chinese Buddhist context as determined by the kind of note to note and essentially mathematical relationship underlying the European concept of musical harmony. In fact, the Chinese conception of harmony derives not from the abstract musings of a mathematically inclined musician, but from the hands-on practice of agrarian sagacity. The distinction can be fleshed out by considering that the graph translated as "harmony" (*ho* 和) is composed of the radical for "growing grain" (*ho* 禾) and the character for "mouth" (*k'ou* 口). To begin with, the choice of growing grain rather than harvested or edible grain (*mi* 米) prohibits our understanding harmony as a unilateral relationship under the general rubric of satisfaction or the momentary meeting of a need. The temporality proper to harmony is not the instantaneous one of paired notes or the filling of an empty belly, but rather a seasonal and hence cyclic timing—a temporality of ongoing and practical care or appreciation. Growing grain requires at one time and in one locale the draining of fields and at others steady irrigation. It entails attending not only to the ever-changing qualities of soil and sky, but of our coordination with the unseen, with the myriad aspects of the worldly Tao. Harmony is in this sense not a kind of individually negotiable ratio, but a truly global relationship—the dynamic wedding of plant and human communities in the context of mutual nurturance or furthering.

Thus, while a discursive understanding of communication would have us bias our efforts toward achieving certainty and self-consistently building upon that solid foundation, taking harmony as our guide orients us toward focusing on the entire narration of which each 'one' of us is but an abstraction. What is valued is not, then, an unremitting adherence to principles or to the kind of truth which admits of no actual plurality, but personal fluency—an ability to respond in virtuosic timeliness, free from both hesitation and any reference to set patterns or habits of conduct, be these perceptual, emotive, or active. Moreover, since the Chinese conception of harmony is quite literally communal and not abstract or ideal, communication can never be conceived hierarchically, as a transmission from 'me' to 'you' which connects us only by first establishing a power gradient. Instead, communication must be seen as irreducibly mutual appreciation or envaluation.

In short, if concursive meaning is always lived and never grasped, any systematic approach to attaining communicative virtuosity will involve the practice of relinquishing any horizons presently constraining our ability to caringly and creatively respond with change or challenge. In more properly Buddhist terms, communicative virtuosity should be seen as incomparable skill in ending suffering.[10]

Dangerous Intimations: Communication and the Place of Suffering

Now, if all this is true, it would seem that the Chinese and later Ch'an alliance of harmony and improvisation, of order and the unexpected, entails our recognizing and accepting as part of our methodology that communication is always a 'self'-endangering process. That is, whenever we enter into communication, we place our 'selves' deeply at risk. The term *fa ch'an* 法戰 or "dharma combat" provides us with a clue as to the risk-ladenness of the enlightening encounter of master and student. For a tradition ostensibly involved with helping people to attain peace—freedom from affliction and all forms of contrariety—the choice of such a martial term to designate the context of enlightenment cannot be accidental.

As in battle, when truly communicating with the master, a student stands in danger of losing the ability to maintain his or her previously chosen heading. Indeed, since the underlying bases of all our accustomed navigations—that is, our assumption of beginnings, of the reality of causes, of the objectivity of identity and difference, and so on—are not universal, everything familiar and comfortingly secure is in danger of being submerged, even eroded. Drawn into and immersed in the confluence of living sociality, the movement of our narrative is continually opening to interruption, to being forced to take an unexpected twist in order to remain viable. And in its most dramatic realization, this twist manifestly folds us into a kind of Mobius strip or Klein bottle so that inside and outside, 'self' and 'other,' even 'the Buddha' and all 'sentient beings' are longer experienced as self-identical and hence mutually differentiating, but in a very real sense as one-mind.

In keeping with our discussion of suffering in the first chapter, however, this necessarily entails our seeing communication—and therefore sociality—as the paradigmatic source or topos of suffering. Claiming that Ch'an enlightenment is social and that its realization occurs in communicative encounter is to say, then, that the place of suffering is not different from the place of enlightenment, that samsāra and the *bodhimandala* are one and the same. Indeed, Ch'an is nothing other than the attainment of this absence of identity and difference in our continuously present responding with "others."

Moreover, as hundreds of Ch'an anecdotes attest, the dangers of *fa ch'an* have never been merely abstract. Ear-splitting shouts and threats were commonplace and physical abuses of one sort or another were hardly rare. Nor, as we shall see when we turn more directly to the task of understanding the system of Ch'an practice and the unique role therein of the master-student partnership, should the relationship of master and student be seen as primarily formal or inherently hierarchic. That is, it is never just the student, but the master as well who is at risk. Stories abound in which Ch'an masters have not only been shouted at or struck by their students, but even had their legs run over with a cart full of vegetables as a challenge to their teachings about emptiness.

By bringing the danger of enlightening communication to the forefront with the use of so-called "shock tactics," Ch'an resolutely closes off the option of remaining aloof or disengaged. As the paradigm of all enlightening communication, the encounter of student and master reveals the necessity of dropping every pretense, every hope of security and safety if we are to truly awaken. This, of course, signals nothing short of our willingness to enter unrestricted intimacy with others, to forfeit all safe havens, all reservations. And yet, this is clearly not enough. Mere willingness to be placed at risk is like standing up in front of the assembly in response to Lin-chi's request for a challenger, a worthy opponent in dharma combat. Successful communication comes only when we can discard everything which separates us, everything which promotes our discourse. We must, in short be able to respond without any hesitation no matter what occurs, realizing in conduct the Ch'an injunction to "accord with the situation, respond as needed" (*sui-shih-ying-yung*). Discerning how this realization occurs—how, in other words, the sociality of Ch'an enlightenment is brought uninhibitedly into play—is nothing other than discerning the nature of Ch'an practice.

Part II

Practice: The Embodiment of Enlightenment

Chapter 5

Intimacy and Virtuosity:
Entering the Gate of Ch'an Practice

For most of us, the mention of practicing Ch'an conjures up a welter of images centered on the priority of meditation. We begin perhaps by envisioning a lone hermitage ringed by wind-blown pines, perched on the side of a mountain so lonely and remote that only wraithlike pieces of cloud wander its valleys. Within the thatched roof and stone walls of the hut, apparently unaware of the changing seasons and the daily advance of the sun, is a man or woman, head shaved and dressed in gray or saffron-colored robes. Seated cross-legged on a small cushion, eyes barely open, hands folded into a cradle-like mudra, the meditator trains with the aim of eventually becoming a buddha, an enlightened one. Less romantically, we may see a group of such men or women, seated all alike with their backs to one another in a nondescript building at the corner of a downtown intersection. Concentratedly following their breath, they simply sit, perfectly still, surrounded with an aura of impenetrable silence and the sweet heaviness of sandalwood incense.

In both cases, our imagery reveals a belief that the practice of Ch'an involves an at least temporary withdrawal from the tumult of daily life, a commitment to an inward journey that is apparently incompatible with satisfying the demands of career and family. Influenced perhaps by the stress in Indian Buddhism on leaving the home life as a prerequisite for fully "entering the stream," we tend to think of practicing Buddhism and especially Ch'an as an essentially private or internal affair. It is the disciplined cultivation of various noble dispositions (physical, mental, and moral), the acquisition of which is intended to finally bring about our awakening as buddhas. Recalling in addition the example of Bodhidharma's nine years in cave-dwelling solo retreat, we are quite naturally inclined to identify meditative training, and in particular sitting meditation (Ch *ts'o ch'an;* J *zazen* 坐禪), as the primary means by which each of us can eventually and quite apart from any association with others experience enlightenment.

Now, if we accept as legitimate this identification of practice with an individually undertaken course of meditative training that culminates in the experience of enlightenment, the characterization of practice as opening up horizonless intimacy cannot but be dismissed as fundamentally mistaken. If, as the imagery above suggests, practicing Ch'an is something that we ultimately carry out on our own, the total absence of others—far from being a cause for lament—may actually work very much to our advantage. And if for no other reason than this, the suggestion that enlightenment itself be conceived as social and not private or experiential in nature will appear to be misguided, if not ruinously misleading. It may well be that the Mahayana ideal has always been that of total immersion in the flux of daily life and never a private and necessarily transcendental retreat from it, but we find no inconsistency in thinking of this ideal as something realized after the fact of enlightenment. Parinirvana may indeed be forfeited in consideration of others, but the basic experience of awakening is understood as indispensable—an experience attained by way of meditative and moral training.

There can be no doubt, of course, that there is a strong relationship between meditation and the practice of Ch'an. Even discounting the story of Bodhidharma who was, after all, neither born nor trained in China, frequent references to sitting meditation in the indigenous literature of Ch'an certainly suggest that its usefulness is undeniable. What none of these passages indicate, however, is that sitting meditation is either a necessary or sufficient condition for the realization of enlightenment. To the contrary, meditating for the purpose of becoming a buddha is as often as not ridiculed—a labor as vain as diligently polishing a clay roofing tile in order to make a mirror.[1] Indicating why this is so here and in the following two chapters will not only provide us with a convincing rationale for maintaining the sociality of Ch'an enlightenment, it will open up the possibility of at least intellectually realizing the meaning of Hui-neng's statement that "it is precisely Buddhist practice that is the Buddha." (PS 42)

The Diversions of Experience

There is nothing closer to us than our experience. Experience is the ever-changing and yet perfectly continuous context of conscious-ness—that in terms of which we are assured not only of the fact of our existence, but apprised of its depths and breadth. At least, this is the conventional wisdom. So profound is this alleged closeness that the absence of experience is taken as tantamount to an absence of the self. Thus, a comatose patient may be wholly incapable of relating with his or her family, friends and surroundings, but we will accept the likelihood of their continued presence with us on the basis of evidence (in the form of EEGs, for example) that they are still having some kind of experience. The complete lack of such evidence is taken as signifying the departure of the 'soul,' of he or she who once called this inert and yet still living body their own. Whether to heaven or hell in the context of some Christian narra-tive of the afterlife, or to Brahman or a further incarnation in a Hindu one, this departure amounts to an effective loss of every form of sentient relation. Losing experience is losing our place—that central vantage from which everything manifestly reveals itself as happening around us.

Significantly, however, being what is closest to us does not mean that experience is identical with us. Even if we are avowed materialists who deny anything like a soul, our experiences are still spoken about and thought of as objective—'things' we may have or not have, recollect or forget, cherish or dread. Underlying this con-ventionally acknowledged difference between who we are and what we experience is, it would seem, the premise that we are enduring and autonomous individuals who in some sense link all of our experiences. For most of us, the fact that experiences can be accu-rately anticipated and recalled stands as sufficient proof that in some very real way we precede and outlast them. And so even if the most arduous and vigilant introspections never uncover anything like self-subsistent, enduring selves, we typically continue assum-ing they exist. After all, we have the objective evidence of experi-ence itself as an ultimate and ostensibly incontrovertible warrant for doing so.

It is, indeed, by virtue of this supposed difference between who we are and what we experience that self and other can be made and kept distinct. In the absence of such a premise—as in Chinese culture as we've been articulating it—the dislocation of self and experience is likely to be seen as pathological, a tear in the fabric of our given-togetherness that forces all others outside of and hence apart from us as 'friends' or 'enemies' we have or have lost. Kept at the imperceptible distance of experience, others are 'things' we may either possess or dispossess.[2]

I have bothered to go into this digression because in a very real way our attachment to experience is an attachment to our sense of self—our sense of being just here in the midst of all that is happening. Because it amounts to an implicit denial of karma (in its communal, Buddhist sense) and a commitment to the objectivity of individuating self-identity, maintaining this attachment profoundly influences our presuppositions about enlightenment. On the one hand, if others are reached only through experience, experiencing remains crucial to the bodhisattva's project of enlightening all beings. This means, of course, that our enlightening efforts will ineluctably revolve about the self as the axis of all that happens. When the Buddha insists in the *Diamond Sutra* that a bodhisattva should not only save all beings, but do so while realizing that not a single 'being' is saved and so while living as one whose mind does not dwell on anything at all, he can be seen as cautioning us against just such a preoccupation with the discursive, narrative dictates of experience.

In short, our conventional wisdom commits us to a belief that should enlightenment be attained, it will manifest and be proven first if not foremost in experience. As long as enlightenment is envisioned as a transformation of the self, as something that happens to us as concrete individuals, then at the very least it must mean a transformation of our experience as well, even if nothing tangible or measurable ever comes of it. But if who we are is not construed as the pivot about which all experience revolves, but as conduct, the so-called "great matter" of enlightenment will hardly be able to exert that peculiar gravity whereby its realization could be mine and mine alone. And if this is so, the conception of practice as a way of transforming my self and my experience must also come under serious question.

From a Buddhist perspective, experience is best understood as occurring with the contact of a sense-organ and an appropriate sense-object. Consciousness may be seen, then, as a higher order system arising on the basis of subsystems which by themselves entail nothing at all like vision, hearing, thinking, and so on. That is, consciousness is seen as relationship. It is by nature something always already shared. Moreover, unlike his realist, Indo-European counterparts, the Buddhist does not assume that the particularity of, for example, eyes and visual objects indicates their ultimate independence or even their self-subsistence. Like all things (*dharmas*), eyes and the objects they come into contact with are empty (*śūnya*). Having no permanent or substantial ground, they arise interdependently, and the visual consciousness which comes about as a function of their systematic contact must be seen as having no essential foundation. Because nothing at all has a permanent self, experience cannot be seen as implying either a pre-existing, experiencing subject or an independent object. If we remain steadfastly, even stubbornly committed to 'having experiences,' we must do so on grounds that remain entirely elusive.[3]

Far from being an innocuous figure of speech, our conventional commitment to 'having experiences' severely distorts the movement of our narration. To begin with, under its auspices we will tend to see as 'things that happen' only what we can comprehend, what we can achieve closure with respect to—even if only by naming and making the unknown into an absence we conveniently fail to inspect. Since comprehension is a function of closing off inquiry—that is, of projecting relevance horizons allowing us to determine that some "thing" 'is'—experience, and hence what happens, will become a function of discrimination. Not only does this drastically limit the creative potential of any given situation, it sets up the precedent for confronting the world (and thus ourselves as persons) as sources of acceptance and rejection, grasping or aversion. In short, by taking experience as something independent which we can either embrace (have) or resist (not-have), we unavoidably and altogether earnestly put ourselves in the position of making karma.[4] Secondly, due in part to the lived structure of having and in part to our identification with the projection of horizons as a crucial component in decision-making, the convention of 'having experiences' will—as suggested above—inevitably place us at the central focus of everything that happens.

The epistemological problem is one to which we will presently return, but more immediately the issue here is that when the bias toward experience is extended to encompass enlightenment, we find ourselves quite naturally thinking that becoming a buddha is something we will know via experience. Enlightenment becomes a goal, something to be sought and eventually made our own. We may admit that until we do so, everything we say about it is mere conjecture. We may even admit that once we experience enlightenment, we will not be able to communicate or pass on what we have experienced to others, no matter what language we avail ourselves of. But the implication we take for granted is that whether by practicing or by some unspecified form of grace, we can arrive at the point where we will be able to directly verify our expectations regarding enlightenment.

It may be that on this basis we conceive of practice as a kind of clearing process—the mirror cleansing recommended by Shen-hsiu, for example—by means of which we make room for the experience of enlightenment. While this is not wholly untrue (at least in the Buddhist sense of 'true'), it is nevertheless misleading. First, by continuing to assume that we are independent selves—at the very least something other than our experiences—who must find a way through to the attainment of enlightenment, we do not imagine that awakening as a transformative exuberance burgeoning throughout our entire narration and thus as not requiring either the acquisition or discarding of anything at all. To the contrary, we think of it as a state of consciousness which each of us quite separately earns and enjoys on the basis of making hard decisions about what we will and will not do. A function of our choice and hence of our discriminations, enlightenment becomes a karmically determined event. In so imagining, and no matter how altruistic our intentions may be, we remain hopelessly entangled in 'I,' 'my,' and 'me,' even when we are astute enough to think of enlightenment as necessarily entailing some kind of ego loss. The bias toward centrality that comes with a commitment to the foundational nature of experience is such that even when we consider what it is like to lose the boundaries of our self, we imagine it from the perspective of a distinct somebody who undergoes the experience of ego-loss. Thus, contrary to the admonitions of every Ch'an master from Hui-neng to Lin-chi, we continue to think of practice as a vehicle for transporting ourselves from our current state of suffering to the extinction of that suffering in nirvana.

As long as we persist in envisioning practice as a means of ridding ourselves of unsatisfactory traits and experiences while positively cultivating those that are more in keeping with what we think is best for us, the driving metaphor of our imagination continues to be that of having and not-having.[5] Self-ishness flourishes and our discriminating between 'good' and 'evil,' 'pure' and 'impure,' 'samsara' and 'nirvana' continues unabated. Making distinctions in the hope of guiding ourselves through our presently unenlightened mix of experiences to a state we imagine to be much, much better, we see ourselves as beings who move in and through the world and who can at least dream of transcending all of our obstructions, all of the resistances we meet in pursuit of our goals. By imagining that someone attains enlightenment, we make it into something separate from us about which we can achieve at least enough closure to distinguish it from everything else. In short, as long as we are determined to maintain the paramount importance of experience, far from dissolving those features of our narrative which bring about the possibility of identifying ourselves as relatively enduring and existentially lonely individuals, meditative practice will actually reinforce the centrality of the very 'self' the Buddha sought to undermine. For the Buddha, we—the irreducible plurality of 'you' and 'I'—remain the central concern of practice.[6]

From a Buddhist perspective, then, the bias toward experience must be held wholly suspect. Philosophical hair-splitting aside, it is certainly possible to insist that—at least as long as we are conscious—experience occurs. But inferring from this that experience is fundamental would be like asserting that music is basically the organized movement of air molecules on the grounds that air moves whenever we play a musical instrument. Just as music cannot be reduced to the fact of molecular kinetics, Buddhist enlightenment cannot be reduced to either (subjective) experience or its (objective) counterpart of behavior. In a word, the realization of enlightenment is not a matter of 'fact'—something that can be 'pointed out'—but one of meaning. As such, it cannot be the possession of any single individual but marks the transformation of an entire narrative, a revolution of conduct.

Focusing on experience cannot but raise the specters of 'self' and 'other'—a self-justifying diversion into 'knowing subjects' and 'known objects.' Bluntly stated, it is a way of forgetting who we really are, of dismembering our narrative into a plurality of mutually exclusive characters clustered around the centrality of our own ego. Seeking the experience of enlightenment is at the most profound level our greatest adversary, the most dear and hence virtually intractable of the 84,000 delusions that block the liberating realization of our true nature.

Now, it should be evident that if focusing on experience leads to the distinction of self and other (or more generally of subject and object) it must signal the erection of a boundary between here and there, between what 'is' and 'is-not'—a boundary or interface which entails the resistance or blockage of a free flow of energy through our narrative as a whole. Selfhood (especially in the form known as self-consciousness) marks the point at which the free development of meaning has in greater or lesser degree been arrested.[7] In Buddhist terms, the existence of selves is a function of karma, of the systematic deformation of character through the creation and maintenance of set patterns of bodily action, speech, and thought—in a word, through the creation of an 'identity.'

If this be granted, and if enlightenment is the orient (and not the result of) practice, practice itself cannot be seen as a generator of experiences but instead as the transformation of narrative movement or conduct. Specifically, practice marks a profound and unremitting shift of orientation away from the division of self and other—what was referred to above as horizonless intimacy.

Intimacy and the Meaning of a Truly Social Life

Having just finished eating the alms gathered that morning in his walk through Sravasti, the Buddha washed his bowl and settled himself in the midst of the bhikkus enjoying the shade in Anathapindika's park. Among those gathered under the luminous canopy of the park's many banyan trees was Subhuti, one of the Buddha's foremost disciples and a man of formidable intellect. Having also just finished his breakfast, Subhuti rose from his place and approached the master. Walking once around Gautama, he bared his shoulder in respect, settled himself on the sun-dappled grass, and after a brief pause asked how a bodhisattva should live, how he should orient his thoughts. Without any hesitation, the Buddha responds by saying that bodhisattvas must realize that even though they liberate all sentient beings, not even a single being will have been liberated (DS 3).

At one level, the Buddha is here rehearsing a formula that will appear again and again throughout their discussion that day: a 'sentient being' is not a sentient being, we only refer to her as "sentient being." But he is also enjoining Subhuti to drop the premise that liberation—or, for that matter, anything else that happens—necessarily entails the existence of someone who is liberated. Subhuti initially seems satisfied with this injunction to drop the assumption that the question "who is liberated?" has an objective answer, but before long he feels compelled to ask about liberation itself. If no one is liberated, then what sense can be made out of freedom—what is it? If it were something felt or known in the sense of a literal comprehension, then someone would be freed and that has already been denied. Is liberation something wholly objective, then? And if so, what could that possibly mean?

The Buddha is delighted with Subhuti's question and, no doubt smilingly, replies that when he attained ultimate enlightenment (*anuttara samyak sambodhi*), he didn't get a single thing (DS 22). That is, ultimate enlightenment is not an experienced goal—something received or attained at the terminus of some more or less long period of training. But if that is true, and if enlightenment is not a comprehensible fact—something we can grasp—then what are all of the Buddha's followers doing? If enlightenment amounted to an exalted state of consciousness or of moral perfection or an all-encompassing wisdom—something definite, something known or at least knowable—then practice could be taken to be the means to arriving at that end. The proclivity for Ch'an masters to answer their students' requests for a description or definition of enlightenment with an injunction to practice would make good hermeneutical sense: attain enlightenment and then you'll know first-hand, in experience, exactly what the sutras 'mean.' But if a buddha cannot be known by any 'mark' (Skt *laksana*, Ch *hsiang* 相), by any specific characteristics, and if there is no attainment (no subjective acquisition) and nothing attained (no experience), what is the point of practice?

We can begin answering this by returning briefly to the epistemological problem mentioned above. It has become almost canonical in the Indo-European tradition to consider experience as the bottom line of epistemology, usually with the result that the problem of knowledge comes to be seen as the reconciliation of experience and reality, of opinion and fact. That the Chinese never formulated such a problematic is significant for understanding the meaning of practice in Ch'an. To begin with, even if the Buddhism first brought to China from south Asia almost unilaterally endorsed the notion that practice (*bhāvanā*) amounted to a progressive cultivation of moral clarity (*śīla*), concentration (*samādhi*), and insight (*vipassanā*) leading to an eventual culmination in the attainment of wisdom (*prajñā*), this would not automatically entail the Chinese seeing practice as primarily a means of generating favorable experiences. Whereas the Buddhist Sanskrit term *prajñā* has the technical connotation of "knowledge of the waning of influxes" (*āsravaksaya-jñāna*) and implies the achievement of a state of consciousness untrammeled by defilements of any sort, the Chinese explained *prajñā* as either *hui* 慧 (intelligent, clever, quick-witted, wise) or *chih-hui* 智慧 (realization + quick-wittedness, or prudence). Wisdom, as the Chinese understood it, was not a matter of knowing about the nature of things and how they have come to be, or even one of realizing the cessation of unhealthy influences—both of which impute a knower who is separate from what is known—but of unconstrained and yet profoundly sensitive skill. Perfection here is not so much a matter of finalization or completion as it is a wholeness or roundness that remains vibrantly responsive.

As was discussed earlier, the conception of knowledge in Chinese culture has more to do with ready responsiveness than with the achievement of closure that serves as the guiding metaphor of the Indo-European imagination. For the Chinese, knowing the meaning of a word like *jen* 仁 is not a matter of being able to discourse on the virtues of being humane or authoritative, but rather the ability to conduct oneself in appropriate ways given a world of ever-changing circumstances. In short, knowledge has to do with the realization of lively concourse with others. For the Chinese, then, knowledge implies community and human relatedness to a degree nearly incomprehensible from the standpoint of a typically Indo-European approach to epistemology. In the end, displaying the meaning of *jen*—or, for that matter, of *prajñā*—will not mean a move to a more abstract dimension in which we appear as ideally disembodied knowers undistracted by the vagrant concerns of body, time and place, but an immersion in the unique convolutions and interdependence of our day to day lives—that open-ended narration of which each of us is a crucial (if ultimately unprivileged) part.

The difference between knowing how to act and knowing what something is can admittedly be blurred into extinction by simply suggesting that knowing how to act *is* knowing what something is— namely, the best course of action given the situation. That is, we can reintroduce the primacy of an independent experiencer of knowledge by making 'knowing how' into a species of 'knowing that'—a shift of emphasis that is entirely natural for us.[8] But the Chinese did not make this move. Without denying the ostensibly private character of feelings and thoughts and our ability to mask them—that is, our ability to lie or misrepresent our selves—the epitome of knowledge in (especially) Confucian China continued to be wholly embodied expressions of meaning (*li* 禮—usually translated as 'ritual action') and not subjective experience. What is most significant about this for understanding the peculiarly Ch'an approach to Buddhist practice is the refusal to shift the locus of knowledge out of the public sphere into the private. As ritual action, *li* serve to establish appropriate human relations—even when these are relationships between the living and the dead—and must, therefore, be seen as irreducibly interpersonal. Far from being thought of as a fixed code for individual action, *li* were seen as analogues of cosmic patterns that served to appropriately orient conduct (narrative movement). In this sense, the Chinese conception of knowledge can be said to be basically communal—a conception which, as Roger Ames has put it, "precludes the myth of the solitary knower" (personal communication, 1993).

This, however, did not mean that *li* acted as societally maintained curbs on personal freedom—a set of rigid prescriptions for behavior which we elect to perform simply to avoid conflict with those around us. Rather, they represent concrete modes (in especially the musical sense of the word) of knowing, of responsiveness, which are learned to be sure, but which are not thought of as ultimately distinct from us. To the contrary, they should be seen as essentially underdetermined modes of relationship which can be wholly realized only through their personalization. Granted the relational view of self proper to Chinese culture, as lived patterns of human relatedness, *li* are at least as fundamental in our constitution as persons as are the shapes of our bodies or the fantasies and desires we can readily identify as 'mine alone.'[9]

Given the focus in Chinese culture on the interpersonal and not intrapersonal or intrapsychic dimensions of knowledge, it would only be natural for Chinese Buddhists to see practice as epistemically significant, as promising a deepening of their relationships both with one another and the foreigners who acted as emissaries for the Buddhist tradition. The locus of the meaning of practice would not be seen as the private spaces within our minds or hearts, but the open field of personal relationships, and instead of producing insights or revelations—the stuff of Indian mysticism and arguably much of the degenerated Buddhist traditions of South and Central Asia—practice would have been expected to open up novel and more integrative dimensions of conduct. Thus, Ma-tzu speaks of the path of Buddhism not as a means of arriving at some particular experiential end, but quite simply as "responding to opportunity and joining things" (*ying chi chieh wu* 應機接物) (TTC 45.406), where "things" (*wu* 物) are understood not as substantial entities, but interpenetrating patterns of living disposition.

In the Confucian tradition, self-cultivation—precisely this sort of integrative expansion of conduct—was typically conceived as occurring under the rubric of the five relationships: father-son, elder brother-younger brother, husband-wife, ruler-minister, and friend-friend. Cultivating one's self meant nothing short of rectifying these relationships in a virtuosic manner, and at least initially, the same would have held true for the earliest Chinese Buddhists. But as the doctrine of no-self was more profoundly assimilated, the emphasis on perfecting set relational patterns—not to mention the societal tendencies they can often encourage when ulterior motives and a concern for expedience come into play—would have diminished markedly. In short, knowing what was meant by "no-self" (Ch *wu-wo* 無我, Skt *anātman*) would have eventually forced Chinese Buddhists into seeing their task as not identifying themselves with any particular role, but rather as a fount of unhindered responsiveness. Having no 'self' would mean living as if we were free to adopt any place in the schema of the five relations, and not just those few given to us by the exigencies of our birth as male or female, first or last son, aristocrat or peasant. In a passage that neatly captures the anarchic gist of Ch'an practice, Huang-po remarks that once you embark on the path of making fewer and fewer distinctions in responding, you will eventually arrive at a point where there is no place to anchor. This, he says "is conducting yourself as all the Buddhas have. Then, in responding without having any fixed perspective, you are bringing forth your heart.... This is known as 'supreme enlightenment'" (T 2012.383b).

Thus, unlike the Confucian sage who remains firmly embedded within the definitions of his place and develops a virtuosity akin to that of a be-bop stylist and not a master of free jazz, the Ch'an ideal eventually comes to be epitomized in Lin-chi's famous "true man of no rank." Practice is not carried out in order to achieve something, but must be seen as opening up in unhesitating and unhindered responsiveness. As Pai-chang put it, the gate of Ch'an enlightenment is *dānapāramitā*—the perfection of offering.[10]

With the introduction of the themes of responsiveness and offering into the body of practice, we have set the initial precedent for exploring the relationship of Ch'an enlightenment and intimacy. But before doing so in earnest, special care must be taken to not carry along any last vestiges of the centrist biases associated with taking experience as basic. With the shift from seeing practice as the means of attaining one or another form of experience to seeing it as a direct transformation of conduct or narrative movement, it is no longer possible to consider practice something that enables 'you' and 'I' to relocate ourselves from a present characterized by suffering to one free from crisis. The thrust of Ch'an is that practice is not a vehicle at all—the proverbial raft discarded once we have gained the other shore. Since persons have no identifiable location, conceiving of practice as a means of changing our place or circumstances is unintelligible. Huang-po goes so far as to say that "the Tao (path) that has no location is called Mahayana mind. This mind is not present inside, outside or in-between. In actuality, there are no 'locations'" (T 2012.382c).

By denying the truth of goals, Ch'an renders cultivation irrelevant and forces us to admit that none of us will ever arrive at the experience of enlightenment. As the transformation of conduct or narrative movement, practice transports no 'one.' Instead, it must be seen as the meaning of a re-orientation of our entire narrative away from the duality of 'self' and 'other,' 'have' and 'have-not,' toward increasingly harmonious integration. In a word, it is never a single individual who practices, but only persons, entire worlds.

This is particularly hard to accept given the stubbornness with which we typically hold onto our identities as concrete individuals. At an intellectual level, it is easy enough to allow that a narrative understanding of persons provides a corrective to the biases that normally drive us toward taking ourselves to be autonomous individuals—a kind of "Copernican revolution" by virtue of which the concept of person is finally freed from the violence of the one-many dichotomy.[11] Once this revolution is carried out, it is impossible to regard either practice or enlightenment as functions of individual effort. Instead, they are effectively decentered, seen as transformations of an entire story and not merely of a single character or ego-center within it. But, just as the Copernican revolution didn't alter our daily perception of the sun circling the earth, rising in the east and traversing the sky to set in the west, our intellectual grasp of a decentered reality does not alter our impression that we initiate and carry out our practice. We persist in thinking, at least hoping, that we will be the beneficiaries of our commitment.

Nothing could be further from the truth. When Subhuti is told that while a bodhisattva liberates all sentient beings, not a single sentient being is liberated, we are at first tempted to think that the Buddha is contradicting himself. The idea that liberation could occur without some 'one' being liberated is rationally repugnant—it means that there is some attribute with nothing for it to qualify; a mass, for example, with nothing that is massive. And yet, this is precisely the Buddha's point. Liberation is not of the self, but from it. The only way to bring suffering—a narrative interruption—to an end without making some karma which will eventuate a return to the same meaning configuration is to dissolve the source of the suffering, the 'I' who views the world through the projections of attachment and aversion. Thus, in his *Essential Gate for Entering the Path*, Pai-chang says that the principle of liberation "is just letting things come and not selecting anything" (HTC 119.425a).[12] Ma-tzu makes much the same recommendation:

> When you're in the midst of either good or bad states of affairs, simply don't check anything. This is called being a cultivator of the Tao. Grasping the good, rejecting the evil and viewing emptiness as entering meditative stillness are all classed as 'over-doing-it.' (TTC 45.406a)

Any activity on our behalf (even where that explicitly includes others as in the case of altruism) insures that 'we' remain. That is, we continue creating the conditions which give rise to a sense of identity and with it the manifestation of attraction and resistance. Making use of the systems-theoretical model, this amounts to saying that because an individual identity—as a higher-order system not reducible to the sum of its (bodily, emotive, intellectual, and even spiritual) component parts—is open, it can persist only by taking in and retaining some form of energy. 'Selves' are, in this sense, possible only when there is some blockage to the free flow of energy through our world/narrative. But this is as much as to say that selves are possible only when there is suffering. Ending suffering is losing our 'selves.'[13]

Liberating a sentient being means taking off the mantle of both conceptual and felt distinctions by means of which he or she is individuated or made into some 'one' existing apart from others even while in the closest contact with them. In the vernacular of the Buddhist tradition, this mantle is popularly referred to as "karma"— the matters by which we are bound and which can be dissolved only by the antidote of what Ch'an calls "no-'mind.'" As with the sailor who has a definite port of call in mind and can therefore speak of favorable and ill winds, it is only to the extent that we indulge in identifying with some abiding form, that we can intelligibly speak of things going 'well' or going 'awry.' Without this identification, there is nothing to resist the spontaneous and interweaving flow of events—the natural course of our narration.

In a practical sense, what this implies is that the flow of our narration can be objectionable only insofar as the lines of force within it find some resistance around which they can tighten. Without a central ego which takes as its vocation the avoidance of 'ill' and the pursuit of 'happiness,' suffering is quite impossible—an insight which almost invariably leads to us pondering just what we can do about lessening (if not altogether eliminating) the influence of our egos. We want to be able to do something about our predicament, and that is part of the problem. Perhaps the most central one.

In the most general sense, karmic entanglements are never loosened by intentional activity.[14] Like knots which only tighten further when meddled with, karmic bonds can only be undone by providing them with no purchase, by eschewing the process of deciding what we want and do not want to have in experience. As a means of opening us up to this most crucial aspect of the practice life, Ch'an has traditionally employed the imagery of sea and sky as metaphors for the mind that is Buddha. A mind that is like the ocean or the empty sky does not resist anything. No matter what something looks like, no matter how objectionable we might typically think of its form as being, the ocean and sky unhesitatingly accept it. Moreover, neither the sky nor the ocean can be tied up or bound. No amount of ingeniousness will enable us to keep water in a net or to bind the sky. Nor is it possible to use air or water to block objective movement. A wall of water or air may have great force when it is itself in motion, but at rest, not even the weakest thing is incapable of penetrating and passing through it. The initial method of Ch'an is thus realizing an oceanic mind—a mind that is as clear as space.

Notably, there is a tradition in the Mahayana that immediately upon attaining enlightenment, the Buddha entered what is referred to as the "ocean-seal samadhi." In the terms we have been articulating, this is as much as to say that the initial, narrative impact of enlightenment—its characteristic transformation of conduct—is the realization of an oceanlike harmony of self and other. Now, the Sanskrit term "samadhi" originally referred to a state of concentration or meditative absorption, suggesting that its nature is mental or internal—a cessation of distraction and a fixation of the mind. For the Chinese, however, the term carries a much more dynamic meaning since mind is not understood as the locus of experience as much as it is a particular constellation of narrative dispositions. That is, mind is seen as a constellation of dispositions for the realization of certain kinds of dramatic relationship by virtue of which some characters, settings, and occurrences are much more likely to arise together than others. Mind is thus not located in the body or even in the universe as a whole, but should be seen as the characteristic realizing of a world.

Now, while it is true that a samadhi is said to occur when the mind is *ting* 定—the typical translation of which is "fixed" or "settled"—since mind is seen in dispositional terms and not as a locus or generator of experience, being settled doesn't indicate a lack of movement, but rather certainty of direction or dramatic development.[15] Moreover, since the prevailing conception of *ting* within the Ch'an tradition is that of meeting (*tui* 對) your environment with no-mind (*wu-hsin* 無心) (HTC 119.420b), and since *tui* carries the connotations of confronting, correcting, and immediately responding, *ting* itself must be understood not as a kind of stolid imperturbability or fixation on a set destination but as maintaining a clear direction, an unswerving orientation in conduct.[16] Since we are to greet all things with no-'mind', *ting* cannot be construed as a contrary of improvisation, but that continuity of concern which allows us to respond in manners which are neither rigidly ordered or merely chaotic. Ch'an meditation (*ting*) is not, therefore, typified by silent repose, but rather by a dynamic and unreservedly confident (*hsin* 信) meeting with whatever comes one's way. "Just like right now, whether walking, standing, sitting or lying down, responding to opportunity and joining things is entirely Tao" (TTC 45.406a).

For the Ch'an practitioner, the Buddha's ocean-seal samadhi is not a kind of dispassionate regard for all things, but a wholly dynamic opening up to and drawing in of all things. And so, while Matzu remarks that, "being constantly calm and extinguished (*chi-mieh* 寂滅, nirvana) is called making the ocean-seal samadhi," this calmness and state of extinction is understood as a dynamic absence of impediments to integration with others and the achievement of a common enlightenment. Ma-tzu goes on to say that,

> Taking in all things (*she-i-ch'ieh-fa* 攝一切法), it (nirvana) is like 100,000 streams equally returning to the great ocean. All are designated ocean water, and so savoring one taste is to take in all tastes. Abiding in the great ocean is then the turbulent confluence of all streams.

That is, abiding in nirvana is entering into samsara, the mutual suffering that occurs when narratives initially interrupt or break into one another. "For this reason, a person who washes in the great ocean uses all the waters" (TTC 45.406a–b). In short, whoever cleanses his or her own mind thereby cleanses the minds of all other sentient beings—skillfully accomplishing the work of the bodhisattva. "If you want to obtain the Pure Land, you should purify your own mind" (PS 38, quoting the *Vimalakirti Sutra*).

Entering the ocean-seal samadhi is thus to incorporate the karma of all those we meet into our own narrative. It is to allow the sediments deposited by the habituation of intent and experience to be eroded and finally absorbed without remainder. To use a common Ch'an phrase, when our conduct comes about from the clarity of no-'mind', our individual actions are—like words written on water or in the air—without form or trace. In this sense, as a bodhisattva the practitioner of Ch'an receives whatever comes into his or her life without attaching to it, without either averting or holding onto it in any way. And for this reason, the Chinese often referred to the ocean-seal samadhi as the "ocean mirror," and to its associated level of understanding as the "great, round mirror wisdom."

The mirror metaphor has had special currency in East Asian Buddhism because mirrors remain untainted by what they reflect and therefore seem an appropriate symbol of buddha-nature.[17] But for Ch'an, the most salient characteristic is that mirrors don't discriminate according to form, but take on the appearance of whatever presents itself, whatever the circumstances require. In this sense, the mirror is a particularly apt metaphor for the conduct of the bodhisattva who has unlimited skill in means and who—no matter how extreme the situation—can respond immediately and without any reservations, supplying whatever is needed without retaining anything for him or herself. Unlike the typical conception of mirrors as nothing more than surfaces which can reflect who 'we' are and hence foster our narcissistic tendencies, the Ch'an Buddhist conception does away with the reflected 'I' and replaces it instead with an orientation of concern and compassion. This is the significance of Huang-po's denial that buddha-mind is like the moon. "Mind," he insists, "is like the sun constantly circling through the empty sky. Naturally luminous, it does not reflect light, but radiates. . . . [This] is conducting yourself as all the buddhas have" (T 2012.383b).

The practice of Ch'an is not getting enlightenment—achieving some state of mind or some particular complex of experience—but enlightening, living the bodhisattva life, and thereby creating innumerable, pure buddha-lands. And so whatever enters the ocean mirror is received without resistance and then returned purified and without remainder. In the end, this is possible only if we realize no-'mind'—that is, if we relinquish any internal and external blockages

or horizons that arise, retaining nothing which will give rise to the
habits and fixed dispositions by means of which 'you' and 'I' are
identified. True nonattachment is not a kind of impassiveness, then,
but unobstructed responsiveness, boundless giving.

The realization of this campestrial generosity within and com-
plemented by the oceanic inclusiveness of a mind that selects no-
'thing' is what was referred to earlier as horizonless intimacy.
According to the prevailing dictates of the European imagination,
intimacy must be taken to be a kind of discourse. However deeply
the intimate encounter may be internally characterized by the feeling of open-ended sharing and even integration, our usual conception of intimacy entails a sharp divergence between the private and
public—that is, between the protected space within which we can
open up to one another and lose (even if only partially and for a short
time) our sense of separateness and isolation, and that greater sphere
within which we are all equally present and yet undeniably alone.
Thus, the intimate conversation takes place in hushed tones, the
love letter is "for your eyes only," and the lovers' tryst takes place
in a moon-lit garden, a tree-encircled meadow unwatched by human
eyes, or at least in the bustling anonymity of a public park which
insures a de facto privacy—the privacy of being taken as just another
feature of the environment. The poetic, fictive and cinematic depictions of intimacy with which we are most familiar all involve a
disjunction of the personal and the public, of the inner and the
outer. Intimate partners take one another into themselves, but in so
doing at least initially disregard those around them by either physically or psychologically distancing them. That is, our usual
construal of intimacy involves the projection of a horizon marking
off 'us' and 'them,' the sphere of completely open vulnerability and
that of regulated self-protection.

To be sure, such a separation of the spheres of intimacy and
publicity marks the institution of a relatively effective strategy for
overcoming some of the primary sources of suffering or narrative
disruption. By wrapping ourselves in an exclusive mantle of intimacy, we are able to open ourselves enough to feel fully human
without exposing ourselves to the vagrant demands of the general
populace. With our chosen partners, we establish the possibility and
usually the acknowledged goal of relating in an unmitigatedly social
fashion, allowing our uniqueness to blossom freely and with gratitude. With all others—and this is admittedly a function of degree
and not absolute boundaries—we tend to fall into a societal manner,
meeting them not as our "better halves," as long-lost parts of our

selves, but as individuals with whom we have only external and ideally contingent relations. Thus, the intimate relationship becomes a refuge, a kind of second skin into which we can withdraw when the pressures of our day-to-day interactions with others threaten to derail our preferred—that is, our customary—flow of experience. In our intimate life, we feel we can really "be who we are," dispensing with the hide-and-seek gamesmanship of public life. And so, we see no inconsistency between being a crack military strategist and a loving father, between being a tender spouse and a hard-nosed litigator, between being a publicly cold and analytic business consultant and a privately passionate, even reckless lover.

That this disjunction of the public and private is generally effective as a means of holding suffering at bay can be seen in the simple fact that when an intimate relationship falls apart—when the sanctity of the space of shared self-hood is violated and then torn asunder—we as often as not take refuge in our jobs, our hobbies, in the tumult of the public life, even in the self-divesting upheaval of religious conversion. The break-up leaves us feeling raw, exposed in the way that only a wound can expose us, and our natural tendency is thus to retreat into that part of our life where we are relatively invulnerable, where our societal armor is best maintained. Like an injured fox seeking out the uterine closeness of its burrow, we return to the birthing sites of the 'self,' the places where our incompleteness isn't mentioned even if it's noticed, where we are apparently individual and safe.

Intimacy in this sense depends on a sense of trust. We approach each other with careful reserve and will begin fully opening up to one another only once we have determined that we pose no threats to each other. In other words, we become intimate only once we have gotten to know one another, when we have achieved enough of a sense of closure to be willing to expose our incompleteness. Failing this, we remain aloof, having decided in effect that the potential danger to our selves is too high to warrant the kind of vulnerability that intimacy demands. Trust which is not childlike—that is, which is not unconditional—is necessarily based on a calculation of risks to the integrity of the reflexive discourse by means of which we identify who we are. As such, trust must be seen as part of the project of affirming and strengthening the self.

By contrast, the ocean mirror of practicing Ch'an is ultimately oriented toward the advent of an intimacy free of all 'self'-ishness— an intimacy which is not born in an accentuation of the discourse of public and private, but in horizonless concourse. Whereas a selfish

entry into intimacy is burdened with a concern for potential loss—
of the familiarity of our present way of life, our independence,
youth, wealth, or secrets—practitioners of Ch'an have already recognized their own emptiness, the absence of anything which they can
definitively call their own. Eschewing the possessiveness and discrimination that comes with the assertion that "I am,"[18] they are
able to open up fearlessly and without reservation. Only in this way
is it possible to follow Ma-tzu's advice to "take in all things (*she-i-
ch'ieh-fa*)," according with the situation and responding as needed
(*sui-shih-ying-yung*).

Perhaps the greatest exemplary of this mode of conduct is—for
the Chinese Buddhist—the bodhisattva Avalokitesvara or Kuan
Shih Yin (literally, "perceiving-world-sound"), whose ability to see
any situation clearly and respond as needed is symbolically mani-
fested in her depictions as the thousand-eyed, thousand-armed god-
dess of compassion. As the great master of love and sympathy
(*t'zu-pei-ta-shih* 慈悲大士), Kuan Yin not only hears the cries of the
world, she incorporates them. She quite literally feels them as
her own (Ch *pei* 悲, Skt *karuṇā*) and responds with the all-
embracingness of a healing love (Ch *tz'u* 慈, Skt *maitrī*), a love that
mends what has been sundered. Recalling that suffering is best seen
as narrative interruption or the blockage of the free and creative
orientation of our conduct—the experience of intractability or (what
for the Buddhist is the same thing) unreality—the healing which
occurs with Kuan Yin's attendance to our needs and desires should
itself be seen as the dissolution of those horizons by means of which
'distance' comes to be seen as ontically grounded separation or
severance. Needs and desires, after all, can only occur when some
apparent limit (*ching*) segregates 'us' and 'what we lack,' when
'what-I-am' is effectively cut off from 'what-I-am-not'. What Kuan
Yin accomplishes with her wish-fulfilling gem is not necessarily the
closing of some objective difference or distance, but the erasure of
whatever has been imposed on our relations with others (our narration) to give us the illusion of discontinuity, of painful cleavage,
of intractability. In short, Kuan Yin's work is the restoration of
intimacy.

For the Chinese,[19] intimacy (*ch'in* 親) is not primarily conceived
in terms of a dyadic and typically exclusive relationship. While
ch'in—like the Latin *intimus* (a superlative form of "within") from
which the English "intimacy" derives—does imply nearness, this is
seen in terms of the closeness or affection of kinship. Given the
Chinese construal of personhood in terms of a field of relationships,

kinship cannot be understood simply as a matter of blood or lineage, but of shared feeling and the dovetailing of unique contributions in the constitution of the harmony known as family (*chia* 家). Kinship in this sense is not something given with birth, but achieved and maintained—an orientation of conduct by means of which each member of a family realizes that virtue (*te* 德) which is uniquely his or her own. Thus, the term *ch'in* means not only being close, but "being related," "relative," "affection," "self," "in person," and "family." Intimacy does not, that is, join individuals in some special way, but marks the harmonious functioning of an entire family or clan and ultimately of the entire world. It is not psychological in nature, but social.

Virtuosity and the Perfection of Offering and Appreciation

Most importantly, then, seeing practice as realizing unimpeded intimacy not only has the effect of challenging us to give up any set dispositions we discover in our conduct but of doing so in such a way that we do not lapse into random and ultimately 'self'-serving or 'self'-defeating activity. Instead of making consistency (logical or otherwise) our principle and establishing the precedent for a crusade to cleave 'right' from 'wrong' at every available opportunity, we are invited to valorize flexibility and refrain from calculating the probable returns on various courses of action. In a word, we are asked to quit trying to control what happens. Instead of regarding others through the prismatic lens of self-determined and ultimately self-serving trust, we are urged to allow our conduct to be *wu-wei*—that is, fully improvised, without any precedent or ulterior motive. Only in this way can we, like Kuan Yin with her wish-fulfilling gem, freely pass through the gate of Ch'an enlightenment and embody unobstructed *dānapāramitā* or the perfection of offering.

But this is far from easy. As long as we are not entirely free of doubt, we are constantly searching for something or someone to validate our decisions, to warrant our actions and intentions, to guide us toward our chosen ends. And so, when we resolve a difficult situation by acting in a certain way, a precedent is set for acting in that way whenever similar situations occur. This, we think, is what it means to learn from experience. But for the practitioner of Ch'an, the appeal to *yu-wei* 有為 (action on the basis of pre-existing dispositions) is a form of dependence which makes it impossible to accord with every new situation and simply respond as needed. Instead, we will interpret what is happening now as an instance of a much more general flow of experience and will react on the basis of what we 'know' to expect from it. Whether this interpretation is scientific, religious, political, mythic, or entirely idiosyncratic is irrelevant. Nor is it relevant whether our precedented behavior leads to 'success' or not since any consistently maintained course of intention/action will give rise to conditions which apparently call for more of 'the same.' That is the law of karma, the process by means of which we are bound up as selves.[20] True intimacy is forestalled by the projection of an interposing, analytic framework.

Thus, one of the more common teachings in Ch'an is the need to "know when to keep the precepts and when to break them." That is, we are not instructed to rely on the teachings or the sutras or even the Dharma as a whole, but rather on ourselves—on nothing at all. Allowing our conduct to proceed *wu-wei* entails not a frustrated capitulation to "the way things are," but an anarchic and unblemished confidence (*hsin*), since only someone who is entirely fearless can open him or herself up to the improvisational demands of horizonless intimacy. In short, practicing Ch'an as the realization of unimpeded intimacy should be seen as the path of inconceivable skill in means—of unhesitating, social virtuosity.

The themes of intimacy and virtuosity are neatly brought together by Huang-po in his suggestion that "Manjusri should be regarded as the pattern (*li* 理), Samantabhadra as the practice (*hsing* 行). The pattern is that of unhindered, pure emptiness. The practice is that of inexhaustibly departing from forms" (T 2012.380a). To begin with, on an abstract level Huang-po is suggesting that the body or pattern of liberation is interdependence (emptiness, Skt *śūnyatā* or Ch *k'ung* 空)—the absence of any abiding identities, while its vitality is nonattachment ("departing from forms")—relinquishing the horizons which make 'me' different from 'you.' Together, these give rise to the radiance of enlightened conduct. But by speaking of pattern and practice as persons, Huang-po indirectly and yet keenly alerts us to the fact that there is no 'one' who maintains this pattern and performs this practice. Instead, pattern and practice are both aspects (*mien* 面) of who we are—characteristic expressions of our undivided nature, a deft enlivening of the flow of our entire narration. As Ma-tzu put it, "Everything is your own body. Were it not so what kind of person could there be?" (TTC 45.406b).

Moreover, the Chinese transliteration of Manjusri (wen-shu 文殊) has the literal connotation of "killing the classics/the literary embodiment of culture," while Samantabhadra (p'u-hsien 普賢) means "universal capability/versatility/talent." The pattern is thus avoiding the reduction of "right conduct" to acting in a manner consistent with the precedents set by others for situations we never actually meet. Killing the classics is destroying the basis for a reliance on and placing of our confidence in any societal codifications of behavior. In effect, it means leaving all prescriptions behind and living a fully social life. But this is possible only if we are also able to respond in any direction at any time, if we are—like Samantabhadra—the embodiment of unlimited versatility. Giving up the relatively successful and stable structure of societally approved behavior is advisable only when we are so skillfully and roundly attuned to the world that no matter how unexpectedly we are jolted out of the normal flow of our narration we can respond without deliberating, realizing a new and more openly diverse harmony. Otherwise, we shall fall into hesitation and doubt and drown in utter confusion—either alone or while dragging along whoever tries to lend us a hand. Seeing pattern as Manjusri and practice as Samantabhadra is thus to regard Ch'an as relinquishing all boundaries as they appear and responding directly and confidently to the needs of others—in short, the marriage of intimacy and virtuosity.

While the Indian tradition took the absence of any substantial core at the center of a banana tree as one of its guiding metaphors for emptiness and later fell prey to a tendency to regard the latter as some sort of central and transcendent reality,[21] Chinese Buddhists tended to understand k'ung (literally, a "hollowness") in terms of the open quality of the sky or space. Thus, for Huang-po and the Ch'an tradition generally, emptiness is understood as expansiveness, as oceanic receptivity, and interdependence is conceived less in terms of an external relation characterized by mutual reliance as in terms of unobstructed interpenetration.[22] In this light, it is interesting that Huang-po repeatedly claims that enlightenment (the realization of wu-hsin, no-'mind') is a "silent bond and that's all (mei-ch'i-erh-i 默契而已)."[23] Recalling Ma-tzu's suggestion that we see Tao as "responding to opportunity and joining things" (ying-chi-chieh-wu), Huang-po's mei-ch'i makes it quite clear that the path of liberation is not—as is the case in the Upanishadic tradition—one of gradually extricating ourselves from the samsaric net of human relationships. To the contrary, liberation must be seen as implicating us ever more deeply in the lives of those with whom we come into contact.

This would seem to be the meaning of Huang-po's use of *ch'i* 契, a word which originally referred to the notches or tally marks made on a piece of bamboo when the terms of a trade agreement had been set and which was later extended to signify any mutually established bond or contract. The general sense of *ch'i*, and hence of Ch'an enlightenment, is that of entering into an uncoerced relationship of shared obligation or responsibility with others—committing ourselves to an explicitly concursive mode of conduct. At the same time, it is clear that Huang-po did not want to encourage us to think of this as a purely voluntary act in the sense of a course of action 'you' and 'I' choose by and for our 'selves.' Hence his pointed qualification of this bond as *mei* 默 (silent/dark/secret)—something that is tacit or unspoken and hence not necessarily a function of having reached a self-conscious decision.

The significance of this cannot be overemphasized. Our experience of ourselves as enduring, self-conscious entities is in large part a function of the language-mediated fission of the unique world of our narration into distinct (eternal) 'universals' and (relatively short-lived but definitely located) 'particulars.' As far as Ch'an is concerned, "It is in establishing names that differences come to be" (HTC 119.423b), especially the difference between us and that about which we discourse. Whenever we speak, we take up a position or view (*dṛṣṭi*) from which we can say that something is or is-not, and so 'we' remain part of what is spoken even if no mention is made of men and women, of selves and others. Unlike music-making where it is possible for everyone involved to both sing and listen simultaneously, speech establishes a clear duality of actor (speaker) and acted upon (listener)—what in Chinese Buddhism is referred to as *neng-suo* 能所—and therefore sets up a guiding precedent for the identification of our 'self' as the generating nexus of experience. Thus, Huang-po remarks that "when the route of words and speech is severed, the practice of mental states is extinguished" (T 2012.380b). Instead of moving from experience to experience, we realize the lack of any objective marks separating us from everything else. By departing from all forms, we silence the ego and enter into a profound rapport. As a "silent bond," Ch'an liberation can be seen as the advent of true religion—the recovery of our original nature as persons.

Now, it should be clarified that Ch'an does not have a problem with making distinctions as such—after all, there is a distinction between what brings about harmony and what further exacerbates an ongoing break in our narration. But Ch'an does deny the ultimate basis and practical utility of the kind of lasting distinctions we establish through language. It is habit and not the power of making distinctions that is problematic, and precisely because it inhibits the wondrous functioning or superlative usability (*miao-yung* 妙用) of the latter. And so, while Lin-chi claims that as soon as he opens his mouth he has made a mistake—that even the intention to talk about Ch'an is evidence of error—he was famous for demanding that his students unhesitatingly engage him in conversation. If they paused to think about their reply or to consider the meaning of his remarks, Lin-chi would as often as not yell at or strike them with the demand that they "Speak, speak! Give me one true word!" Cutting off the route of language is not, therefore, the equivalent of becoming speechless, but is refusing to follow the dictates of linguistic convention, imagining that 'you' and 'I' are not aspects of a seamless whole just because a river of words and concepts apparently separate us. Just as a knife can be used to carve a buddha-statue or to murder a rival, language can be used as a liberative technique—something the *Vimalakirti Sutra* makes quite clear (see especially T 475.540c, 553c). What is not permissible if this is to occur is that we take what language refers to as anything other than a set of more or less stable conventions which can be dispensed with when necessary.

Thus, Pai-chang makes it clear that the great, round mirror wisdom is nothing other than the emptying of all duality by being able to be confronted by various sensations without giving rise to aversion or attachment—that is, without falling prey to habitual judgments of like and dislike.

> If you're able to enter the various sense-fields and realms, excel at being able to make distinctions without giving rise to disruptive thoughts and remain free and comfortable (*tzu tsai* 自在)—that is the wisdom of wondrous contemplation and examination. If you're able to make the various senses accord with circumstances, respond to need and comprehend entering correct reception (*shou* 受), there's no duality and that is the wisdom of perfecting what has been made. (HTC 424a)

Crucially, the failure to understand that such practice is not something done by and for one's 'self' not only makes it impossible to stop acting *yu-wei*, it disposes us toward seeing our relationships with others as individually dispensable and collectively necessary only for ease in satisfying certain of our (typically material) needs. Because we take it for granted that it is 'you' and 'I' who will with sufficient effort attain enlightenment, we feel compelled to determine which risks are worth taking and which seem destined to result in a loss of identity—something that the Ch'an Buddhist can only see as amounting to a forfeiture of liberation. 'Practice' will then only continue to inculcate marks of differentiation.

As long as we are unwilling to place ourselves deeply at risk, not only is true intimacy forestalled, we will effectively divert our experience away from precisely those configurations most likely to demand a completely unprecedented break with our accustomed range and orientation of conduct. In short, we will avoid the kind of adversity on which virtuosity thrives. Unlike skills which are developed gradually and are able to be used more or less at will, virtuosity is not the direct result of effort and intention. Nothing is more familiar to listeners of jazz than the wholly unsatisfying pyrotechnics of performers who possess skills of the highest order and so little inspiration or musical feel that their playing seems predictable at best and mechanical at worst. Notes are played seemingly for their own and not a profoundly musical sake, and no matter how impressive this is technically the improvisations so generated fail to draw us into intimate relation with the musicians and the world they are creating. To the contrary, the music as often as not draws too much attention to itself as an object for our appraisal and serves in the end only as mediation. Especially in the context of Chinese culture, this kind of thorough immersion in *yu-wei* is seen as improper not simply because it is typically productive of uninteresting and uninspiring music, but because the display of technical brilliance for its own sake is conducive only to our further standing out from and ultimately apart from one another.[24]

As a minimal condition, then, virtuosity arises only when we realize a shockingly creative and unexpected union of an actual crisis—be it political, social, intellectual, or even dramatic—and those formless qualities of concern and capability which will open up its truth. In short, virtuosity has no abiding nature. Just as the completely amorphous liquid known as water has no existence apart from a continuing union of two hydrogen atoms with single atoms of oxygen, there is no virtuosity in the absence of an always unique union of adversity with a concerned and unconstrained versatility. If unconstrained versatility—the supreme attainment of technical expertise or skill—is untempered by concern and left undirected due to the absence of concrete adversity, it would result in nothing more profound than the momentary pleasures of masturbation. The fact that we can speak, for example, of certain musicians as being occasionally capable of great displays of virtuosity may suggest that it is a thing individually acquired and then possessed. But this is nothing more than an illusion produced by the peculiarities of our grammar with its scission of subject and object, of agents and their acts, and taking it seriously is no more advisable that is trying to quench our thirst at a mirage. True virtuosity always occasions intimacy. Far from being a function of individually possessed talent, it is irreducibly social in nature and hence necessarily communal.

In a Buddhist context, truth is neither the timeless or eternal nature of things nor a correspondence between the world and our judgments about it. Rather, it should be seen as an entirely dynamic and corrective reorientation of narrative movement away from habitually restrictive channels into the signlessness of living freedom. Given this, and allowing that virtuosity has the function of opening up the truth of what initially seem to be intractable crises, it is possible to see the bodhisattva life as an ongoing manifestation of virtuosity. That is, the bodhisattva takes as his or her labor the initiation of unprecedented breaks with the ultimately discursive dictates of karma.[25] The business of the bodhisattva is not to disseminate information about nirvana and samsara, to deliver awe-inspiring gospels of enlightenment, or even to convey sentient beings to the nether shore, but to enter into unbounded and chartless concourse.

Practicing Ch'an thus depends on our being subject to narrative patterns—that is, forces both 'natural' or 'external' and 'psychological' or 'internal'—operating counter to our customary and hence preferred dispositions and the typical (habitual) actions they spawn. In the absence of such challenges, virtuosity simply cannot arise. It is possible, for example, for a jazz saxophonist to spend years diligently working on his or her chops and to acquire a degree of technical proficiency seldom achieved by others on the instrument. Given a standard tune like "My Favorite Things" to perform, he or she can elect to navigate the interpenetrating harmonic and melodic spaces by playing note for note the exact changes originally penned by Rogers and Hammerstein, and in so doing will certainly be lauded as an exceptionally competent player. But as long as this is the case, as long as the sax player is dedicated only to following musical prescriptions, he or she will never manifest true virtuosity. This comes about if and only if he or she elects to respond in an unprecedented way to the contours set for the musical space referred to as "My Favorite Things"—usually by striking out into previously unknown musical terrain. This may mean little more than improvising off of the established lead lines in such a way as to imply and then elicit from the rest of the ensemble previously unheard and unconceived harmonic and rhythmic motifs. It may, however, involve using the set structure of "My Favorite Things" as a kind of doorway through which the sax player leads his or her fellow musicians, destination unknown. Listen, for instance, to John Coltrane's several recorded renditions of the piece. Especially in the more improvisational forms of jazz, virtuosity entails opening up the horizons of a piece and giving birth to entirely new worlds.

Now, just as has been the case with every other type of true exploration, this extension of the limits of the known makes us vulnerable to unforeseen and in principle unforeseeable crises. If the sax player is unequal to the task of immediately resolving a dissonance or conflict of harmonic and rhythmic tempos, the performance will either disintegrate into noise or simply have to be yanked violently back into the most familiar of changes. As anyone who has participated in or listened to jazz improvisations knows, when the magic is happening there is no limit to what can be played, no ceiling to the musical heights ascended. When the magic fails—usually because someone stops actively and responsively listening—there is no limit to how abysmal the session can get. The same, of course, is true in our 'personal' relationships. The opportunity for realizing horizonless intimacy arises only when we allow the relationship to get far enough out of our individual control that our usual roles dissolve in an unprecedented and unpredictable dance of mutual attunement.[26]

And so, as the process of systematically relinquishing all impediments to social virtuosity, the practice of Ch'an must be seen as a committed flirtation with failure. The practitioner of Ch'an, far from retreating into the insulating solitude of the mountain cave or the deep forest glade, takes as one of his or her primary tasks the resolute courting of disaster, traditionally and specifically at the hands of his or her master and more generally in the tumult of daily life. Making him or herself maximally open to the possibility of interruption, diversion or conflict, practice is not directly a cultivation of peacefulness or quietude, but a radical exposure to risk. Practice entails unreservedly endangering one's 'self.'

In Ch'an, this self-endangering comes about as a joint function of refraining from acting on the basis of our ingrained likes and dislikes and engaging in truly social communication. The written records of the Ch'an tradition are luxuriant with injunctions to not discriminate—for the Chinese, to not conduct ourselves differently in the face of—good and evil, the pleasing and the unpleasing, the desired and the undesired. The point is not to achieve a kind of psychic numbness or imperturbability, but rather to both stop averting the dependent arising of what we refer to as ill and cease chasing after that which we think of as good. We are asked, in other words, to accept our karma—the conditioned and regularly patterned deformation of experience—rather than trying to escape it.[27] Doing otherwise only makes more karma, further binding us by identifying as 'me' the recipient of the consequences of past deeds.

Normally, we try to avoid ill and pursue good, thinking that who we are is totally and without remainder present at this point in time. We seem to feel that if we can avoid an unpleasant result now, that we stand a good chance of avoiding it forever. The Buddha was, however, clear in his denial of this reasoning. In fact, no intentional act is without experienced consequences. All that is in question is the timing, the precise moment at which the energy we intentionally diverted from its natural course will come full circle. And this is a matter of conditions over which we ultimately cannot exercise complete and direct control. While we may deflect this 'return' by so altering the present conditions—typically either through some form of ignorance or strenuous self-control—that the time is no longer ripe, we cannot prevent the eventual recurrence of appropriate conditions. In actuality, we as often as not make it possible for this karma to appear only at those times when we are least vigilant in our discriminations. That is, we make ourselves liable to what will be lamented as unforeseeable accidents or instances of 'bad luck,' often coming in strings. In respect of what we prefer, we will often contrive to bring about conditions which will foster the appearance of what we think is good, and in so doing further enmesh ourselves, deepening the experiential ruts into which we have diverted the flow of our narration—the behavior of our friends and family, the dispositions of our enemies, the prevailing political, economic and cultural climate, the condition of the ecosphere and so on. Thus, while the gods could be said to have the best of all possible incarnations, being entirely free of pain and unpleasantness, the Buddha insisted that they could not attain enlightenment. That possibility he reserved only for human beings—beings who can engage their suffering with unbridled virtuosity.

Insofar as concourse or communication that is truly social is itself a placing of the self at risk, it should come as no surprise that

Ch'an—ostensibly a "transmission beyond words and letters"—is of all the Chinese Buddhist schools the one which has placed the relationship of student and master at the very crux of both its doctrinal corpus and its practical injunctions.[28] For example, in the transmitted tradition of Indian Buddhism, a student ideally hears the dharma and then goes off on his or her own to gain insight into it through solitary meditation—a pattern which we still see operative in the not yet completely sinified teaching style embodied by Hui-neng in the Platform Sutra. But a Ch'an disciple who does not immediately engage the patriarchs of the tradition in lively, communicative improvisation is reviled as a mere "hearer" (*srāvaka*) or, in Lin-chi's less than gracious terminology, as a "worthless shit-stick" (T 1985.496c). Indeed, when a student has exhausted the ability of a given teacher to awaken a recognition of their own nature, they are not typically instructed to go off by themselves to practice and become a *pratyeka* or self-enlightened buddha. Instead, they are urged to travel and see this or that Ch'an master, often with the warning that this new counterpart will not be so grandmotherly and patient. The student is literally told to walk into communicative crisis.

To take an example from the oral tradition of Korean Ch'an, there was once a monk who had been practicing meditation with great zeal and diligence for many years but who had still not divested himself of his impediments to awakening. Thinking that the life of the monastery was distracting him from penetrating the great matter of enlightenment, he decided to ask his master for permission to go off on a long, solo retreat. The master made a show of deliberating for a few moments and then nodded. The monk was sent to stay in a hermitage owned by an elderly widow—an acquaintance and, it would seem, a long-time accomplice of the master. There, the monk redoubled his efforts at meditation, convinced that he would soon be able to break through the clouds of his delusion.

Every morning, the old woman would send her granddaughter up the winding trail to the hermitage with food for the monk. And every morning she would return full of praises for the depth and uninterruptedness of his discipline, recounting how he never so much as lifted an eyebrow when she entered and how on even the coldest mornings he always wore the same thin robe. Fall turned to winter, winter to spring, and when wildflowers began to dot the sunny side of the valley, the old woman decided to give the monk a chance to demonstrate his attainment.

She instructed her granddaughter to try engaging the monk in conversation, to speak about herself, her dreams, and her worry that they might never come true. The monk had remained silent throughout the young woman's visit, and she again had nothing but praises for their guest. Grandma, however, was clearly disturbed. Go back tomorrow, she said, and this time be more persistent. Sit right beside him and tell him that you have come to love him and that you wish he would marry you. If he still doesn't respond, try kissing him and ask what he's going to do about it. With some trepidation, the granddaughter did as she was told and was profoundly impressed when the monk remained steadfastly in meditative repose, even when she brushed her lips against his cheek. Asking him what he was going to do, he quietly and somewhat poetically said, "a burned-out log in deep winter snow."

The girl took this as a great virtue and happily reported the whole encounter to her grandmother, who responded by storming up the hill, pulling the monk out of the hermitage by his ear, and sending him tumbling down the path with a well-placed kick, reviling him as a worthless impostor while she set the hut on fire, burning it completely to the ground.[29]

In holding himself like an ice-encrusted, fire-hollowed log, the monk is acting out an image of nirvana as quiet extinction—as the complete absence of even the possibility of the arising of passion. The burned-out log, firm outside and hollow within, represents his (still Indian-influenced) conception of attaining emptiness or selflessness. Looking like good material for a fire, the log is in fact quite useless, and while the monk may look to the young girl like good material for a husband, he is in fact impervious to temptation. Almost as if he were not a man at all, he remains aloof from her charms, rigidly adhering to his precepts. This he takes as Buddhist virtue. But in the old widow's eyes, this is simply a convenient story absolving the monk of the difficulties involved in really dealing with whatever comes in front of him. By saying he is like a burned-out log in winter snow, the monk is saying that he has nothing to give her granddaughter, no help, not even a word or two of real understanding. Having nothing to offer, the monk has nothing to lose and so is in no position to be able to enter into an intimate relationship. Far from being able to respond with virtuosity, he is able only to put her off, to deny her access. In a word, he separates himself from her, looking on the outside like a sincere Buddhist practitioner, but inside as desolate and bereft of real compassion as the site of a burned-down cottage.

By identifying himself with the cold indifference and uselessness of the burned-out log, the monk not only asserts his disparity with the girl, he ruthlessly cleaves their narrative into 'his' and 'hers,' reducing it to a discourse which will carry him further along the path of sagely and meditative stillness and leave her to be swept along the way of the commoner. Taking meditation as his practice, the monk refuses to be drawn into the girl's life or to take her fully into his own. Their relationship remains wholly societal—she is just someone who brings his food, nothing more or less. But his distinction of 'sage' and 'commoner' is ultimately destructive of the very foundations of the bodhisattva life. Not only does it leave the young woman's needs unanswered, it secures the monk, insuring his safety—the safety of his 'self,' his identity as 'monk.'

In refusing to relate intimately with the girl, the monk enforces their difference, projecting a horizon within which he does his 'practice' and outside of which she carries on in the life of a layperson. In refusing to accept responsibility for her feelings, he blinds himself to the meaning of their meeting and the shared karma this reveals. Finally, in refusing to accord with the situation and respond directly to her need, he makes a virtue out of his unreadiness to realize enlightenment and open up the wondrously unlimited meaning of true sociality.

Chapter 6

Opening the Field of Virtuosity:
Practicing *Tun-wu, Wei-hsin,* and *K'ung*

If persons are seen as narration, the practice of Ch'an may be intensely personal, but it can never be purely individual. As an orientation toward intimacy—the achievement of harmonious nonduality—practice erases the very boundaries by means of which 'I,' 'my,' and 'me' are defined without at the same time eliding our uniqueness, our quite real differences. Thus understood, practice—like suffering and its liberating resolution—is not reducible to or even located in individual behavior. Instead, it must be seen as given directly in *conduct*—narrative movement and meaning.

While it is certainly more comfortable to continue imagining otherwise, this is as much as to say that the value or meaning of Buddhist practice can never be determined by an exclusive analysis of the quality of our own experience. Regardless of the insights or revelations we may obtain, the vows we may take and scrupulously honor, the changes of lifestyle we may undergo, whether or not we are practicing Ch'an can be assessed only with reference to the changing complexion of our entire narration. As the bodhisattva ideal makes quite clear, whether or not 'I' become a 'buddha' is practically irrelevant. What matters is not 'my' salvation or even the salvation of particular 'others,' but the liberation of *all* beings, of the entire world apart from which no one of us obtains.

The root illusion under which most of us labor is the belief—underwritten by an at least tacit acceptance of the priority of being over value—that liberation has something to do with independence. Taken to its extreme, this belief guides us inexorably toward conceiving of freedom as having no necessary connection with anyone or anything else. But granted the validity of our suggestion that

117

virtuosity arises out of the interplay of adversity and care, such a freedom amounts to a rejection of at least certain crucial conditions involved in realizing unlimited skill in means. Bluntly stated, conceiving of freedom as independence is inconsistent with living the life of a bodhisattva or buddha. At bottom, it is because of the fundamental arrogance of such a conception of liberation and the parsimoniousness it implies that the old widow burned down the monk's hermitage. Believing that he could, even had to attain enlightenment on his own, the monk concentrated himself, conserving his energy (*ch'i* 氣), presenting a cold and indifferent exterior. Removing himself from the unpredictable demands of social life, he focused exclusively on his 'spiritual' development. He decided, in short, to not share himself, and—barring the intervention of some 'distraction' like the widow and her granddaughter—the energy he stored up by doing so would eventually have triggered off an experiential breakthrough. This he would undoubtedly have seen as a mark of success. But when his old habits of perception and feeling reasserted themselves—and they almost invariably do—he would have been compelled to try corroborating his initial breakthrough, to relive its wonder. And because this sensation of breaking through is so deeply satisfying, repetition not infrequently leads to addiction—to a compelling desire to possess and so be possessed by it. Left to his own devices, the monk would hoard more and more energy, making his difference from others greater and ever greater.

Stiff and puffed up with the pride that comes from feeling so much energy held in one place at one time, the monk might even become a meditative adept, might attain the classic marks (*siddhis*) of those who have developed supernatural powers. But none of this can happen except at the expense of the rest of his narrative. Making and maintaining any kind of distinction requires the diversion and retention of energy that would otherwise circulate freely and hence be generally available for the creative resolution of unexpected crises. Novel meanings will remain unrealized even as our narrative as a whole stagnates. Stored or blocked energy becomes power, and with that come further distinctions—those who have and those who do not, those who know and those who do not, those who are able and those who are not. It means, in effect, the degeneration of a world, the incurrence of intractability or unreality.

The Mahayana belief that the Dharma will undergo an extended period of decline is thus quite distinct from the Hindu belief in an objective cycle of world ages. The degeneration of the Dharma is not due to factors *beyond* individual control but is precisely the result of individuals gaining and *refusing to relinquish control* of the flow of natural energy, diverting it instead into the continuous maintenance of distinctions—the most harmful being that between the 'enlightened' and the 'unenlightened.' Ch'an is the recognition that this age will come to a close only when each of us realizes that no 'one' is ever truly enlightened and that the greatest service we can perform is to carry out Lin-chi's famous injunction: "If you meet the 'buddha', kill him" (T 1985.500b).

Forgetting the 'Self': *Ch'an* Overtures

It is in this spirit that when answering a question about the five kinds of dharma bodies, Pai-chang concludes that "not having attainments and 'evidence' is precisely 'evidence' of the Buddhadharma dharma body" (HTC 119.422b). Having no 'attainments' and no 'proof of achievement' in practice is simply the wondrous function (*miao yung* 妙用) of the great ocean mirror samadhi in which nothing is rejected and nothing retained. By contrast, "if someone possesses 'proofs' and 'attainments,' [we should] regard them as evidence of his/her being an arrogant person (*tseng-shang-man-jen* 增上慢人) with false views" (HTC 119.422b). For the Chinese Buddhist, people like this literally "add on" (*tseng-shang*) "slowness" (*man*). By advancing themselves, they necessarily retard the natural course of events, inhibiting others through their own acquisition of power. Standing out is always done at someone else's expense. In contemporary slang, we simply say that an arrogant person is "a drag"—someone who robs every situation of the energy necessary for opening up its truth.

In the same way that the success of a musical improvisation is a function of how sensitively all the musicians involved listen to and play with one another, whether or not we are actually practicing Ch'an is never simply a function of our individual streams of consciousness (our solos), or even of the general level of expertise we bring to playing out our karma (our chosen instrument). Rather, it depends on whether our playing accords with and augments the contributions of everyone else involved in our narration. Practicing ch'an, far from enforcing a depreciation of all that is not 'me' and 'mine,' arises only with a profound appreciation of others. And so, it is quite possible to experience a marked increase in our individual level of distress upon entering the practice life in earnest. Eschewing all arrogance means a spontaneous reorientation of our narration away from the gathering of power toward releasing as much previously blocked energy as possible for the benefit of others and so for the vitality of our relationships with them.

This humbling of the 'self' typically leaves the ego feeling deflated if not completely baffled—certain that something is unpredictably and perhaps uncontrollably getting out of hand. At this stage in the realization of Ch'an, doubts arise about the efficacy of practice, about the trustworthiness of the master, about the whole project of realizing enlightenment. And yet it is only if the practitioner is able at this point to refrain from reinforcing his or her distinctions and resist the desire to wrest back control of events that the true meaning of Ch'an can manifest.

In other words, the sincere practitioner must be willing to 'do' nothing at all and simply allow his or her life to proceed unchecked. Anything else amounts to holding on (obsessive attachment) and holding off (the arrogance of aversion). Like a piece of improvised music, practice is something other than the sum of its individually experienced, factual or behavioral parts, and there are times when the part 'we' play in it seems so infinitesimal as to be no part at all. To extend the musical analogy, practice sometimes puts us in the position of playing a simple rhythmic pattern again and again, subtlely opening up the field of time and space on which we find others soloing, expressing the infinite degrees of their freedom. There is no glamour in this "repetition," no exalted sense of individual accomplishment, and yet it is precisely what is needed at times for the music to come fully to life. When this happens, our simple contribution is heard in a completely new and always unanticipated way, becoming something much more sublime than we could ever have imagined. In the same way, as long as we are fully engaged in practicing Ch'an, even though we may from an objective point of view be doing nothing out of the ordinary, the meaning of our activity—our conduct—is undergoing continual transformation. Even though we are doing nothing special, our relationships become progressively more open and truthful.[1]

In this light, Ma—tzu's declaration that "ordinary mind is Tao" (*p'ing-ch'ang-hsin-shih-tao* 平常心是道) (TTC 45.406a) cannot be reduced to a bit of histrionic iconoclasm. Rather, it must be recognized as a practical reminder that the true Tao of Buddhism is always right in front of us and that there is no need to pick and choose our experiences, to guide ourselves out of ignorance. To the contrary, it is picking and choosing that lies at the root of our confusion and continued bondage. We have all had the experience of trying to act differently or better only to discover that it does no good—our relationships still falter and collapse, we encounter the 'same' difficulties again and again, the same sense of being stuck. Even though we change jobs, move to another city, make new friends and lovers, we find ourselves repeating the 'same mistakes,' suffering the 'same injustices.' In Buddhist terms, our karma remains undigested no matter how much we change our circumstances.

According to Ch'an, this impasse is resolved only when 'we' relinquish control and allow our narration as a whole to open up. Then, even if we don't do anything differently, our relationships become progressively clearer (*ming* 明), less sticky, less characterized by misunderstanding and feelings of loneliness, frustration, or conflict. This is the meaning behind Ma-tzu insisting that ordinary mind—the mind of a buddha—is "not making anything (*wu-tsao-tso* 無造作), not affirming or denying, not grasping or rejecting, not annihilating or eternalizing, not being 'common' and not being 'sage'" (TTC 45.406a). In short, ordinary mind is realizing the *complete relaxation* referred to as "no-'mind'"—the relinquishing of all karma-generating and necessarily discursive dispositions.[2] Then:

> whether in robes (lay life) or cassock (ordained life), sitting and rising follow one another and the precepts and cultivation are an added perfume that accumulates in pure karmas/deeds. . . . Neither cultivating nor sitting is the Tathagata's pure and clear ch'an. Right now if you see this principle and are truly correct, you won't create any karma and will pass your life content with your lot. . . . If you're simply able to be like this, what worries are not penetrated? (TTC 45.407a)

Strictly speaking, striving to bring about such an unmitigatedly relaxed condition is inconceivable. Arguably, the original function of conception is making distinctions useful in our ongoing efforts to control experience, promoting satiety over hunger, ease over difficulty, happiness over sadness. For this reason, conception inevitably implics a point of view, an 'agent' or 'experiencer' who will engineer and benefit from the regulation of his or her environment. But in "rejecting phenomena so as to promote the order of things, people don't realize that it is 'mind' (set dispositions) that obstructs (hinders the opening of) horizons, and the 'order of things' that obstructs phenomena" (T 2012.382a). Making no distinctions is thus tantamount to doing nothing at all for our 'selves'—a way of neglecting the center of gravity around which our karma revolves like a vast system of comets. If the center does not hold, the events, people and things which we have captured and been drawing back lifetime after lifetime are all at once liberated.

It should come as no surprise, then, that when he was asked for the significance of the term "middle path," Pai-chang replied that it means "boundaries" (*pien* 邊). After all, "if there were no boundaries (no horizons), from whence would the 'middle' come to be?" (HTC 119.424b). If we didn't project likes and dislikes—external or objective 'things' we crave and detest—there could be no 'middle path.' All that would remain is the campestrial generosity of an oceanic mind which selects nothing. Realizing horizonless intimacy through systematically relinquishing all impediments to social virtuosity, the practitioner of Ch'an undertakes refusing nothing on principle, projecting no distinctions which will cause the narration of which they are a part to splinter into mutually exclusive subjects and objects. "When a bodhisattva's mind is like the empty sky, every-'thing' is entirely relinquished"—that is, no horizons remain, no possibility of marking some 'thing' or 'individual' off from everything else and saying what it 'is':

> Then, there is nothing to grasp, nothing to push away. In accordance with the situation, you respond to things and 'agent' and 'acted upon' are both forgotten. This is great relinquishing. . . . [it is] like a blazing torch right in front of you so that there's nothing further of 'delusion' or 'enlightenment.' (T 2012.382a)

With no shadow of 'self' remaining in what lies before us, enlightenment—the meaning of practice—is simply the realization of true (*cheng* 正) and clear (*ming*) relationship with others.

The Modes of Ch'an Practice

It has already been suggested that Ch'an practice should not be reduced to or even identified with meditative discipline—an individually navigated path from lesser to greater control over body, emotion, thought, and so on. At the same time, if practice is indeed best seen as liberating intimacy, it clearly cannot be associated with

reckless abandon, or worse yet with the cultivation of some ada-
mantine capriciousness. Seen as "according with the situation, responding as needed," Ch'an practice occurs as the virtuosity of the
middle path between control and caprice, between having (yu) and
not-having (wu).

The thrust of Indo-European rationality has been to deny such
a path, to exclude the ambiguity out of which 'is' and 'is-not' or
'having' and 'not-having' are abstracted as mutually exclusive and
yet mutually entailing opposites. According to such a rationality,
whether some thing 'is' or 'is-not' is given. What is contingent is, if
anything, our knowledge of this fact. Crucially, this means that the
'thing' persists as the necessary object of our knowing. Rationality
of such a mint is, in short, the rationality of an ineluctable subject.

By valorizing a mind that dwells on no 'thing,' Ch'an is in this
restricted sense of the word quite irrational. Ch'an arises with a
refusal to entertain the middle path as an axis described by linking
the points between 'is' and 'is-not,' 'having' and 'not-having,' 'good'
and 'ill,' 'enlightened' and 'unenlightened.' Such an axis, after all,
only recreates and sustains the centrality of the self as a ghostly
trace lying between objectively ideal contraries. Such contraries
evidence as nothing more than impediments or blockages to the free
flow of our narration, to the increasing virtuosity of our conduct.
Dwelling on no 'thing' manifests as realized nonduality, the blossoming of a decentered reality—a world which takes care of itself
and in which conduct or dramatic relationality is irreducible.

In such a world, the middle path can never be construed in
terms of compromise—a construal possible only under the auspices
of inescapable subjectivity—but as the relinquishing of horizons,
the untraceable elision of all segregating boundaries for our narration. That is, if the Buddha and the masters of Ch'an have been
honest in declaring that they attained nothing with the realization
of enlightenment, and if it is precisely Buddhist practice/conduct
(hsing 行) that is the Buddha, practice is just getting nothing at all.

For heuristic purposes, and because there is some historical
warrant for doing so, we can explore the nature of this relinquishing
along three interdependent dimensions of meaning or ramification
in conduct: readiness, responsibility, and relevance. Roughly, these
three correspond to the explicitly social turn of Buddhism exemplified in Hui-nengs so called "sudden teaching," and the appropriation
by Ch'an of on the one hand the Yogacara teaching of mind-only and
on the other the Madhyamika teachings of emptiness. These teachings constitute the narrative threads woven together in the realiza-

tion of Ch'an by the lineage extending from Ma-tzu through to Lin-chi—the harmony creating modes of the true Buddha-dharma dharma body.

Tun-wu: *Relinquishing All Horizons to Readiness*

It is clear from Huang-po's characterization of the great relinquishing (ta she 大捨) as "according with your situation and responding as needed" that it is not merely a putting away or release—a kind of rejection—but entails in addition an offering or giving, a spirit of concern. In fact, the Chinese term *she* not only suggests parting with something, but includes the sense of bestowal, the giving of alms. And so, the great relinquishing can be seen as an unhindered embodiment of *dānapāramitā*—as freely entering the gate of Ch'an enlightenment. Since what we are giving up in this great relinquishing are not the tools of our trades, our food or our relationships with others, but rather set all forms or distinctions (*hsiang*), our offering is not of anything in particular but rather of the energy that has until now been bound up in the habitual maintenance of 'self,' 'other,' 'good,' 'evil,' and so on. With the release of this energy, we signal our manifest readiness for creating a pure land—for living the bodhisattva life.[3]

This suggests that the central doctrine of Ch'an—the teaching of *tun wu* 頓悟 or what is usually translated as "sudden awakening"—is not a declaration of fact about the nature of enlightenment or the speed with which it is attained, but is rather a verbalization of the core practice of Ch'an. If enlightenment is not to be identified with any particular experience but is instead given in conduct or narrative movement as a great relinquishing, taking *tun* as a primarily temporal indicator would seem wholly inappropriate. In fact, Hui-neng—traditionally regarded as the first proponent of the "sudden teaching"—makes it quite clear that it is not the dharma which is sudden (*tun* 頓) or gradual (*chien* 漸), but people who are keen (*li* 利) or dull (*tun* 鈍). (PS 16) That is, the distinction being made is dispositional, not temporal.[4] Some people are slow—reluctant to entirely divest themselves of the discriminations which retard the natural digestion of their karma—and effectively inhibit the clearing of their narrative, deferring enlightenment by continuing to make decisions and act on the basis of their habits for 'what works.' Others are *li*—people who are willing and clever enough to presently reap the fruit of their deeds, to accept and digest their karma and free all the energy which has until now been kept bound up in them.[5]

Thus, *tun-wu* seems best translated not as "sudden awakening," but as the "readiness for awakening," where the ambiguity of who awakens—me or you—should be taken as a reminder that liberation is found in conduct itself, in the nonduality of intimate narration. In fact, the character *tun* 頓 has the primary connotation of bowing the head, putting in order, preparing. It designates the process of humbling oneself through the expression of an unalloyed willingness to serve. Like a servant accepting his or her instructions, a bodhisattva not only stops resisting the situation, but offers it his or her unconditional assent.

According to Pai-chang, "*Tun* is the readiness to do away with misleading thoughts"—thoughts that lead us to neglect what is right before us. "*Wu* is awakening to the absence of anything to be attained"—and, by implication, of anyone who attains. The recommended method for accomplishing this is *ting* 定 or "responding to circumstances with no-'mind' (*tui-ching-wu-hsin* 對境無心)" (HTC 119.420b), with no set or habitual dispositions. In short, far from indicating a flash of insight or an instantaneous achievement of liberation, *tun-wu* should be seen as wholeheartedly placing ourselves in the service of our entire narration or world, as relinquishing all horizons for readiness.[6] And so, even today Ch'an masters will challenge beginning students by asking them: "Twenty-five-hundred-years-ago Buddha, present-day Buddha, and you . . . are they the same or different?" If the student answers "the same," he receives thirty blows. If he says "different," he still receives thirty blows. If he tries "both the same and different," he is hit sixty times. And if he says "neither the same nor different," he is dismissed as unworthy even of the stick. In short, the student is challenged to resist all judgment, all decision, and hence all reliance on the segregation of self and other, of knowing and known. He or she must truly—that is, correctively—respond with the situation. At the very least, this means undoing the dualism of the master's question.

Nowhere is this more forcefully articulated than in the teachings of Lin-chi. Adamantly insisting that he has nothing to give anyone, Lin-chi constantly challenges his students to develop the confidence (*hsin* 信) needed to be able to become the master of any situation, to be able to caringly respond without any hesitation with whatever comes their way. Any form of seeking is a waste of time that only makes more karma and more deeply enmeshes us in the habits already strangling our original nature. Any hesitation or doubt is a blockage to the free flow of energy on which the resolution of narrative interruption depends:

> If you doubt even for an instant, the demon Mara will enter your mind. When a bodhisattva has even a moment of doubt, the demons of birth and death take the advantage. But if you're able to stop thinking (attain no-'mind') and moreover don't search outwardly for anything, things just come and are illuminated (*chao*). (T 1985.499a)

Dispensing with all the usual worries that impede our readiness to respond freely to the needs of others, "there is nothing that is not profound, nothing that is not liberation" (T 1985.497c). As Hui-neng puts it, when the mind dwells on no-'thing', the Tao freely circulates (*tao-chi-t'ung-liu* 道即通流) (PS 14) and there is nothing special that needs to be done. So even if we are unable to see our own natures, we need only "give rise to *prajñā* and illuminate (*chao* 照) with it and in the briefest instant all delusive thoughts are eliminated" (PS 31). Nothing else is necessary.

Relinquishing our horizons to readiness is thus the practical or functional equivalent of giving rise to *prajñā*—defined by Hui-neng as *chih-hui* 智慧, where *chih* is wisdom or being capable of conducting oneself in an appropriate manner and where *hui* carries a range of connotations including favor, benefit, conferring kindness, according with, and being gracious. As both Lin-chi's and Hui-neng's use of the term *chao* ("to illuminate" or "reflect," but also "to look after" or "care for") suggests, *prajñā* is the radiantly careful offering of all that comes our way—the realization of the great, round mirror wisdom that receives everything without any discrimination and which without any hesitation or holding back brightly reflects or returns it. Wisdom is thus another designation for what we earlier referred to as the "Copernican revolution" by means of which who we are ceases to be understood in terms of individualism and hence duality. *Prajñā* is not knowing-about, then, but should be seen as directly releasing others by emptying the 'self,' rendering it incapable of acting as the (illusory) center about which the cosmos spins. Seen in this light, the great relinquishing cannot be a 'self'-generated experience of releasing what is no longer desired, but is realized only as an understanding kindness or wise beneficence (*chih-hui*). Accordingly, *tun-wu* cannot refer to any kind of 'self'-serving sacrifice, but only to a luminous offering of profoundest and hence most intimate compassion.

Wei-hsin: Relinquishing All Horizons for Responsibility

Now, in addition to this great relinquishing, Huang-po also refers to middle and lower "levels" of relinquishing and it is important to ask whether these three form a comprehensive and necessary system—with relinquishing our horizons for readiness as the chief—or if they represent a hierarchy of independent and disparately valued types of Buddhist practice. In other words, are the three relinquishings an integral system of practice or are they to be seen as separate practices appropriate for people of different roots or capacities? Huang-po's use of the terms "middle" and "lower" would certainly seem to suggest the latter interpretation, but granted the often remarked upon tendency among those uninitiated into the true meaning of Ch'an to identify practice with sitting meditation and the realization of emptiness, it is possible that Huang-po's hierarchy is really nothing more than a corrective or cautionary device. That is, it need not be understood as reflective of an actual superiority or independence of "great" relinquishing as opposed to the "middle" and "lower" forms.

At the very least, it would seem to be the case that we would be disinclined to offer our distinctions and ultimately our 'selves' up to others if we had no reason to believe that this would help to correct or alleviate their difficulties. That is, unless we had reason to feel in some way responsible for the needs of others—unless we saw a connection between or interdependence of our distinctions and their ills—the great relinquishing would occur in a vacuum and prove futile except as a means of either disemburdening ourselves of karmic baggage and attaining an individual liberation or of satisfying a need 'we' have to feel helpful. In either case, 'you' and 'I' would remain central to the practice of Ch'an and the act of relinquishing our horizons for readiness in the service of others would not lead to unimpeded, liberating intimacy, but to precisely the kind of egotism that Subhuti was explicitly warned against by the Buddha. In short, if our readiness to humble our selves in the service of others is based on a distinction of their suffering and its causes and our own, we will not yet have grasped the true principle of Ch'an. The great relinquishing can arise only on the basis of a relinquishing of all horizons for responsibility.

This, in fact, seems to be the import of the middle level of relinquishing. Huang-po says, "If on the one hand you practice the way, manifesting virtue, and on the other hand you turn around and relinquish it and have no hope in mind—that is the middle relinquishing" (T 2012.382a). The key phrase here is "manifesting virtue" (*pu-te* 布德). One of the primary focuses in the conceptual matrix of Chinese culture, *te* has a constellation of meanings ranging from virtue, power, energy, and conduct, to bounty and the repayment of kindness. All of these connotations must, of course, be understood in the context of a relational metaphysics where dynamism or change is taken as irreducible and basic.

In the existence-biased metaphysics of the Indo-European traditions, change is a modification of being and what is most real is what remains, what endures. Accordingly, in such traditions, virtue is acquired by and secondary to the individual who acquires. Power or virtue and the degrees to which we possess them are in this sense seen as separating us from others, setting us at odds. The reverse is true in the Chinese traditions generally and in Chinese Buddhism in particular. Contrary to the conception of energy or power as a value-neutral, individually deployed component of all change or motion, *te* is seen as arising with the intensification of our narration. Far from segregating us, *te* draws us into more profound and harmonious intimacy. For the Chinese, the association of *te* and the arrogance of 'power' is simply contradictory.

Thus, in the explicitly humanistic context of the Confucian tradition, *te* is said to be accumulated whenever we articulate our persons by doing our best, living up to our word, and taking excellence in adapting to what is appropriate as our primary concern. Neatly phrased, "*Te* is never isolated, but necessarily has neighbors" (A IV.25). With the intensification of *te* we come into progressively deeper, more extensive and mutually nurturing relationship not only with other men, women, and children, but with heaven (*t'ien* 天) and all that lies below it.

Lao-tzu takes this basic notion to its conceptual limit and claims that with an abundance of *te* we become like new-born infants—persons who as yet mark no difference between 'self' and 'world', mine and yours (LT 55). Just as newborns simply do what is natural without entertaining intermediary 'shoulds' and 'should-nots' and carving the world up into what can and cannot be done, someone with an abundance of *te* is free from all ulterior motivation. In the Ch'an tradition, this is encapsulated in the famous injunction to simply eat when hungry and sleep when tired.

Unlike the Indo-European virtue or power, *te* implies an ease or naturalness which is not only unresisting but which meets in turn no resistances. One of the effects of this return to naturalness is, of course, a lack of discrimination between what is 'me' and 'mine,' what I have done and am responsible for and what has and must be done by others. With an increase of *te*, energy flows into and through us with less and less impedance—the consequence of which is the linking of our particular manners of being in such a way that our fates (*ming* 命) become interdependent. In keeping with this principle, Lao-tzu later remarks that, "The person of *te* takes charge of the tally (*szu-ch'i* 司契)"—accepting full responsibility for carrying out the system of obligations symbolized by the tally, while "the person without it manages the collecting"—is concerned only with what they can get (LT 79).

For the Taoist, the communion of a particular *te* with the *tao* is a function of "acting naturally" or what we have referred to as conduct without precedent (*wu-wei*)—conduct that is spontaneous and complete (*tzu-jan* 自然), disemburdened of hope, uncontaminated by the calculated divisiveness of ends and means. Not making anything, the person of profound *te* expresses the *tao* with unselfconscious virtuosity, freely improvising with—and hence becoming inseparable from—whatever comes his or her way.

To summarize, in the Confucian and Taoist traditions that provided the ritual and conceptual contexts for the Chinese appropriation of Buddhism, manifesting *te* entails an active extension of our naturalness and responsibility for what happens. In this light, Huang-po's constant reference to enlightenment as a "silent bond" (*mei-ch'i* 默契) takes on a more dynamic and explicitly narrative cast. Since realizing the great, round mirror wisdom means receiving and reflecting whatever comes our way, a buddha can be seen as a focus of universal energy—a person through whom all things flow unimpeded. Like the ocean which takes in all water no matter how clear or muddy, a buddha in effect refuses to disown any karma or narrative movement—refuses to say: "That belongs to your story, your tally, is your doing, your problem and not mine." Like the Confucian or Taoist person endowed with great *te*, a buddha is best seen as a liberating and harmonizing focus of both energy and the conduct in which it is articulated—in short, a person through whom the interdependence and intimacy of all things is quietly and unprecedentedly realized. Unlike a selfishly centered individual who constantly divorces himself from others by claiming that 'they' are to blame for this or that state of affairs, a buddha realizes everything as the wondrous functioning (*miao yung* 妙用) of onemind.[7] No matter what happens, it is entirely oneself (*tzu chia* 自家, literally "one's own family"), one's own doing (*karma*) (TTC 45.406b), and so one's own responsibility.

As Huang-po puts it, when we realize that we are one-mind, "wriggling beings and all the buddhas and bodhisattvas are a single body and do not differ" (T 2012.380b). But if the least shred of ego remains, this body will inevitably seem to be 'mine' and the energy flowing through it will seem to need directing—a vector along which we can extend our 'selves,' perhaps even for the 'good' of 'others'. In short, we will fall prey to the lures of power and persist in acting *yu-wei*, beset by both precedents and goals. To the precise extent that we indulge in this decision-making—in asking which course of action is right and which ones wrong—we sunder the one-mind and continually give birth on the one hand to the two-mindedness of doubt and on the other to the disparity of 'here' and 'there,' of 'mine' and 'yours.'

In the end, and no matter how altruistic our motives may be, this means that our attention will necessarily be directed first to resolving our own doubts—to making further distinctions of one sort or another—and not responding directly to the needs of 'others.' Instead of integrating all things, our effort will serve only to define our means and our ends and so intensify our separateness and the fragile certitude of our discriminations. The very conceptualizing done in trying to determine or identify what is best for others necessarily places us at a distance from them, be it spatial, temporal, or metaphysical.[8] Hence the insistence in Huang-po's middle relinquishing that we literally disown the virtue we focus—actively departing not only from the distinction between 'what is' and 'what might be' that lies at the root of all that is merely hopeful, but from the illusion that 'we' can engineer the betterment of circumstances thought of as not our own. Only in this way can we free up the energy hitherto expended in the continual maintenance of our 'selves.'

By relinquishing our horizons for responsibility we not only take on the karmic burdens of others and realize an intimacy with them that is so thorough as to render all distinctions between us purely conventional, we begin to understand that nothing separates who we are from all that comes to be. Ultimately, we are responsible for the entirety of our narration—our world—and not only for whatever we have consciously contrived to bring about in this life. It is in this spirit that Ma-tzu insists that "the three realms are only mind" and that "everything that is seen as form is [actually just] seeing mind" (TTC 45.406a). In short, our dispositions are implicated in everything that happens. There are no 'things' existing apart from our intention and doing.

Since both Shen-hsiu's verse and Hui-neng's famous rebuttal were written on walls destined to be painted with scenes from the *Lankavatara Sutra*, the watershed between the so-called Northern and Southern (gradual and sudden) schools can arguably be traced to differences in the meaning of the Lankavatara's central doctrine of mind-only (*wei-hsin* 唯心). Whereas Shen-hsiu takes the separate or independent existence of pollutants as given and sees our task as practitioners to be the continual cleansing of our minds so that they can function in an enlightened manner, Hui-neng denies the validity of any discrimination between our nature and these 'dusts.' After declaring that buddha nature—the original nature of our own minds—is constantly pure and clear, he seems to raise his hands in a gesture of rhetorical dismay and asks, "Where is there dust?" (PS 8). While Shen-hsiu implicitly affirms a kind of dualism, seeing mind and dust as sufficiently distinct for the latter to be able to be said to cover or obscure the former, Hui-neng realizes that this effectively cuts us off from ourselves. By divorcing ourselves from the 'dust' of the world we perform the root scission from which the disparity of 'you' and 'I' is born.

As understood in Ch'an, the Yogacara teaching of mind-only (*wei-hsin*) is not a move into subjective idealism, but realizing that we are a single family, a single body of harmoniously interplaying parts. But this understanding is not just an intellectual acceptance of our interdependence. It is conducting ourselves *as* one, manifesting our *te* without indulging in the selfish interrogation of "what's in this for me?" *Wei-hsin* is a mother waking in the middle of the night just before the first cries of her infant and without thinking offering her breast. It is the conduct of the man described by Mencius in his argument for the inherent goodness of human nature—a man who sees a small child about to fall into a well and who rushes forward to save her without any hesitation or thought of who the child belongs to or who is to blame for the impending accident.

Thus, when asked how laypersons in particular are to practice Ch'an, the pivot of Hui-neng's response is that we must cease making differences between what we are responsible for and what we are not.

> A true cultivator of the Tao does not see any errors in the world. If you see wrongs in the world, it is your own wrongs that are affirmed. We are to blame for the wrongs of others just as we are to blame for our own. (PS 36)

In short, there is no aspect of our narration in which we can legitimately claim to have had no part. As persons in the full narrative sense, splitting up responsibility for the ills of this life is tantamount to a willfully induced schizophrenia which not only fractures our world (interrupts our narrative), but makes it virtually impossible to truly communicate with one another, to enter into unhindered concourse. This is the profound impetus behind Huang-po's claim that, "All the Buddhas and all sentient beings are just one-mind (*i-hsin*), and beyond this there is no other teaching." This one-mind "rises beyond all boundaries, calculations, names, words, traces and attitudes. It is [your] present body/self and that's all" (T 2012.379c).

K'ung: *Relinquishing All Horizons for Relevance*

Now, one of the standard accusations aimed at Buddhist proponents of the doctrine of mind-only is that it leads to affirming the independent existence of mind and forces us into an admitted subjectivity seemingly incompatible with the Buddha's teaching of selflessness. This indeed follows logically, but only where the relationship between mind and 'things' is seen as linearly causal and not karmic. To be sure, if 'things' are the effect of mind and if mind is not effected in return by 'things,' the doctrine of mind-only would amount to a substantialist reduction—an assertion of 'what really *is*'. Whether this is called 'mind' or 'buddha-nature' or 'substance' is finally irrelevant. The practical danger in each case is the profound ignorance involved in allowing our own minds to settle on one 'thing' as ultimately or unconditionally real. But if it is understood that nothing can be identified as the basis of reality—that all things are impermanent and hence in constant evolution, unborn and yet having already come to be—what matters is simply the manner in which things come together, the quality of their interdependence. What is real is not 'mind' or 'matter,' but the values embodied in the orientations and movement of our narration—what we have referred to as conduct.

Given this, it is significant that Hui-neng is said to have attained enlightenment upon hearing Hung-jen reading the passage of the *Diamond Sutra* in which the Buddha tells Subhuti that we give birth to a pure and clear mind by having "nothing on which the mind dwells (*wu-suo-chu* 無所住)" (T 235.749c). Only in this way can we avoid identifying mind and making it into some 'thing' opposed to all others—the imagined, central axis on which the world turns. Dwelling on any 'thing' means and end to improvising, a resistance of the impermanence of things, a projection of horizons within which alone a 'thing' may come into being. Such a willful imposition of constraints on our concourse with others cannot but selfishly divert the natural circulation of energy into the creation of karmic patterns. We may initially take this selfish action as evidence of our freedom, but in fact it can serve only to more and more deeply enmesh us in ignorance. As the *Diamond Sutra* makes clear, the only sure way beyond bondage as a distinction-generating and generated self is the refusal to accept any limit to inquiry as final— to eschew any appeal to the dichotomy of 'is' and 'is-not.' In short, the possibility of successfully relinquishing all horizons for responsibility depends on the practice of emptiness (*k'ung* 空).

According to Huang-po, the lower [level of] relinquishing occurs when "you extensively cultivate a great many excellent qualities in the hope of attaining something and upon hearing the dharma realize emptiness and are then unattached" (T 2012.382a). For example, you may wish to acquire a good birth in the next life and to that end cultivate a kind and generous attitude, having been convinced that this is the best route to achieving your end. While there is nothing inherently wrong with acting kindly and generously, taking it as an inviolable principle of appropriate or correct behavior is to make it into something fixed and inflexible which cannot but limit our ability to respond to others as needed. There are times, for instance, when a parent must show stern disapproval and refuse to be leveraged by pleading and tears into bending the rules "one last time." In other words, complete virtuosity—living the bodhisattva life—can arise only when 'good' and 'evil' are emptied, when our conduct is constrained by no set forms and we are free of all predetermined ends. Ultimately, of course, this is nothing other than the practice of the middle path—the avoidance of the conflict which necessarily comes about as a result of opposite thinking or the maintenance of set views (*dṛṣṭi*).[9] Huang-po's lower or primary level of relinquishing can thus be seen as the realization (*chih* 知) of the Madhyamika doctrine of the emptiness of all forms.

We can begin exploring the practical implications of this by noting that insofar as the problem identified by Huang-po is not the selection of a false view of things, but the selection of *any* view as an abiding pretext for our conduct, the lower relinquishing is not a weeding out process—the removal of unwanted or wrong views and forms—but a realization of the unobstructed mind-ground (*hsin-ti* 心土) of our original nature. As Huang-po makes quite clear, "mind is originally emptiness" (T 2012.382a), and the root problem of views is not a function of content, but of the horizon-making structure of having a view at all—the fixed segregation of knowing subject and known object, the 'one' who grasps and 'what' is grasped.

Given that we develop views as distillations of and then guides for the strategies by means of which we have coped with the various challenges of being human, and given that the primary inspiration for the Madhyamika doctrine of emptiness is the Buddha's declaration of the selflessness of all things, it cannot be consistently maintained that views and the concepts on which they pivot are inherently bad or misleading. For example, marking a distinction between food and poison is not intrinsically problematic, but is so only when it becomes a fixed barrier to further inquiry or creativity—a barrier that may make it impossible to discover medicinal or more generally therapeutic uses for what has until now only been associated with harm. As long as our concepts remain flexible and heuristic in nature, they simply represent dependently arisen forms of inquiry which may be judiciously used in the service of our creative intelligence. Hence Huang-po's suggestion that the lower level of relinquishing occurs in the context of "extensively cultivating a great many excellent qualities."

However, in the event that we lose sight of the conventional nature of conception, it is possible for our concepts and the views depending on them to harden into habitual and rigid (i.e., absolute) forms of discrimination, often below the threshold of conscious experience. Such habitual forms of thought, feeling, and behavior are referred to in the early Buddhist tradition as *samskāras*, the fourth of the five *skandhas* or "aggregates" included in the psychophysical system of human being. Often translated as "dispositions," but perhaps more forcefully and accurately rendered as "impulses," the early tradition did not see *samskāras* as simple inclinations or paths of least resistance, but as drivers of confused (*musa*) or ignorant (*āvidya*) reactions. Thus Nagarjuna remarks that *samskāras* lie at the very basis of both confusion (MK 13.1) and ignorance (MK 26.11).

Interestingly, the Chinese use the same character (*hsing* 行) to stand for *samskāra* as they use for practice and conduct, graphically indicating that the problem with the former is not a matter of nature or content, but habituation—their function as regulators of conduct. There are two important implications of this. First, instead of being seen as different in kind, *samskāras* and enlightened conduct are understood as qualitatively distinct—the former orienting conduct toward regularity, the latter toward spontaneous responsivity. *Samskāras* are not seen as problematic because they are not useful, but only because they tend to reinforce and even to precipitate societal and not social orientations in conduct. Secondly, since the conception of conduct in China is inseparable from a consideration of the relational context in which it arises, *samskāras* are not seen as drivers of individual or private activity, but as compelling distortions of interpersonality.[10]

Such compulsions are not, of course, equivalent to views, but do constitute a primary condition for their arising. If we take the twelvefold chain of dependent origination to heart, it would seem that the fossilization of the forms of inquiry into set dispositions is itself dependent on ignorance (*āvidya*) which may be rendered as a not-seeing of the mutual relevance of things. Thus, we find Nagarjuna stating that, "When ignorance ceases, there is no occurrence of dispositions. However, the cessation of that ignorance takes place as a result of the practice of that [non-occurrence] through wisdom (*prajñā*)" (MK 26.11). Since Nagarjuna asserts that when self-nature exists (or is taken to exist) the practice of the path is not appropriate (MK 24.24), and since he invariably associates self-nature with a commitment to the reality of both identity and difference (see MK 14.7), the practice of the non-occurrence of dispositions can be seen as vigilantly relinquishing all discriminating boundaries as they arise. Moreover, insofar as Nagarjuna elsewhere alerts us to the dependence of discrimination on obsessive or habitual thinking (*prapañca*) (MK 18.5), and since he claims that *prapañca* ceases in the context of emptiness, emptiness itself should be seen as the relinquishing of all fixed distinctions—what in Ch'an is referred to as *wu-nien* 無念 or non-thinking.

That the culprit is not thinking in the most general sense, but habitual thinking is suggested by the use of *nien* which means thinking in the sense of remembering or recalling and also means chanting—the regular repetition of set phrases or verses for the purpose of inculcating a fixed frame of mental or spiritual reference. Thus, Pai-chang claims that "*wu-nien* is the absence of errant thoughts. It's not the absence of corrective thinking." This he goes on to define in terms of thought which does not posit 'being' (*yu*) and 'nonbeing' (*wu*) (HTC 119.421a). Indeed, corrective thinking is free of all duality and is "the enlightenment (*bodhi*) of thought." Asked whether *bodhi* can then be attained, Pai-chang replies that it cannot and is taken to task for talking about the enlightenment of thought. He responds by noting that it is as if *bodhi* were falsely established and designated by a written character when in fact it can neither be attained nor thought about. "Just this absence of thinking is called 'truly thinking of bodhi as the absence of anything to think about.' The absence of anything to think about is in all situations to have no-'mind'" (HTC 119.421a).

That is, non-thinking refers to the practice of emptiness (*k'ung*)—a departure from formal and habitual mental constructs, not from mentation or the having of dispositions in general. Hence Hui-neng's warning that "if you do not think of the myriad things, but always cause your thoughts to be cut off, you will be bound (and not liberated) by the Dharma" (PS 31). Emptiness is not the blank insentience of a stone or a burned-out log, but a compassionate refusal to ignore what is immediately present by interposing a deflecting screen of stock concepts, memories, and regularity-tempered views. Moreover, since the Chinese Buddhist understanding of thinking was not that it was primarily a psychological process but a phase in our conduct, the attainment of correct thought—thought that has been made true by the practice of emptiness—should be seen as the realization of harmonious conduct or what Huang-po has termed "one-mind" or *i-hsin*. Errant thought, then, cannot be construed as thinking which doesn't somehow match with an objective reality that it is *about*, but as the manifestation of dispositions which interrupt the free flow of narration.

Now, while it is the case that *prapañca* ceases in the context of emptiness, according to Nagarjuna's Madhyamika so does selective relevance. "Everything is relevant for whom emptiness is relevant. Everything is not relevant for whom the empty is not relevant" (MK 24.14). In the context of the Ch'an articulation of emptiness as *wu-nien*, this means that obsessive thinking (*prapañca*) ceases when we stop selecting (HTC 119.425) and checking what occurs—that is, when we relinquish control and with it the 'self' whose likes and dislikes that control is intended to serve. Instead of trying to decide what is relevant to achieving our aims and what is not, insuring thereby a continuing role for the ego as an arbitrator of alternative courses of action, with the practice of emptiness or *wu-nien* we relinquish all horizons for relevance and shift our attention entirely toward our narration as a whole—that is, not toward 'self' and not toward 'other,' but toward the intimately creative realization of true relationship.

The System of *Ch'an*

Thus far, we have articulated a chain of dependence whereby Huang-po's great relinquishing can arise only on the basis of the middle form, and that form only on the basis of the lower. But if these three are to be seen as a comprehensive *system* of Ch'an practice, the dependencies cannot be uni-directional. After all, if that were the case, we would have nothing more than a simple series, not a system as such—a whole with characteristics not entailed by those of its parts taken together or in isolation.

As has just been suggested, it is possible to look at emptiness as the practice of relinquishing all views and not merely this view or that. In terms of the two-truths doctrine of the Madhyamika, engaging in creating the distinctions needed to decide which views are (for example) workable is certainly pragmatic, but it is true or corrective only in a conventional sense—that is, at the level of *saṃvṛtti*. Granted that conventions serve to coordinate the conduct of a given community within a given context, while *saṃvṛtti* may involve seeing in a new and liberating way and hence extending of the range of what we have hitherto considered relevant, it is not necessarily critical of prevailing conditions. In short, conventional truths are specifically oriented toward the institution of new horizons that may serve only to enhance or shift the focus of existing societal norms and not to encourage the spontaneity of *wu-wei*.[11] By comparison, *paramārtha* (the ultimate fruit) is the coordinative and hence communicative working of truth into *all* contexts, the relinquishing of all limits to what is considered relevant—whether in resolving a crisis or in carrying out our day-to-day affairs. Since the position of the Madhyamika is that all things are empty or dependently arisen and hence not-born and not-annihilated, there can be no question of *paramārtha* amounting to finally ending ignorance or suffering once and for all. The middle path is not a destination-oriented project, but a continuous, unlimited endeavor.[12]

But by itself, the emptiness of all things might lead one to feel that *all* differences are somehow equivalent precisely by being empty. That is, the relevance of all things may be seen as a generic, universally attributed quality which encourages us to say that nothing is of particular value since all differences have been either rendered unimportant or entirely obliterated. To borrow a phrase used in description of Hegel's logic of the identity of opposites, such an understanding of and attachment to emptiness results in "a night in which all cows are black." Emptiness perversely comes to mean that nothing matters in both the sense of "there is no matter, no ontic foundation for the play of experience" and "there is nothing which is of any special value." Instead of expressing the bodhisattva life, practicing emptiness becomes a justification for a spiritual hedonism of the sort the Beat Generation was (rightly or wrongly) accused of purveying, and of which Nagarjuna was himself keenly aware (see MK 13.8). At the very core of this attachment is an egoistic retreat from fully responsive engagement with the world—a pernicious misunderstanding of the teaching of no-self which allows one to feel free because all things are dependently arisen and because ultimately there is no one to own responsibility for what happens. Emptiness becomes a justification for withdrawing from the demands of intimate sociality. As the logic of attachment to emptiness would have it, if Hui-neng is right and there is originally "no 'dust'," there cannot be anything we need to do. No matter what ills appear in the world, they lack any self nature. What need could there be to bother about them?

As an authentically Buddhist practice, the Yogācāra affirmation of mind serves to true or correct this errant understanding of emptiness. It is possible—based on the Madhyamika claims that there is neither self-production nor other-production—to assert that there is no one who bears responsibility for what comes to be. But when all things are admitted to be functions of mind-only, it follows that there is, after all, a source or focus of responsibility. The disambiguation by means of which all dharmas have come to be is neither accidental nor a matter of objective necessity. Thus, in the *Lankavatara Sutra* there appears what is apparently an anomalous denial of the theory of no-self (Sagatham 765ff.) and an affirmation of an ego-soul—what in later Ch'an came to be known as one's "true self," Huang-po's "one-mind."

Now, in order to avoid this true self being substantialized as a personal ego, the Yogacara appeals to the *ālayavijñāna* as the bearer of responsibility and the *manovijñāna*—the maker of discriminations based on *vāsanā* (habit-energy, Ch *hsi-ch'i* 習氣)—as the source thereof (LS II.53). Thus, one is not individually responsible for the entire world in a megalomaniacal sense, nor is it merely that one is responsible in the manner of a purely subjective, epistemic solipsism. Especially in the *Lankavatara*, the tension created here between individually and universally owned responsibility is played out quite effectively. At times, it seems that idealism is being asserted ontologically—the mind creates the world, and at other times epistemically—the mind creates by making distinctions in what precedes thinking.

In either case, however, responsibility is not allowed to be diluted in the Madhyamika solution of dependent origination or emptiness. The Yogācāra steadfastly maintains that enlightenment is not a matter of mere insight into the way things have come to be, but rather entails our ceasing to act on the basis of habit-energy. At least in Ch'an, this is in the end understood as one's own responsibility. No Buddha or bodhisattva can dissolve the habits of perception, cognition, speech or action of even a single sentient being. Nor will they disappear by themselves. But, because habit-energy has been plaguing us over the entire course of beginningless time, the question naturally arises of how long it will take to clear the obscurations away, to purify the *ālaya*, the tacit repository of our karma.

As the exchange of Hui-neng and Shen-hsiu evidences, this question focuses a deep and extensive problematic in Yogācāra. If it takes time to clear the storehouse consciousness as Shen-hsiu implies, then enlightenment is a goal, an object. And under the perspicacious gaze of *prajñāpāramitā*, this objectivity is seen as a sign of nothing short of the forfeiture of enlightenment. Indeed, precisely as long as we see nirvana as something to be attained, just so long will it remain unattainable. Hence the *Heart Sutra's* declaration that there is no 'suffering,' no 'origination,' no 'stopping' and no 'path,' no 'attainment' and no 'thing to attain.' The gradual path to enlightenment implied by the Yogācāra is, however, not countered by Ch'an only with a head-on rejection of the self-nature of habits themselves along Madhyamika lines, but also by recognizing that time is no more an objective barrier to liberation than any other dharma. For Ch'an, enlightenment is not something which can be blocked—whether by so many moments of time or by so many fixed habits of thought, speech, or deed—but only resisted. The key is not constant effort (*hsi* 習), but readiness (*tun* 頓).

These sorts of mutual corrections between the three forms of relinquishing could be amplified at some length, but what has been noted thus far would seem to provide warrant enough to regard Huang-po's hierarchic terminology as nothing more than a rhetorical device intended to correct the thinking and conduct of a particular audience. In fact, none of the three relinquishings can stand alone, but instead depend on one another in much the same way that the five *skandhas* (aggregates) exist only in relationship with one another and never independently. To use the analogy often employed in explaining the interdependence of these five constituents of each human being, practice is like a bundle of reeds which will topple over unless each form of relinquishing leans against all the others. In the absence of this support, none of them can stand. Cultivated by itself, each form of relinquishing leads in one subtle way or another to the revitalization of the ego.

Thus, the transition from the lower to the middle to the great relinquishing represents neither a kind of horizontal doctrinal shift equivalent to the transition from, say, Neo-Platonism (mind-only) to positivist materialism (no-mind), nor the step-by-step articulation of a progressively refined method and theory of liberation. The "gateless gate" of Ch'an practice appears only when we relinquish our horizons on all three dimensions—readiness, responsibility, and relevance—and so it does not depend on any particular form of relinquishing being the first or last. Moreover, since practicing Ch'an consists entirely of relinquishing horizons, and since the experienced world is a function of our individual and cultural projections of such limits, we are always capable of beginning. There is no need to traipse off in search of any particular 'this' or 'that,' nor any need to worry about which step comes first and which second. We must simply begin, and "all by itself there is no place that is not the place of enlightenment" (T 2012.380c).

One of the advantages of seeing the practice of Ch'an as a self-correcting system arising out of the interplay of the three forms of relinquishing is that it enables us to shed valuable light on the claims made earlier in this chapter that practice is not something any one of 'us' can do—that it can appear only when 'we' loosen our control over experience. Quite apart from the fine points of philosophical hair-splitting, it would seem that we *do* have a role in inaugurating if not directing the process by means of which practice is realized. It is, after all, 'you' and 'I' who must be willing to divest our 'selves' of their horizons and allow our narration to proceed unchecked. Unless 'we' decide to cultivate wider and more open horizons, our current strategies for grasping and rejecting will not only continue operating but will strengthen with each passing experience. That is, once an ego has developed, it will quite naturally and effectively maintain itself in the face of all but the most severe crises.[13] It may well be that liberation is not a goal at which 'we' arrive, but it is nevertheless also the case that if liberation is to be won, it is precisely 'we' who must be willing to sacrifice our 'selves.'

It is for this reason that Pai-chang, having just announced that the principle of liberation is "letting things come and not selecting anything" (HTC 119.425a), then insists that no one, not even the Buddha himself, can save us. "Sentient beings must liberate (*tu* 度) themselves." That is, unenlightened beings are themselves responsible for salvation. Although we have to exert ourselves if we are to realize liberation, this exertion is simply not-acting (*wu-wei*) on the basis of our likes and dislikes. In short, if a buddha-land is to appear right where we stand, 'we' must get out of the way.

One way of conceptualizing this process is to see each of our 'selves' as a system of baffles (distinctions) which either block or deflect the free circulation of energy in a consistent manner—feeding some physical, emotional, and conceptual subsystems and starving others as seems appropriate for the maintenance and survival of the pattern as a whole. While some of these baffles serve to hold or funnel energy into the pattern as a whole (for instance, what Ch'an refers to as "attachments"), others (our "aversions") divert potentially disruptive kinds and amounts of energy away from 'us.' With the passage of time, a sediment of memories is deposited about the baffles which have proved successful and it is these that form the stable basis of our identities. Thus, the ego or 'mind' which generates these baffles through acting *yu-wei* is like a heart (*hsin* 心) which can exist only as long as there is a balance between its diastolic (attachment) and systolic (aversion) functions. If either of these functions fails, the heart-mind eventually disintegrates—our identity dissolves.

Thus, while it is entirely true that the practice of Ch'an has nothing to do with cultivating this or that quality or this or that store of merit and ultimately entails the dissolution of both 'actor' and 'acted-upon'—a dissolution, that is, of the pattern of *neng-suo* 能所—it is 'we' who must initially desist from all seeking.[14] This apparent paradox can be effectively resolved precisely by seeing practice as a self-correcting system that emerges out of the dynamic interplay of the three forms of relinquishing.

While each form has its own method and aim and can legitimately be talked about in terms of (for example) our cultivating ever more inclusive horizons, practice itself embraces and yet transcends the set of all these means and ends in much the same way that water is something other than a simple collection of hydrogen and oxygen atoms or a living organism something other than an aggregation of various kinds of organic molecules. Even though a living organism is never present when such molecules are entirely absent, a man or

woman cannot be reduced to a particular pattern of organic molecules without the loss of at least some of the properties unique to
being human. Likewise, as a self-organizing and self-maintaining
system, practice never occurs when there is no relinquishing of
horizons to readiness, responsibility, and relevance, but it cannot
be reduced to them without losing what is unique about a
bodhisattva's way of life. 'You' and 'I' may initiate the process out of
which the practice of Ch'an emerges, but once practice begins in
earnest and not merely as an idea 'we' are entertaining, it has in a
very real sense a life of its own.

To appeal once again to an analogy with biological systems,
practice embraces and yet transcends our efforts to relinquish horizons along the dimensions of readiness, responsibility, and relevance just as the human body includes and yet cannot be reduced
to a summation of the forms and intentions (and hence karma)
of the once-independent cells symbiotically bound up in its
psychophysical organization. A bodhisattva or buddha is not a sentient being in much the same way that a living human body is not
a mere collection of cells. Something radically novel appears when
the constituent cells are in proper relationship—what we refer to as
"a human being." Likewise for a bodhisattva who is not any one
sentient being or even a collection of any number of them since the
self-other dichotomy has been entirely relinquished. A bodhisattva
is a person, an entire world, who emerges as the narrative interplay
of a potentially unlimited number of individual characters or
'selves.' That is, a bodhisattva is pure conduct.

The practice of Ch'an is not systematic, then, in the sense of an
orderly or logical procedure which 'you' and 'I' can carry out to
attain the goal of enlightenment. Instead, it is best seen as a higher-
order phenomenon which emerges with the organized interplay of
the three forms of relinquishing and yet is itself formless. In much
the same way that any self-organizing system is a novel pattern of
relationships which—while emerging through the integration of
previously existing patterns—nevertheless manifests entirely novel
properties, practice marks the realization of unprecedented narrative possibilities. In short, it should be seen as the realization of
conduct that is truly *wu-wei*.

Thus, while 'you' and 'I' cannot practice individually, each of us
can and has for at least the span of this lifetime been resisting its
manifestation by positing order as standing over and against the
unexpected, imagining that this is the best way to lead happy and
fruitful lives—both private and public.[15] We refuse to trust ourselves

enough to let go of our tenuous control of experience and allow our narration to open up in unchecked improvisation.

As a system, the practice of Ch'an takes place at a higher level of organization than the ego and yet unless the ego is willing to relinquish the control it has wrested in self-preservation—from the hands of 'others,' from 'society,' from 'brute nature'—enlightenment remains nothing more than a dream, a pleasant fantasy. What emerges with practice has, from 'our' perspective, no form, no beginning, no end. It is not something we can comprehend. We may refer to it as Hui-neng's "original nature," as Ma-tzu's "everyday mind," as Huang-po's "one-mind," or as Lin-chi's "true man of no rank," but in actuality we can never succeed in objectifying it since it has no substance, no abiding nature. What emerges with practice is just spontaneously Buddhist conduct—narrative movement which embodies unlimited social virtuosity in the realization of a horizonless and liberating intimacy. It is for this reason that Hui-neng remarks that "it is precisely Buddhist practice that is the Buddha" (PS 42). Having no 'self,' no attachments, no aversions, there is nothing to stand between us and the Buddha. Enlightenment is not something received or attained, but an offering of centerless and unalloyed responsiveness through the realization of who we truly are as persons—an authorless narration into which all things are being constantly taken up and completed.

Chapter 7

The Techniques of Unmaking: Energy and Awakening in Ch'an

Seen as the embodiment of horizonless intimacy, the practice of Ch'an may be spoken of as the true meaning of sociality. With the systematic realization of the three forms of relinquishing, our narrative opens up as the spontaneous emergence of a pure and centerless buddha-land in which neither identity nor difference has any ultimate foundation and hence in which habit and prediction find no abiding purchase. 'Sentient beings' and 'buddhas,' 'commoners' and 'sages' all disappear, leaving behind only the fluid and wondrous functioning (*miao yung*) of one-mind. Practice is not, therefore, a way of *becoming* a 'buddha'—a present means to a future and superior end—but should simply be seen as the virtuosic expression of our true and original nature (*cheng-pen-hsing* 正本性), as unhesitatingly conducting ourselves *as* buddhas.

Strictly speaking, then, there is nothing we need in order to practice Ch'an. And yet the public records (*kung-an* 公案) of the tradition are filled with instances of students being rejected out of hand, asked to go back to wherever they had come from, even kicked repeatedly down the monastery steps. If Ch'an practice really arises as an unprecedented level of narrative integration and flexibility out of the system of the three relinquishings, these refusals would appear to be inexplicable. After all, if "everyone's entire body is the Buddha" (T 2012.383a), on what grounds could anyone be considered unworthy or incapable of entering the gate of Ch'an? If Hui-neng is right and there is no dust to obscure the mirror of our original nature, what could possibly impede us?

Since we attain nothing in conducting ourselves as buddhas, but simply express our true nature as boundless and responsive offering, all that should be necessary to enter the practice of Ch'an is our willingness to wholeheartedly engage in lively and unrestricted concourse with others. Like all forms of conduct, enlightenment is not something any 'one' of us can do, but must be seen as a spontaneous transformation of our narration in which each of us creatively participates to the exact extent that we relax the 'self'-protecting and 'self'-serving boundaries (*ching* 境) established by our opinions and views. And so the difference between wanting to *become* a buddha and conducting ourselves *as* one finally pivots on 'your' and 'my' ability to let go, to divest our 'selves' of their hard-won control over experience. Only then can our narration naturally (*tzu-jan*) orient itself away from that societal disintegration which spawns ostensibly self-contained and other-regulating egos and move instead toward the realization of true community.

But, conceding that this is true—that relinquishing our 'self'-control is the first and most crucial step in alleviating suffering—is not the same as actually letting go. Indeed, while the readiness to disenfranchise our 'selves' is unconditioned in the sense that it cannot be forced or inhibited by others, the karmic or intentional structure of the 'self' acts as a kind of labyrinth through which this readiness must pass before coming to fruition. In most cases, it simply gets lost along the way, its meaning truncated, and we find ourselves seeking this or that experience as confirmation or proof of our progress in becoming 'self'-less.

This is as much as to say that depending on the density of the distinctions or evaluations which channel and inevitably retard the free circulation of energy throughout our narrative, true practice may remain nothing more than an ideal or potential. Hence Hui-neng's admission that manifesting our readiness to awaken is not simply a function of our *decision* to open ourselves to liberation, but of whether we have keen or dull roots (*ken* 根). While not even a hair's breadth separates samsara and nirvana, unless the pattern of discriminations out of which our 'selves' emerge can be extirpated, their disparity may not be able to be bridged even by stringing together worlds as numerous as the sands of the Ganges.[1]

In fact, every student of Ch'an must eventually discover that they lack the wherewithal to make good on their intent to abandon their 'selves' precisely because this intention provides a failsafe anchor for the very 'self' it aims at relinquishing. In other words, if the Buddhist road to hell is paved with our good intentions, it is not because they or even we were ultimately insincere or misguided, but because they perform the same karmic function as any other intentions—our continued fixation as 'selves.' It turns out that the hardest thing is not accomplishing great deeds or even having profoundly mystical experiences, but not seeking, making, or getting anything at all.[2] The real problem, then, is that the intent to practice or attain enlightenment—to relinquish all of our horizons for readiness, responsibility, and relevance—is the very thing which makes this impossible. The apparent paradox and indeed the great irony is that 'you' and 'I' must decide to forfeit all hope of enlightenment for enlightenment to occur. At least for the Ch'an tradition, this is the true meaning of the bodhisattva vow.

The single most important question we can ask of Ch'an, then, is not "how are we to practice?" since 'we' never will, but "how can our 'selves' be sufficiently attenuated for the unprecedented conduct characteristic of the bodhisattva life to appear?" That is, even as we form the intention to relinquish our horizons to readiness, responsibility, and relevance, we must ask what techniques can be used to dismantle ourselves as intentional beings, as repositories of the 84,000 kinds of discrimination. Failing to do so, the path of enlightened concourse will remain obstructed, our narration characterized by selfishly unresolved conflicts and dishonored commitments.

As a preliminary to articulating Ch'an's approach to the attenuation of 'self,' it is useful to note that in the writings and recorded talks of the lineage running from Hui-neng through Ma-tzu to Lin-chi, there is no suggestion that this dismantling is understood as a piecemeal affair. To the contrary, since no exceptions are granted to Pai-chang's principle of not selecting anything, Ch'an would appear to insist that we avoid taking on the task of choosing which distinctions to eliminate with the same unremitting vigilance we maintain in not grasping after or rejecting any particular sensations, thoughts, or situations. This being the case, relinquishing our distinctions—especially that between 'self' and 'other'—cannot amount to a logical procedure of identifying some conceptual, perceptual, or emotive opposition and then "turning our back on" or negating it. Such a *via negativa* may appeal to our calculative dispositions and their fascination with identity-biased rationality, but it will never do more than produce an infinitely regressing series of meta-distinctions—'self' giving way to 'not-self' which gives way to 'neither ('self' nor 'not-self'), which in turn leads to 'not ('neither ['self' nor 'not-self']')', and so on. As Yung-chia's elaborate dialectics was intended to show (see T 48.2013), such a strategy for achieving no-

'self' is finally 'self'-promoting to the precise degree that it gives 'us' something to do or make (*tso* 作).

To repeat, we cannot free ourselves from all discrimination by fiat. Since discrimination is the very basis on which we are able to act *yu-wei*, purposely entering the gate of Ch'an would amount to nothing short of pulling our 'selves' up by 'our own' bootstraps. An essentially arrogant project, not only will the most Herculean effort fail to lift us over the threshold, our persistence will effectively forestall if not entirely block the opportunity for 'others' to cross over.

Two important implications follow from this. First, relinquishing our 'selves' in order to realize the practice of Ch'an must be accomplished indirectly. That is, such a relinquishing cannot be a simple putting away or cutting off of what we have identified as our 'selves' since these acts of discrimination constitute subtle forms of seeking that cannot but reinforce the existence of a 'seeker'—usually one fatally attracted to 'emptiness' and sustained in direct proportion to the depth and extent of its negative projections. Secondly, if this relinquishing is not ultimately something that any 'one' of us can do alone or that will happen all by itself—the system of distinctions we know as our 'selves' usually being quite competently self-maintaining—it would appear that successfully abating the 'self' means having a partner, a counterpart with whom we can enter into lively and mutually 'self'-effacing concourse.[3] In a very general sense, then, the realization of Ch'an practice would appear to pivot on making effective use of what we can refer to as the complementary methods or techniques of indirection and partnership.

Indirection: Meditative Discipline as Energy Work

If the influence of the 'self' is to be sufficiently curbed for our narrative to unremittingly manifest the practice life, 'you' and 'I' must be deceived—convinced that 'we' are maintaining our central role as 'free agents' even as we are undermining the basis of our control. In a very literal sense, we must be tricked into enlightenment.

One of the seemingly odd facts about the Ch'an tradition is that while it ceaselessly espoused a doctrine of radical spontaneity and freedom from all forms of societal constraint and idealized the unhesitating, indefatigable virtuosity of a master musician or poet, the daily life of a Ch'an monastery was highly organized and formal. From what we can gather, each day included significant periods devoted to chanting sutras, sitting in meditation, and performing the kinds of repetitive manual labor common in unmechanized, agrarian communities. In fact, from the available evidence it would appear that at least after Pai-chang's codification of a specifically Ch'an set of rules for the monastic life, monks and nuns in the T'ang were significantly less free to do as they pleased than were their Indian forebears. For example, whereas the Indian monk or nun was forbidden to earn his or her keep and relied on begging for each day's sustenance, after Pai-chang it was taken as law that "a day without work is a day without eating."

In short, Ch'an seems to have promoted a kind of double life—a life concerned on the one hand with opening up in uninhibited and unrestricted improvisation, and on the other hand to cultivating a mundane regularity which varied only according to the climatic demands of the changing seasons. Thus, while all the masters of the tradition vigorously denied the dependence of Ch'an on any form of cultivation, each underwent and required his students to undergo extensive periods of meditative, moral, and manual training.

This apparent inconsistency is, I believe, related to the need to fool the 'self' into relinquishing control of experience, of the perceived movement of our narrative. That is, Ch'an makes use of a regulative orientation of day-to-day life precisely as a means of undermining the sociality of selfish conduct and preparing us for the transition to truly social life. In much the same way that fire is used to fight fire, Ch'an avails itself of the regularity of a societally oriented life in order to curb and bring about the atrophy of the very 'self' who enters into and promotes that life. Understanding how this indirection works and its relationship to meditative discipline will require us to explicate the basis of what has until now been an unqualified appeal to seeing the 'self' as a pattern of distinctions which characteristically and relatively constantly diverts the free circulation of energy or ch'i 氣.

Ch'i, *Narrative Movement, and the Restraints of 'Self'*

In both the Taoist and later Confucian traditions, the notion of *ch'i* provides a linkage between the quality of human life and that of the

rest of the cosmos. Carrying connotations which we would associate with "blood," "breath," "vital force," and "spiritedness," *ch'i*
primarily designates the dynamic in world process, its inherent and
unlimited vitality as opposed to its organization or form (*hsiang*
相).

Thus, Chuang-tzu states that "human life is a coming together
of energy (*ch'i*)," and that understanding this energy is the key to
sagely conduct. By characterizing the Taoist sage as someone who
"makes absolutely sure that things can do what they are supposed to
do" (1968, 93), who "follows along with things they way they are"
(p. 94) and "supplies all their wants out of total emptiness" (p. 128),
Chuang-tzu makes it clear that understanding energy leads to or at
least allows us to do what Ch'an later formulates as "according with
the situation and responding as needed." This principle holds true
for Chuang-tzu because:

> The ten thousand things are really one. We look on some as beau-
> tiful because they are rare or unearthly; we look on others as ugly
> because they are foul and rotten. But the foul and rotten may turn
> into the rare and unearthly, and the rare and unearthly may turn
> into the foul and rotten. So it is said, You have only to comprehend
> the one breath (*ch'i*) that is the world. The sage never ceases to
> value oneness. (1968, 235–36)

In short, Chuang-tzu sees all opposites as nothing other than
momentary articulations of what is essentially a single movement.
Like our own breath, the vitality of *ch'i* is circulatory, and so while
it may appear to us here as rising or good (*yang* 陽) and there falling
or evil (*yin* 陰), in actuality the natural movement of *ch'i* is always
full and round. Differences are never absolute, then, but must be
seen as a joint function of the spontaneous circulation of *ch'i* and
our orientation or perspective on it. For this reason, while the
apparent polarity of the movement that is *ch'i* is held to be responsible for the articulation of the ten thousand things, it is also seen as
their unification or harmony. Hence, Lao-tzu not only remarks that
"the myriad things carry yin and embrace yang"—that is, maintain
differences—but that "the interfusion of [their] *ch'i* is harmony"
(LT 42).

In the sky, *ch'i* manifests as the orbiting of the planets and stars
and the quality of their light, as the rising and falling of mists and
clouds, the play of emotion witnessed in the shifting directions and
intensities of the wind. In the forest, it appears as the movements

and characters of the deer and the tiger, as the personalities of the fir and the willow, as the spirit of a waterfall spreading the muscular, granite thighs of a sun-washed mountainside. In human beings, it is not only the circulation of the blood and the rhythm of breathing in and out, but the determinant of the roots of their character—what makes one man a passionate musician and another a coldly vicious warrior.

In short, *ch'i* is not a kind of primordial matter or pure force— something that can be comprehended in a purely quantitative or factual terms—but must be seen as an essentially qualitative expressiveness. A large part of the difficulty in understanding the Chinese arts and sciences—medicine and geomancy in particular—is that they do not take 'being' (or even 'beings') and 'absolute measurement' as the basic categories from which everything else is to be deduced. That is, they do not take change or motion to be a definite and calculable alteration of some (ostensibly unchanging) thing with respect to a fixed frame of spatial or temporal reference. Instead, the Chinese have traditionally seen as basic a complex and open-ended system of irreducibly relative or contrapuntal values. While these values are usually spoken of as permutations of *yin* and *yang*, they do not constitute a set of opposing Manichean principles out of which all things are formed, but an unbroken continuum onto which we project divisions for purely conventional purposes. The structure of the world of Chinese thought is not digital but analogic; not calculative but narrative.

Contrary, then, to the Indo-European tradition where some permanent order or source of order has almost always been assumed to underlie and unify the transformations constantly taking place in the world of experience, the Chinese have traditionally seen the unity of all things as a function or expression of change itself—the indeterminateness of ungrounded vitality. The harmony of all things is not provided for by substance, form, a divine being, or even the laws of 'nature,' but by changeability.

Nowhere is this more profoundly illustrated than in the *I Ching* (IC), where the world is said to be engendered when Great Ultimate (*t'ai-chi* 太極) gives birth to the two exemplars (*yin* and *yang*) which in turn generate the four models which then generate the eight trigrams. The eight trigrams—or more properly, the configurations of changeability which they symbolize—determine good fortune and misfortune, and these in turn "create the great field of action" (IC, Great Appendix II, 11.5–6). Far from seeing the Great Ultimate as a kind of Aristotelian "unmoved mover," the Chinese identification of *yin* and *yang* as modes or aspects of *ch'i* makes it clear that the latter is finally indistinguishable from the *t'ai-chi* out of which all things emerge. *Ch'i* is not only embodied *as* the ten thousand things, it is the unbridled vitality flowing through and enlivening them.

Significantly, the eight trigrams not only map out the cardinal points of the natural world—heaven, earth, thunder, wind/wood, fire, water, lake/mist, and mountain—they symbolize parts of the body, organic functions, psychological qualities, emotions and mental functions, parts of the life cycle, family relationships, principles of nature, and positions in time and space.[4] Combined in the sixty-four hexagrams, they are said to exhaustively describe the dynamic order of the cosmos. Thus, the quality of any situation—whether it be auspicious or baleful, progressive or regressive, pleasurable or painful—is inseparable from the transformation and movement of *ch'i*. At bottom, every success and failure, all joy or suffering are a function of how well the various *ch'i* in the situation circulate, blend, and complement one another.

And so, whereas the traditionally trained European medical doctor starts with a symptom and looks for an underlying mechanism—a pinpointable cause for disease in some dietary deficiency, organic malfunction, or invading virus, the Chinese doctor attends to the patient's entire bodily, psychic, and social situation until he or she discerns a pattern of energic disharmony. Rather than the so-called "fixed" organs, skeletal structure, or viruses present, what is most important in both diagnosis and treatment are the fluids and energies flowing both in the patient's body and out of it into his or her environment, family, and friends. Therapy does not consist primarily of manipulating organic structures, but of bringing the whole energy configuration back into balance—restoring the harmonious blending of the various *ch'i* which constitute a living human being. Whether this is done by stimulating various of the energy conduits or meridians in the body with acupuncture, prescribing herbal concoctions, or revitalizing a moribund family relationship through the timely performance of some ritual or *li* is not particularly relevant. What every method aims at is either removing a blockage—opening up the patient as a whole person so that *ch'i* can flow through them freely and spontaneously, or adding one or another quality of *ch'i* to the patient's system in order to redress a debilitating imbalance. For the Chinese, health and disease, pleasure and pain, joy and suffering are functions of the balance and imbalance of *ch'i*.

But since all the modalities of worldly existence are a function of various balances and interfusions of *ch'i*, each of our lives is part of the continual circulation of the blood and breath constituting the cosmic process. Given that all things are thus organically related, if we are out of balance—that is, if our energy is not well-blended or is blocked from flowing in natural accord with our *tao*—not only will we suffer as individuals, all things will be adversely affected.

Balancing someone's *ch'i* is not, therefore, a simple matter of treating their body, but necessarily involves opening all of their relationships to the free circulation of energy. In short, it is a matter of harmonizing their entire narrative. Thus, the *Kuan-tzu* (KT, circa 300 BCE) indicates that:

> When the quintessential is present and of itself vitalizes, the outside of you flourishes. Stored within as the fount and source, floodlike it harmonizes and calms. It constitutes the depths of the *ch'i*. If the depths do not dry up, the four limbs are firm. If the fount is not drained, the nine orifices allow clear passage. Then one is able to exhaust heaven and earth, and spread over the four seas. (KT 2.102, tr. Rickett 1965, 163, H)

The particular relevance of this to the Ch'an project of realizing the bodhisattva life is made clear in the "Inward Training" chapter of the *Kuan-tzu*. There, the presence of this world-balancing flow of energy is said to be possible only when we are free of restlessness, when the "heart/mind is fixed within" and the senses clear and distinct. Once a stable heart or mind arises, every part of the body is filled with the straightforward and complete "energy of the mind." This energy cannot remain within, however, but takes shape and appears on the outside as well.

> It can be known from the complexion of the face. When people meet someone whose appearance and mind are full of positive energy, they will feel happier than if they had met their own brother. On the other hand, when people meet someone with negative energy, they will feel more hurt than if they had been confronted with arms. (KT 13.5b, quoted in Hidemi 1989, 57)

It follows that since the basic structure of our personality depends on the configuration and quality of our energy, and since our personality directly affects others and their responses to us, reconfiguring our energy is the key to transforming our lives.

In full agreement with this understanding of the relationship between the quality of our energy and the responses of others,

Huang-po tells us that we should not try "to control other people," but should "see things as reflecting [our own] demeanor (*mien* 面)" (T 2012.382c). Failing this, we are no better than "idiotic dogs" barking at the wind blowing through the grass and trees because they seem to be attacking or challenging us. Ultimately, it is our own energy—our habits (*ch'i hsi* 氣習) or demeanor (*ch'i hsiang* 氣象)—which directs and restrains the movements of the people and things confronting and often countering us.[5] As Hui-neng is said to have answered when he overheard a group of monks arguing about whether it is the flag that moves or the wind—"You are all wrong. It is your mind (your present configuration of energy) that is moving" (Hoover 1980, 64).

What this implies, of course, is that the quality of our entire narration and hence the meaning of our conduct can be transformed indirectly. Although the 'self' typically considers experience to prove otherwise, a positive and lasting course of personal development does not necessarily depend on our acting *yu-wei*, on the purposeful application of our wills. To the contrary, simply by balancing our own *ch'i* and opening up to its free circulation through us, not only our own lives but the lives of those around us are naturally (*tzu jan*) ameliorated.

Thus, Chuang-tzu informs us that there are times when a true sage—someone who understands the one *ch'i*—can:

> without saying a word, induce harmony in others; just standing alongside others, he can cause them to change until the proper relationship between father and son has found its way into every home. He does it all in a spirit of unity and effortlessness—so far is he removed from the [customary] minds of men. (1968, 281)

Importantly, the key to the sage's influence is his effortlessness and ability to divorce himself from the customary minds of men—that is, from their habitual dispositions, the typical structure of their precedents for action. In a word, the key is conduct that is *wu-wei*— the realization of true spontaneity (*tzu-jan*) which is at once true harmony.[6]

In a passage the spirit of which is later and enthusiastically taken up into the corpus of Ch'an, Chuang-tzu supplies a crucial clue as to how this spontaneity comes about through what the *Kuan-tzu* referred to as stilling or fixing (*ting* 定) of the heart. In the context of arguing that a man can be without what is essential to 'man,' he says that:

judging 'it's this, it's not' is what I mean by the essential to man. What I mean by being without the essential is that the man does not inwardly wound his person by likes and dislikes, that he constantly goes by the spontaneous and does not add anything to the process of life. (tr. Graham 1989, 195–6; Watson's translation in Chuang-tzu)

Uncannily reminiscent of the Buddha's claim that 'is' and 'is-not' are the barbs on which mankind is impaled, Chuang-tzu identifies the source of our discomfort and our loss of spontaneity as the formation of distinctions leading to likes and dislikes—in short, to our immersion in horizon-mediated seeking.

Holding distinctions wounds us by biasing our body-mind system in such a way that *ch'i* is blocked from circulating freely. Whether this wound comes from rejecting or from attaching to some quality of change or some object of intellectual or sensual desire does not matter. Regardless of their 'impeccability,' our intentions divert or stem the natural flow of energy by means of which all things are nourished. Our intentions—and in the end our 'selves'—can be played out only at the expense of others. As soon as we take a stand on our likes and dislikes, we lose our natural ability of responding spontaneously and develop instead a relatively unchanging complex of stock reactions—a familiar habitus of feelings and desires. In a word, we engender our 'selves.'

As what is "essential (*ching* 精) to 'man'," this complex of stock distinctions is what identifies us as particular individuals.[7] But in establishing the central perspective from which we perceive a horizoning world 'around' us and on the ground of which we decide how and when to act, it is also what curbs and directs the movement of our narration—the quality and orientation of our conduct. And so, in a reversal of the usual roles granted to the world and the 'self,' the Taoist and the Ch'an Buddhist agree that ultimately it is never things which restrain the 'self,' but the 'self' which—as at least Chuang-tzu makes clear—controls or restrains all 'things' through systematically perverting the free circulation of *ch'i*. In fact, as A. C. Graham puts it, "In renouncing control of the *ch'i*, selfhood dissolves; yet paradoxically in ceasing to distinguish myself from what all the time has been acting through me, I become for the first time the true agent of my actions" (1989, 198)—what we have been referring to as a person or that which precedes the splintering of 'subject' and 'object', 'self' and 'other'. With the dissolution of the 'self', our conduct opens up in an unprecedented effortlessness and our narration—that is, our entire world—regains its creative and ineluctably apt spontaneity.

Sitting Ch'an as the Atrophy of 'Self'

As long as we are involved in seeking, we inhibit spontaneity. Searching for 'this,' we neglect 'that.' Selecting one path or one aim, all others are cut off. When matters are like this, we so impose on the world that nothing can move unimpeded in a natural expression of its *tao*. Since for the Chinese, all things are specific configurations of *ch'i* or vital energy, imposing an order on the world—on our narrative—is seen as blocking or diverting the free flow of energy in the great harmony (*ta ho* 大和) which naturally obtains when nothing interrupts its "self-soing" (*tzu-jan*). Spontaneity cannot, therefore, be directly cultivated. We cannot *make* ourselves or anything else act without precedent (*wu-wei*). To the contrary—and unlike the farmer who pulled up all of his rice plants trying to help them grow—'we' must refrain from doing or making anything.[8]

In pre-Buddhist China, it was already well-established that learning how to let things grow by themselves was something indirectly accomplished by balancing our *ch'i* through a regimen of concentrated breathing and sitting which were said to have the effect of "fasting the heart/mind." The locus classicus for this is a passage in the *Chuang-tzu* where Yen Hui is criticized by Confucius for still taking his 'mind' as his teacher. Yen Hui is nonplussed and asks what else he can do, to which Confucius replies, "You must fast!" Unlike bodily fasting before a sacrifice, fasting the heart-mind involves "unifying our attention" and refraining from listening with either the ears or the 'mind.' Instead, we must listen with our *ch'i*. "Listening [usually] stops at the ears, the 'mind' at what tallies with it, but *ch'i* is empty and waits on all things. The Tao gathers in emptiness. Emptying is the fasting of the heart" (Chuang-tzu 1968, 58–59).

Listening with our *ch'i* is attending to where energy is already and naturally flowing, not to where our limited senses and our distinctions orient us. Especially when we listen with our 'minds', we hear only what is predetermined, only what falls within the particular horizons for relevance we're presently projecting. Only because these horizons exist is it possible to speak of the tally being met, our expectations fulfilled. On the other hand, *ch'i* is said to be empty precisely because it has no preferences, no fixed biases. Without these and the horizons on which they depend, there is no possibility of ever being filled—no likelihood of ever coming to an 'end,' a point at which things have gone far enough.

Ch'i "waits on all things" because it has nowhere it is trying to go, nothing it is trying to avoid. Without aim or identity, *ch'i* moves without being moved and acts without acting. In this sense, it exemplifies conduct that is *wu-wei*—narrative movement that happens all by itself, unauthored and unrestricted. Thus in the fifth-century Taoist text, the *Hsi-sheng Ching* (HSC), it is not only said that "when energy departs, the living die; [and that] with its increase and decrease, there appears radiance or disease" (HSC 11.5–6), but that "if the five elements did not overcome each other"—if their natural flow were not blocked or imbalanced—"then the myriad things could all be complete" (HSC 11.9). How is this radiant harmony brought about? "Constantly empty, doing nothing, being aware and serene and cultivating your bodily form: thus the myriad things are nurtured" (HSC 25.2).

Fasting the heart should be seen, then, as a means of bringing about the uniquely balanced energy conditions within which it is possible for us to conduct ourselves as if we had no preferences, no aims, and no identity. In short, it is starving our 'minds'—the central constellations around which revolve the greater dispositional networks we identify as our 'selves.' By refusing to nourish the distinctions out of which 'mind' has emerged, we effectively attenuate the 'self' and release the energy hitherto bound up in its structure for the benefit of all things.

Importantly, this fasting cannot be a matter of simply refraining from conscious decision-making and allowing our attention to wander wherever it is inclined to go. As long as the multidimensional complex of distinctions on which our 'selves' depend still exists intact, not focusing on anything in particular is not a way of attenuating the 'self,' but a license for it to run riot. It is for this reason that the minds of beginning meditators are compared to monkeys chattering and swinging through a jungle canopy. Left unattended, the 'mind' simply follows the momentary and apparently randomly ordered whims of its dispositions. Whether these dispositions govern the movement of our narrative and hence of our experience because they are chosen or not is irrelevant: the accidental play of our distinctions is no less 'selfish' than when we feel we are consciously making use of them. In Buddhist terms, it is to be used by our karma rather than using it (by conducting ourselves as bodhisattvas).

In recognition of precisely this problem, when Pai-chang is asked what the method of *wu-wei* is, he replies, "*yu-wei*." Then, after dismissing the *yu-wu* dichotomy as just another dependent opposition, he says that:

> If you're actually talking about true *wu-wei*, it's not taking hold of either '*yu-wei*' or '*wu-wei*.' Why is that? The scriptures say, "If you hold onto the characters of things, then you are attached to 'self.' If you hold onto there being no characteristics of things, then you're [still] attached to 'self.'" For this reason, you shouldn't hold onto 'dharmas' ('things') and you also shouldn't hold onto 'adharmas' (not-'things'). (HTC 119.324b)

That is, it is only in an abstract sense that we can eschew purposeful activity. Whether we take precedents (*yu*) or no-precedents (*wu*) as the basis of our orientation, we are still acting purposefully, still setting the parameters by means of which our narrative is directed.

It is thus not the periphery of experience—the so-called "object pole" of 'dharma' and 'adharma'—that really matters if we are to liberate the energy bound up in the intentional structure of the 'self,' but the status of that center itself. True *wu-wei* arises only when the center itself ceases to hold. But as Pai-chang makes clear, since both 'holding on' and 'holding off' are unavoidably 'selfish,' there is in fact no alternative to taking *yu-wei* as our method, no alternative to using the 'self' to undermine itself. In an apparent paradox, fasting the mind—and hence balancing our *ch'i*—cannot be carried out by distraction, but only through concentration.

In what is perhaps the earliest description of Taoist meditation techniques, the *T'ai-p'ing Ching* refers to the general method of concentration as *shou-i* 守一 or "guarding the one"—a term later taken up in Chinese Buddhism to cover the range of meanings usually assigned to *dhyāna*, *samādhi*, or *smṛti* (Chappell 1983, 100). To bring about *shou-i*, one first had to prepare a meditation chamber, lock the doors, and make sure no one ever entered and disturbed the practice. Once inside the room:

> One should examine oneself. If one finds oneself not able to concentrate properly, one had better leave the room again. There is no way to enforce the practice. Only by gradually attaining concentration and by slowly maturing in the practice will one eventually attain peace ... [then] one should be able to inspect oneself as if one saw one's reflection in clear water. Thereby the myriad affairs will begin to take care of themselves naturally. (in Kohn 1989, 139)

Thought of as a "complete mental fixation on the inner light of the body as the visible manifestation of the cosmic forces of creation"—a fixation (*ting*) which was often accomplished in the initial stages of one's training by focusing as exclusively as possible on either the breath or the inner organs or nexuses where *ch'i* was thought to collect (Kohn 1989, 137)—the attainment of *shou-i* was not important on account of it enabling us to *experience* a connection with universal energy or *ch'i*, but because it enables us to enter into such spontaneous accord with our situation that everything takes care of itself. In this sense, *shou-i* may be seen as the consummate, deliberate activity by means of which we cross the threshold from *yu* to *wu*—the concrete means of relinquishing our 'selfish' control over things so that while 'we' do nothing at all, nothing remains unattended.

That this association of concentration, the liberation of *ch'i*, and conduct that is truly *wu-wei* is not peculiar to the *T'ai-p'ing Ching* but represents a kind of orthodoxy in the Chinese understanding of meditative discipline is borne out in both the *Huai-nan-tzu* (HNT) and the *Kuan-tzu*. For instance, it is unqualifiedly claimed that:

> When the mind can be concentrated on the inside of the body, it can pervade everything just as the One or Tao itself. As long as the mind stays unmoving (that is, undistracted), one will never know what one is doing, nor where one is going. . . . [O]ne knows without studying, sees without looking, accomplishes things without doing anything. (HNT 7.5a; Hidemi 1989, 64)

That is, when the mind is so concentrated—whether on the breath, the inner organs, or on the entirety of our own natures—that nothing distracts us or catches our attention, the usual blockages to the free circulation of energy are effectively dissolved and conduct proceeds without precedent. This is nothing short of being "without what is essential to 'man'"—without our likes and dislikes, the preferences or barbs which not only divert or snag the energy flowing through our narration, but which create the conditions that necessitate our 'dealing with' a world which doesn't always 'go our way.' In phrasing that is less facetious than it sounds, when we go fishing for this or that experience, getting a 'bite' almost always means fighting to remain centered and retain control.

Freeing ourselves from these hindrances—achieving unbiased awareness—is for the Chinese a means of allowing energy to freely expand and encompass all things. As the *Kuan-tzu* puts it, "When the mind opens up and energy expands, we speak of the [free] circulation of energy" (KT 16.5a, tr. Hidemi 1989, 49). But since this free circulation is predicated on the absence of all distinctions—all obstructions to fully improvised or spontaneous narrative movement or conduct—opening the mind through concentration must be seen as a way of undermining the 'mind' on which 'self' depends. That is, realizing unbiased awareness through concentrative meditation is incompatible with the maintenance of a centralized 'self.' Hence the *Huai-nan-tzu's* claim that "when energy fills everything"—when we are completely open and offer no resistance to the free flow of energy—"the mind is also present everywhere" (HNT 1.16a, tr. Hidemi 1989, 57). The possibility of locating the 'self' no longer obtains.

What we find, then, in the indigenous (that is, pre-Buddhist) Chinese meditation tradition is a view of concentrative meditation as doing energy-work aimed at dissolving the 'self' and opening up the possibility of conduct that is unprecedented and yet nourishing, free of all predetermined horizons.[9] That is, we are not instructed to perform a "deconstruction" by means of which we directly subvert our customary distinctions, but to simply maintain a constant focus on some aspect (or if our skill permits, of the entirety) of our ongoing experience. Doing so, energy expands both in the sense of radiating outward and accumulating or intensifying.

While this was popularly supposed to eventuate the possession of miraculous abilities in meditative adepts—generally speaking, the ability to defy "natural" law—in its most philosophically relevant formulation, it was seen as leading to the full realization of our inner nature, a nature understood as profoundly connected or one with the cosmos as a whole. According to the *Hsin-hsu* (HH):

> Inner nature is where the energy of the spirit assembles. When inner nature is completed, the energy of the spirit radiates with brilliance and shines out of the body. It then is able to perfectly respond to impulses it receives from other beings. (HH 8.11b)

In short, while concentrative meditation in the Chinese tradition has always been oriented toward the dissolution of the 'self,' this was not equated with an absorption into a featureless or universal consciousness along the lines of Indian yoga, but seen as a practical method for attaining improvisational excellence—a virtuosic ability to respond to any contingency or demand.

While it is too much to say in the context of Chinese medita-tion that experience is irrelevant, the fact that meditation ideally develops us to a point where—while 'we' neither know what we are doing or where we are going—things are freed to take care of them-selves strongly suggests that subjective experience was never taken as the *goal* of meditative discipline. That is, the Chinese meditator no more undertakes his or her discipline in order to have various experiences than a jazz musician plays the guitar in order to move his or her fingers in particularly intricate patterns. Experiences will no doubt occur, some of them quite extraordinary, but they are simply not the point. Whereas Indian yoga traditionally took all activity—be it meditative, intellectual, or practical—as a means of gaining the ultimate fruit of an experienced unity with or nondifferentiation from Brahman, the Chinese seem to have viewed experience as merely an unavoidable component in alleviating the restrictive bias of 'mind'—in cybernetic terminology, as a useful part of the feedback circuit by means of which our world is rendered less inharmonious.

Moreover, since the aim of Chinese meditation is enhar-monization and not any particular quality of subjective experience as such, it also cannot be consistently maintained that the not-knowing which meditation is said to bring about amounts to the kind of absence of consciousness or experience which results with the Indian yogi's attainment of the state of nonperception. To the contrary, it is more like the musician's not knowing exactly what each finger is doing while improvising: finger movements are surely going on, but what matters is the music itself—something which he or she is at once articulating and taken up into or contained by. Indeed, as soon as a musician actively tries attending to where each finger is going and why—that is, as soon as I try to figure out "what 'I' am doing and where 'I' am headed"—the music suffers. Truly great improvisations occur only when 'we' stop trying to *make* music and simply allow it to play through us.

In summary, the fruit of Chinese meditative discipline is just the development of a narration, a life/world, in which *ch'i* is so balanced and unobstructed that all things—and here 'you' and 'I' must eventually be included among them—will take care of them-selves quite independently of the vicissitudes of our subjective awareness. In narrative terms, the fruit of Chinese meditation is not a transcendence of the world, or the experience of ourselves as an eternal and unchanging soul (*ātman*), but realizing who we are as uninterruptedly virtuosic *persons*. Thus, as Donald Munro points out, while the Chinese clearly found a use for terms which suggest aspects of human being which are of a psychic or spiritual nature—for example, *p'o* 魄 ("sentient soul"), *hun* ("spiritual soul"), and *shen* 神 ("spirit")—none of these were given a special metaphysical status (1969, 50). Nor were they taken as needing or warranting either direct cultivation or a purifying disentanglement from physical and hence interpersonal form (*hsing* 性). Even in the later Taoist tradition where immortality became a goal of meditative discipline, this was not conceived in spiritual or psychic terms, but rather bodily terms. For the Chinese, the status of the 'soul' was never of paramount importance, but rather that of our relationships.

In this light, and as a prelude to turning our attention more completely toward Ch'an meditation, consider the following. Ma-tzu, perhaps the most iconoclastic of the masters of Ch'an, not only claims that "all things are liberated" and that "the liberated is true Suchness"—that is, the spontaneously illuminating quality of buddha-nature or conduct that is *wu-wei*—but that:

> A buddha is capable of *jen*. Having skill and wisdom regarding the nature of excellent opportunities, s/he is able to break through the net of doubts snaring all sentient beings and depart from 'is,' 'is-not,' and other such entanglements. Feelings of commonness and sageliness exhausted, person and thing entirely emptied . . . leaping over quantity and calculation, s/he is without obstruction in whatever s/he does. (TTC 45.406b)

By listing *jen* 仁 as the first quality of being a buddha—a person for whom all things are liberation, through whom all things are true Suchness—and by denying that this has anything directly to do with either our positional feelings of being 'common' or 'sagely' or any imputed difference between persons and things, Ma-tzu effectively orients our concern for enlightenment away from what happens *in any one of 'us'* to what happens *in-between*. What is remarkable about buddhas is not the status of their 'selves,' but the quality of their relationships with others.

Composed of the characters for "person" and the number "two," *jen* explicitly refers to the embodiment of true communality. Perhaps the single most important concept in the Confucian corpus, *jen* is nevertheless a term which defied or was purposely denied any precise definition. On occasions when he was asked to describe *jen*, Confucius typically demurred, taking the opportunity to tell instead a story in which *jen* is evident without ever being made explicit. This suggests that *jen* is not only radically underdetermined and so impossible to identify and describe, but that it is manifestly inseparable from the concrete details of our relatedness, our narration. That is, *jen* can only be demonstrated or shown, and only through the quality or tone of some unique realization of harmonious interpersonality.

As Hall and Ames have pointed out, in the context of traditional Chinese thought, *jen* cannot legitimately be defined in terms of either subjective feelings (of benevolence, love, and so on) or of objectively viewed ritual action, but points instead toward that "fundamentally integrative process" whereby the typically disintegrative preoccupations of what we have been referring to as the 'self' are transformed into the "sensibilities of the profoundly relational person" (1987, 115). That is, the central value of the Confucian Chinese view of humanity resides neither in the inner cloister of the 'self' nor in the outer impersonality of the 'public,' but must be seen as an orientation toward what lies vibrantly in-between. By invoking the Confucian concept of *jen* as a leading attribute of buddhahood, Ma-tzu not only makes it clear that meditation is not to be seen as a means of divesting ourselves of our personal/worldly nature, but that enlightenment itself should not be seen as fundamentally private, but social—a function not of experience, but of conduct.

Granted both this and the formal similarity of the original Taoist and Buddhist meditation techniques, it seems reasonable that Chinese Buddhists would have initially seen—and, in the case of Ch'an, persisted in seeing—meditation (*ting* 定) as a way of doing two things: first, indirectly undermining both seeking and avoidance through focusing the mind outside of the pattern of distinctions on which the 'self' is grounded; and, secondly, accumulating/ making available the energy necessary for realizing no-'mind' or unhindered social virtuosity. That is, I would argue that a deeply meaningful parallelism obtains between the Taoist injunction to "observe oneself" so that things can take care of themselves and Hui-neng's claim that the means of entering the bodhisattva life is nothing more complicated than settling (*ting*) the mind in order to concentratedly "see your own nature." In both cases, meditation is not seen primarily as a direct means to the transformation of consciousness—as an activity that necessarily bears experienced fruit— but as an indirect technique for transforming conduct. Meditation is not for the 'self' or for 'others,' but for the whole out of which these have been discriminated.

While it is true that there are few direct references to energy in the classic Ch'an texts and no explicit description of meditation as "energy-work" or "indirection," this is hardly surprising both because these texts contain no practical descriptions of meditative techniques and because there is no need to explicitly mention what is essentially a cultural commonplace—the fact that health, freedom from suffering, and the conduct of those around us are all functions of the balance or imbalance of our *ch'i*. What we do find, especially in the oral tradition, but also in Huang-po's *Essential Teaching of the Transmission of Mind*, is an association of not-seeking, not cutting off others, and gathering the energy needed to be ready to realize our enlightenment—an association which perfectly mirrors the context within which the pre-Buddhist, (largely) Taoist Chinese tradition discussed the meaning of meditation.

For example, Huang-po was once reproached for teaching his students to not seek anything while at the same time insisting that they not "cut off others." His interlocutor's assumption being that if we don't seek anything at all, we can hardly engage in the intentional act of helping anyone and so effectively cut them off, Huang-po countered with the observation that, "If you don't seek anything, you're at rest. . . . Look at the empty space before your eyes! Does it make 'cutting off others'?" (T 2012.382b). That is, just as Chuang-tzu maintained that the emptiness of *ch'i* is intimately connected with its ability to "wait on all things" and just as the *Huai-nan-tzu* associates a concentrated or nonmoving mind with conduct that is *wu-wei*, in an appeal to the skylike quality of enlightened mind, Huang-po allies not-seeking and being wholly open to and supportive of others. In short, the absence of seeking must be understood as tantamount to so thoroughly opening up our narration that everything without exception is accommodated and cared for.

Far from representing a lapse into the blankness of a catatonic's gaze or the unseeing concentration of a yogi who has attained the state of neither perception nor nonperception, not seeking anything is functionally equivalent to not rejecting anything, to not giving birth to or engendering (*sheng* 生) any distinctions. It is having a beginner's mind which has no inclination to push matters this way or that, but ingenuously (and almost eagerly) welcomes whatever comes its way. Living like this, Huang-po notes, has the beneficial effect of "conserving the mind's energy (*ch'i*)" (T 2012.382b). That is, contrary to what happens when we invest our time and effort in controlling the present or in imagining and maintaining a remembered past or a projected future, when we eschew all seeking we are never drained by whatever befalls us, but profoundly and unreservedly enhanced.

Later, Huang-po returns to the theme of energy and tells his students that:

> If you had at all times—whether walking, standing, sitting, or lying down—just learned no-'mind', you would necessarily have actually attained something long, long ago. Because your energy is so low, you're not capable of the readiness to leap over. But if you get in three or five or perhaps ten years, you'd certainly attain an entry and be able to go on spontaneously. (T 2012.383c)

Huang-po does not specify here exactly what his students are to "get in three or five or ten years" of, but it would seem clear that it involves cultivating an understanding of no-'mind'—that is, having no fixed dispositions or patterns of discrimination—and that this has the consequence of alleviating their shortage of energy or *ch'i*. Thus, the great adversary of Buddhist practice is not 'evil' or 'greed' or any of the other distinctions sedimented over the course of our (innumerable) lives, but what the *Lankavatara* refers to as habit-energy (*hsi-ch'i*)—the repetitive diversion of what would otherwise circulate and freely nourish the harmony of all things.

According to the terminology of Buddhist psychology, a mind that is fraught with distinctions is a mind that is both stained (marked with disintegration) and suppurating (Ch *lou* 漏, Skt *āsrava*)—a mind that is not beneficent or apt precisely because the energy needed for creative response is being discharged in continuous acts of discrimination.[10] Like hairline cracks running through a mirror, distinctions disappear as soon as we stop feeding energy into them. As long as we keep up a constant pressure, 'this' side of the mirror is obviously different from 'that' side and whatever it reflects appears shattered. But the instant this pressure is removed, the world regains its wholeness, the mirror shines completely unblemished, and our hands are free to do whatever is necessary. Just so, diverting our attention away from our usual discriminatory preoccupations and focusing instead on one or another manifestation of the *ch'i* which brings about and connects all things, our own energy ceases to be spent on making and maintaining identity and difference. The 'self' begins to atrophy. Things begin taking care of themselves.

In a passage reminiscent of that quoted above from the *Hsin-hsu*, Huang-po indicates that once this leaking has been corrected and our mind regains its natural clarity (*ming* 明) and balance (*ho*

和), no further cultivation is necessary. "Having no-'mind' at all," he says, "is called non-draining (*wu-lou*) wisdom" (T 2012.383b), and once this wisdom has been realized, all horizons for readiness are naturally relinquished and we can "go on spontaneously" in the true practice of Ch'an. No longer bound by the distinction-generated horizons encircling and identifying the 'self,' our minds are then "like the sun constantly circling through the empty sky. Naturally luminous, they do not reflect light, but radiate" (ibid.). And so, whereas the beginning student of Ch'an must be concerned with conserving the energy needed for concentration, Huang-po informs us that when the distinctions or 'selves' that inhibit our responding immediately to others have sufficiently atrophied, Ch'an is no longer "a matter of saving energy. When you arrive at this point, there is no place to anchor. It is conducting yourself as all the buddhas have" (ibid.).

If we are to relinquish our 'selves,' then, all that is apparently needed is a technique for indirectly starving those patterns of distinctions on which they depend. In the case of the catatonic or severely schizophrenic person, self-identity has been shut down or shattered as a survival mechanism in the face of either being forcibly starved of what is needed for normal self-development or being subjected to influxes of energy so great that they threaten to uncontrollably destroy the complex system of the self. In the case of the obsessive or addicted person, self-identity is at once exaggerated and attenuated through a dependence on either an external focus of concern or on a relationship with a substance or activity whereby the addict's energy is systematically drained off into some 'otherness.' At both the catatonic and addictive extremes, true improvisation is impossible. By contrast, the practitioner of Ch'an undertakes a 'self'-regulated course of concentration which leads indirectly to an atrophy of 'self' without rendering him or her incapable of sensitively responding to the needs of others. Instead of locking his or her energy in rigid and purposely impenetrable patterns of either indulgence or denial, the atrophy of 'self' is actually 'self'-affirmed.

As mentioned above, however, this freedom from 'self' cannot be negotiated by simply acting on impulse or trying to randomize our dealings with the world. While we can certainly take the energy flowing into and bound up by our ego-structure and blow it off in unthinking and entirely gratuitous acts—of, for example, debauchery or random violence—not only will each of these acts answer on some level to the dictates of our karma, they can never be truly responsive or creative and in this sense will only block our entry to the bodhisattva life. We may succeed in diminishing the amount of time we are conscious of our 'selves,' but this in no way constitutes real freedom from selfishness—a criticism that can be directed with equal warrant toward the cultivation of so-called 'selflessness' or altruism.

Bluntly stated, while the hedonist may shift the locus of his selfishness to the lower *chakras* and endorse a policy of never checking his physical or sexual impulses, and the altruist may shift his to the higher *chakras* in a bid to render fully conscious every act of other-serving self-denial—neither manages to undermine the tendency to act on precedent. Even if the relevant distinction is as simple as that between what is liked and what is disliked, conduct remains essentially bound by the dictates of 'self'—a manifestation of karma or intentional repetition.[11] And so, while we must starve the constellation of distinctions out of which the 'self' emerges, we must do so without at the same time either creating blocks to the free flow of energy through our narration as a whole or simply transferring the energy hitherto used for maintaining all of our distinctions into one or another set of these. In short, if we are to liberate the energy locked into the maintenance of the 'self,' 'we' must engage in disciplined concentration.[12]

From what we can gather of the daily life of T'ang-dynasty Ch'an, this function was performed by a combination of sitting meditation, chanting, and manual labor. Seen as energy work, Bodhidharma's wall-gazing, Hui-neng's months in the threshing room, and Ma-tzu's years of sitting ch'an were not forms of ascetic denial meant to disconnect them from social life. Nor were they forms of either self or other-induced punishment and humility or a hungry seeking for some experiential proof of enlightenment. Instead, they were understood in Ch'an as unique opportunities to starve the complex of distinctions underlying the manifestation of 'self' or ego without losing the energy bound up in it in random and yet karmically conditioned reaction. They should be seen, that is, as skilled indirection—loving deceptions by means of which 'we' are led to undermine our 'selves.'

Partnership, Shock Tactics, and One-Finger Ch'an

In Hui-neng's vocabulary, this is realizing our "original nature" (*pen hsing*)—something which he clearly states is based on meditation (*ting*) and wisdom (*hui*) and yet that he readily admits not everyone is capable of pulling off on their own. In contrast to the Taoist tradition where no alternative or complement is explicitly mentioned to fasting the heart-mind, Ch'an openly recognizes the possibility that concentrative meditation and insight into the way things have come to be may not suffice for getting us to the point where we can indeed "go on spontaneously" as true bodhisattvas. That is, these techniques may not enable us to practice Ch'an in the sense of conducting ourselves as buddhas. Hui-neng is thus quite explicit that if we are not able to awaken ourselves, we must seek a great teacher who can help us see our true nature. Meeting such a teacher is, he says, "the great causal event, the transformation which allows you to meet Buddha" (PS 31). In addition to the energy-work of meditation, chanting, and manual labor, passing through the gate of Ch'an depends on joining with a master or masters in communicative concourse.

Recalling that in a Buddhist context, communication cannot legitimately be seen in terms of the transferal of information and that concourse is irreducibly improvisational in nature, the student-teacher relationship which Hui-neng refers to as the "great causal event" cannot be seen as mediated, as a function of giving and receiving various teachings. Indeed, while all of the Ch'an masters we have been concerned with thus far apparently gave public talks, none of them credited the teachings so delivered as being anything more than expedient means for "stopping the crying of babies" (TTC 45.408b). Far from being thought of as the crucial turning point at which the student is enabled to actually meet or manifest as Buddha (*chien fo* 見佛),[13] the teachings were seen as entirely topical palliatives. Intended only to sufficiently ease the discomfort of having a 'self' for the student to consistently employ one or another of the Ch'an techniques of indirection, the teachings were certainly an important prelude to opening up to the great causal event, but in no way definitive of it.

Thus, when Ma-tzu is asked what he says when his teaching "present mind is Buddha" has stopped the crying, he replies, "Not 'mind,' not 'Buddha'." Should someone come along who has overcome these two poles, he indicates that he would "say it isn't a thing (*wu* 物)"—that is, something living *in* the world. Finally, if someone comes along from the Middle, Ma-tzu says he would then "instruct them to embody the Great Tao"—to actually *become* the Path, the entire process of liberation (TTC 45.408b). All four teachings are meant to bring the student to the point where he or she will stop feeling sorry for him or herself, leave off thinking and searching, and simply allow their buddha-nature to freely express itself. In no case is the student actually required to do more than absorb and then act on what the master has told them. In other words, the situation in which a master teaches a student simply does not open up the kind of responsive immediacy characteristic of true concourse.

It is for this reason, it would seem, that Huang-po suggests that the teachings are useful and attractive only for those whose energy is not yet sufficient to make the transition from being *born in* this world or that depending on our karma to actually *giving birth to* incomparable buddha-lands:

> When its energy is expended, an arrow falls back to earth, and the target attained in the coming life is not as intended. Once you leap over contention, apparent inaction and the 'gate of reality,' you straightaway enter the land of the Tathagata. [But] because you are not such a person, you necessarily want to turn toward the gates of conversion established by the ancients and extensively study knowledge and distinctions. (T 2012.383b)

That is, only if our energy is insufficient for us to leap over the divisions crazing our narration and see it as a truly horizonless buddha-land, do we grasp after the words of the great teachers. Hoping to find a map showing the way through our distinction-induced suffering—the key by means of which we may unlock the gate barring our passage on the Tao—our very hunger for knowledge and guidance is indicative of our lack of energy, of the extent to which we have isolated ourselves as 'selves.' Turning to the great masters, we hope to find some secret, some shortcut that will all at once allow us to quit taking a stand on the Path and instead to wander it freely and easily. But, as Huang-po points out, "If [we] don't meet a brilliant master who has gone beyond the 'world,' [we] will have swallowed the medicine of the Mahayana in vain" (T 2012.383b). By themselves, the teachings will not help us.

Granted this and taking seriously Ch'an's millennia-long commitment to treasuring the "public cases" (*kung-an*) recounting the largely informal and impromptu meetings of student and master, it would seem that the great causal event is best characterized as catalytic—as the introduction of some narrative element that brings about an unprecedented realization of practice while leaving no mark (*hsiang* 相) on the student, no remainder that is carried off as something acquired through the interaction. Like all catalysts, the master's actions are functionally inert in the sense that they are not taken directly up into the student's practice or enlightenment, but serve only to greatly hasten what would otherwise be a quite uncertain and very protracted affair. Ma-tzu's hitting and kicking, Nan-ch'uan's non-sequiturs, Chao-chou's "dry shit on a stick," and Lin-chi's rafter-lifting shouts are neither transmissions in the sense of insights passed down from generation to generation nor templates for or models of enlightened behavior which are to be meticulously imitated. Instead, they must be seen as timely triggers or shock tactics which explode the preconceptions of their students and allow the energy pent up in their distinctions to be released into the horizonlessness of unselfish response to the needs of others.

As a catalyst, the master's conduct effectively "jump starts" the practice of Ch'an by momentarily opening us up enough that a nondeliberate response can occur. That is, the master forces us into a position where the energy 'we' have been conserving through our concentrative techniques can burst past the 'self.' We find ourselves doing or saying something completely unexpected and unplanned and yet perfectly in tune with the needs of our present situation. In short, we discover 'proof' of the reality of conduct that is *wu-wei*.

Now, reacting without deliberation is, of course, no problem—that, after all, is what we generally do in acting on the basis of established habits. It is only when our habitual ways of dealing with the world and the others populating it prove insufficient to the demands of the moment that we find it necessary to consider alternatives and weigh options. Having "better things to do," in the absence of such demands or challenges, we simply don't bother to engage in any fresh thinking, analysis, or planning. Instead, we quite contentedly allow our conduct to take an almost exclusively societal heading and live our lives essentially by rote. When this proves impossible, our first recourse is typically to reconceive our situation so that one of our systems of habitual reaction will in fact appear adequate, and only failing this will we begin the process of mapping out new patterns of thought, feeling, speech, and action.

What this means, of course, is that we spend most of our lives either reacting to things along habitual lines or actively calculating the most efficient means of doing so. Whether the 'costs' we calculate are counted in physical, sensual, intellectual, emotional, or even spiritual currency does not alter the fact that our primary orientation is toward deciding what is relevant to 'our' happiness and then regulating experience to maximize its recurrence or maintenance. And for the most part, the power of calculative thought is such that 'we' are nearly always successful. To be sure, there are times when both habit and active rationality fail us and 'we' can navigate through a particular impasse only by an appeal to intuition or a retreat into madness. But in general 'we' manage well enough, and these forays into "irrationality" are few and far between.[14]

But, regardless of whether 'we' unconsciously appeal to habit and react to our situation in a nondeliberate way, or consciously appeal to the canons of a calculative rationality, 'we' remain fully within the horizons of activity that is *yu-wei*. What the master-student encounter is meant to bring about is, then, conduct which is immediate or nondeliberate without being habitual, and novel and responsive without being calculative. Otherwise, in the first case, 'we' effectively vanish but only at the cost of fixing our behavior—rendering it fundamentally static. In the second, habit is indeed overcome, but only at the cost of indulging in 'self'-promoting deliberation. That is, partnership with a Ch'an master should be seen as realizing conduct that is both virtuosic and free of 'self'—a concursive interplay which 'we' can witness or experience, but not engineer.

When we approach a Ch'an master asking for admission to the community or for the meaning of Bodhidharma's coming from the West and are answered with a kick, a shout, or a complete non-sequitur, any possibility of reasonable response is cut off. If the timing is right, this has the effect of shocking the meditation-attenuated 'self' into silence and opening up our narration in such a way that the energy we have been bleeding off from our habitual distinctions is liberated in truly creative and unintentional response. That is, 'we' are stopped in our tracks—undergoing at least a temporary dissolution of the horizons normally defining 'you' and 'I' as individuals—and we witness the advent of conduct that is wholly without precedent. At this moment, student and master—Lin-chi's guest and host—become partners in lively concourse.

As documented in the public cases of Ch'an, this is often a cause of jubilation but almost never marks the end of discipleship. Delivered at a moment of maximum vulnerability—when the student is just arriving or turning to leave, or when he or she is bowing or standing before the *sangha* to engage in "dharma combat"—the shock precipitates a flash of content-free readiness in which the possibility of true communication can come to fruition. As Lin-chi makes very clear, this is the result of stealing away whatever it is that 'we' depend or rely on—whether it is form and ritual, the dharma, our experiences in meditation, or our sense of individual identity:

> Sometimes I steal away the man but not the circumstances. Sometimes I steal away the circumstances but not the man. Sometimes I steal away both man and circumstance. Sometimes I steal away neither. (T 1985.497a)[15]

If the theft is successful, we find that the ground of discrimination has been pulled out from under us and that far from being a void or blank absence the resulting emptiness is a bright and limitless responsivity. For a time, 'we' glimpse what it means to attain such social virtuosity that no matter where we stand everything becomes true (T 1985.498a)—what it means to be a person "who can ride all circumstances" (T 1985.499a).

But as the Chinese term (*ch'an-chi* 禪機) for this perfectly timed assault on the 'self' indicates, this moment is unfortunately something artificial or contrived—*chi* having the connotation of both "an opportunity" and "a machine"—and so something put together and destined not to last. For example, in Ma-tzu's case, while he attained a great awakening after years of diligent meditation by way of Nan-yueh's ruse of ostensibly polishing a roofing tile to make a mirror, he then continued to serve as the latter's attendant for ten years before going off on his own to teach. And so, while a well-timed shock from a master can temporarily paralyze the 'self' and spark the advent of real spontaneity in our narration, unless we are sufficiently free of discrimininatory and karmic blockages, the free circulation of energy characteristic of conduct that is *wu-wei* will eventually be interrupted and diverted back into the maintenance of 'selfish' activity. 'We' will regain our usual control over experience. Things will no longer be able to "take care of themselves."

Although we lose our naiveté about the relationship of 'self' and practice in achieving even momentary concourse with an enlightened master, fully entering the bodhisattva life involves our being able to bring about such concourse with all beings at all times and in all situations. That is, we must be able to conduct ourselves *as buddhas*—as the initiators of enlightening partnership and not merely as its beneficiaries. This suggests, however, that while shock tactics as we have thus far described them are in most cases going to prove useful and perhaps necessary in a student's development, they are unlikely to be sufficient to bring about a permanent crossing of the threshold into Ch'an practice. With the reassertion of the 'self,' our concourse with the master degenerates into a discursive relationship which—even if formally adequate—we cannot but see as both qualitatively deficient and undeniably our own doing. That is, we recognize that it is our own 'selves' which interrupt the concourse by means of which our world is transformed into the undivided Suchness of a pure buddha-land.

At this point, continued shocks will prove successively less effective as a strategy for triggering a permanent relinquishing of the 'self.'[16] What is required instead is a means of getting the concentration-enfeebled 'self' to stand down of its own accord—to willingly step aside so that our narration can spontaneously repair itself as unimpeded concourse. In short, what is needed is the regular presentation of occasions for the 'self' to recognize its fundamental and unmistakable incapacity for convincingly and effectively playing the role of bodhisattva.

Once we have witnessed the shock-induced expression of unprecedented conduct in our narrative, the possibility of imagining that 'you' and 'I' are absolutely essential to the resolution of either our own crises or those of others can no longer be seriously maintained. At the same time, however, as long as the challenges we experience to our own competency are intermittent, it is altogether possible to continue disavowing full responsibility for the quality of our conduct. In other words, we can persist in blaming others for the intractability of the problems we have with them, convinced that it is not our inadequacy, but their recalcitrance which keeps us locked into a fundamentally imbalanced and hence discursive mode of relationship.

It would seem that Ch'an's way of dealing with this was to put the student in the position of having to correct their teacher—to cease being a mere guest and successfully play the role of host. To this end, the master would often adopt a particular and unvarying way of dealing with students at this stage. For some, like Lin-chi, this meant always shouting in response to a query. For others, it meant always repeating the student's question, always contradicting the student, or always making the same expression or gesture. Ch'an Master Chu-ti, for example, was known for always answering a question by raising his finger. In all such cases, the master is doing what each of us does countless times each day—reacting to new situations in virtually identical manners, effectively insensitive to their irreducible uniqueness. Instead of demonstrating the kind of improvisational genius idealized in the never-contradicted injunction to "accord with the situation and respond as needed," the master casts himself in the role of a mere sentient being, and the student is enjoined to do something truthful about it—to draw the master into the incomparable freshness of unbridled concourse.

Unlike fellow students or lay people who have yet to realize their own true nature, however, the master will accept nothing short of real spontaneity in response to his shouting or finger raising and for this 'we' must first step out of the way. Since any attempt to 'act spontaneously' entails a discursion of 'me' and 'what I'm going to do,' not only does it commit us to acting *yu-wei*, it places an invisible and yet quite effective barrier between us. Concourse becomes impossible.

A unique demonstration not only of the use of shock tactics, but of the kind of conduct by means of which a student truly ceases being a mere guest in the house of Ch'an is found in the case of the awakening of Chu-ti's personal attendant. As the story goes, Chu-ti's attendant was a young boy who every morning would rise early, make the daily rice, sweep the area in front of their hermitage, and then sit nearby while the master greeted and instructed his visitors. Every day, the same scene was repeated: a monk or layperson would arrive to ask Chu-ti some question or seek some guidance and he invariably responded by holding up his index finger. One day Chu-ti announced that had to visit a friend and asked the boy to tell anyone who came to return the following day. The boy, however, figured that he had seen enough of Chu-ti's method to be able to perfectly well play the role of the host and so spent the whole day greeting visitors with his upraised finger. When Chu-ti returned and asked how things had gone, the boy demonstrated his understanding. Chu-ti pulled out his knife and in a flash had severed the upraised finger, at which instant the boy is said to have attained a great awakening.

When Chu-ti returns and finds that his attendant has taken on his own role—that of the host or master, he immediately adopts the stance of the keen-eyed student—a guest capable of breaking through the obdurate regularity of his host's behavior. Greeted with the knee-jerk reaction of a raised finger, Chu-ti literally cuts off the habit at its root—demonstrating not only his ability to not get sucked into the meaninglessly discursive pattern in which a guest circles the host trying to figure out what the latter's gesture signifies, but also his ability to shock his host into illumination. In short, by allowing the boy to play the role of host, Chu-ti is able to demonstrate not only how a guest overcomes the habits of his host and brings about true—that is correcting or enlivening—concourse, he enables the boy to understand what it really means for him to be a student or guest. Taking on the role of guest, Chu-ti again becomes a master; taking on the role of host, the boy finally realizes what it means to be a guest. And at this unanticipatable moment, guest and host both disappear in the concursive spontaneity of conduct that is truly *wu-wei*.

Thus, unlike the phase of Ch'an partnership in which shock tactics are used by a master *as* master to precipitate a flash of spontaneous conduct for the benefit of the student, by engaging in such a role reversal the master here forces the student to repeatedly confront someone who refuses to open up, who refuses to do anything but reiterate themselves or monkey the actions of those around them. In order to get around this impasse, the student must become a true host—someone capable of bringing about the awakening of others. In a word, the student must go beyond merely attaining awakening and directly realize what it means to be a bodhisattva. As long as s/he tries responding on the basis of what is 'known' or 'understood'—on the basis of what Mead refers to as the 'me' (1934, 175, for example)—the master will either keep repeating him or herself or will simply dismiss the student as unready. Ultimately, the pivotal break by means of which this uneasy discourse is transmuted into concourse can occur only when the meditation-attenuated and shock-prepared 'self' has exhausted all of its options and simply stops trying. Then the student unhesitatingly realizes his or her true "I" in conduct that is completely unpredictable and yet marvelously adept. The famous Ch'an gate (*kuan* 關, literally a "frontier pass") turns out to have all along been gateless (*wu-men* 無門)—a product of our own horizon-bound imagination.

Chapter 8

Morality and Character in the Mastery of Ch'an

Realizing the gatelessness of Ch'an is discovering who we truly are. Whereas we have until this moment thought of ourselves as 'selves'—as the central players on whose thoughts and feelings pivot the action of a myriad separate and only partially overlapping dramas—we now fully understand that each thing interdepends with everything else. Since no 'thing' has any abiding self-nature, there is really nothing which separates us, no barriers but those we create. In short, we realize that we are buddhas—not individual and locatable 'sentient beings' cast at birth onto the stage of an independent and objective world, but unfathomable and enlightening narration.

Thus, in speaking to his students about entering the practice life, Lin-chi says:

> If you want to be able to freely be born or die, to go or stay, to take off or put on (this or that body, clothes, mood, position, etc.), then right now perceive *who is listening to this teaching*. S/he has no form, no marks, no roots or origin and no abiding status. Flexible and lively, her/his responses are established [in accordance with] the ten thousand kinds of things, only the place from which s/he functions is, in fact, no 'place' at all. For this reason, if 'you' search for her/him, s/he retreats ever further away. So s/he is called mysterious. (T 1985.498c, emphasis added)

Functioning from no 'place,' a bodhisattva cannot be identified. Having no form or special qualities, no fixed origin or status, s/he should never be conceived of as 'someone' who acts in this or that ideal fashion, but as virtuosic responding in the absence of any 'one' who responds.

Unlike Thomas Nagel's (1987) purely rational agent who takes up an ideally unbiased vantage from which it is possible to see things "as they are" and arrive at agreements about matters of mutual concern with other such agents, a bodhisattva doesn't dwell anywhere and so cannot be said to have a view at all—even one from "nowhere." Far from being an ineluctable subject standing over and against an objective world making decisions about what to do in or with it, a bodhisattva arises only when there obtains conduct without remainder—the realization of true nonduality in the movement of our narration. And so, far from being disembodied spirit or pure consciousness, buddhas and bodhisattvas have the entire, irreducibly dynamic world as body—what Ma-tzu referred to as the wondrous functioning (*miao yung*) in and through which all things are liberation (TTC 45.406b).

When Lin-chi says that liberation—being able to freely be born or die, go or stay, and so on—is no more distant than right now "perceiving who is listening," he is graphically insisting that we let go of the presumption that enlightenment occurs either 'here' or 'there,' that it is in some sense propagated or transmitted. Were he to ask his students to discern who is seeing him teach, it would precipitate an occlusive focus on their mutually excluding perspectives. Not only would it affirm their differences as teacher and taught, such a request would ground the continued isolation of each student from all the others. Those in front would be obstacles blocking the views of those behind who would block in turn the views of those still further away. Under such circumstances, there arises a constant jockeying, an incessant seeking for the best position, the place of privilege or rank.

By contrast, it is the nature of hearing that the importance of position or perspective is minimized. Whether sitting to the left or right, in front or behind the speaker, we all hear the same words. If anything, it is the constant shuffling for position that makes it hard to hear. Perceiving who is listening to the teaching means coming to attentive rest and stilling our desire to seek advantage. But more importantly, it is also the case that while only the audience can see Lin-chi speaking, *everyone present*—Lin-chi included—*is listening* to the teaching. The freedom of which Lin-chi speaks—the freedom of having emptied the 'self'—means realizing that our true body excludes no one or any thing.

Emptiness and the Anarchic Intimacy of Ch'an Morality

Far from being the culmination of a linear series of incremental changes—an event brought about or caused through the intervention of our will—realizing the virtuosic freedom that is our true nature marks a kind of gestalt shift signifying our having ceased identifying ourselves with any locale, any set of qualities, any set aims, favored experiences or desired statuses. In a word, it marks our personal realization of emptiness. As suggested earlier, in much the same way that the transition from seeing the 'same' drawing now as two women facing one another in profile and now as a single vase is not a shift mediated by a point by point reinterpretation of the dots and lines out of which the drawing is composed, the 'transition' from the life of a sentient being to that of a bodhisattva is not a function of getting closer or straying further away, but an immediate reconfiguration of our narration *as a whole*. That is, the change is not a matter of adding or subtracting anything from our lives or personalities, but of reorienting. The transition is not fundamentally ontic, but axial; not a matter of being, but value.

Now, in a Buddhist context where interdependence is understood as irreducible, no substantial ground or purely objective 'reality' is assumed to underlie our evaluations. In consequence, the claim that transforming the world of sentient being into a buddha-land should be seen as a function of *how we perceive* does not carry any immediately pejorative connotation. In the absence of some objective and independent reality to which we are opposed as fallibly knowing subjects, a change that occurs with a shift of orientation or perceptual gestalt is not inferior to, any less real, or (in a Buddhist sense) any less meaningful than one in which the relevant 'facts' are altered—where we "redraw the picture" instead of just seeing it anew.

From a Ch'an Buddhist perspective there is, indeed, no more inconsistency in my seeing our present as 'enlightened' and your seeing 'the same' present as 'unenlightened' as there is in our having the 'two women' and 'single vase' views of a drawing. The potential of such diversity is in fact one of the conditions of that harmony which arises on the middle path between individualism and collectivism, between selfishness and so-called selflessness. When the world is not seen as objective and singular, but as irreducibly ambiguous, it can only be we who make it 'good' or 'ill' or, better yet, who avoid the dichotomy altogether. The meaning of an event is not inherent, but a function of its irreducibly narrative context.

It is only with this firmly in mind that we can understand the unremitting insistence in Ch'an that nothing needs to be either sought *or* cut off. Living as a bodhisattva does not necessarily involve either getting hold of or getting rid of anything, but a liberating redirection of the manner in which all of the elements of our world are being narrated. What changes are not 'things' or 'people'— the dots and lines comprised by our life narratives—but their meaning. What is transformed with enlightenment are not 'beings', but *how* our dramatic interrelation proceeds, our story.

Were this not the case—if, in other words, it was necessary or even invariably desirable to bring about "real" changes in the circumstances of our world for liberation to be realized—then a bodhisattva would have the infinitely taxing job of acting as a kind of round-the-clock cosmic social worker and jack-of-all-trades. She would have before her at all times a task—something to push or pull into a more fitting position—and would undoubtedly find it useful if not necessary to invent an at least provisional standard for "the way things ought to be." All in all, we would have no alternative but to regard as mere fabrication the Buddha's declaration upon enlightenment that there was no longer anything needing to be done.

Since, however, the real source of suffering as narrative interruption is not ultimately *what* occurs, but a lack of the virtuosity and/or energy to play along with whatever arises, none of these unsavory consequences need obtain. To the contrary, since our narration is interrupted only when responding is truncated or blocked—when the energy generated in concourse is prohibited from circulating freely—and since such blockages always pivot on relatively fixed distinctions, ending suffering is best accomplished through undercutting distinction itself. Working to stabilize and maintain the 'good' and eliminate 'ill,' far from ending suffering, must actually be seen as one of the prime contributing causes of its arising. That is, it is only from the unenlightened perspective of immersion in so-called "objective" distinctions that some factual change—be it material, moral, or spiritual—needs to be brought about for liberation to be realized.[1]

Inverting the usual premises on which altruism is typically undertaken, from the perspective of realized Ch'an, the buddha-work simply does not depend on the presence or alteration of particular circumstances—no more so at least than any other gestalt shift does. Only if we canonize one version is it necessary to render the situation (the "drawing") unambiguous by adding or subtracting certain distinctions which make the other view impossible to maintain. The problem with doing so, of course, is that no matter how 'humane' or 'unselfish' or 'sacred' our motives are, by enforcing any particular bias we in the long run create a progressively rigid world more and more deeply prone to interruption. Once the work of promoting the 'good' and excluding the 'ill' is begun, not only do we find there is always something else needing our attention, it will seem increasingly the case that ever greater efforts are needed to realize ever lesser results. In the worst-case scenario, we eventually enter a living hell—a kind of gridlock in which the distinctions out of which we have built the circumstances of our lives are so dense and command so much of the natural flow of energy through our narration that a nearly infinite amount of time and effort would seem necessary to solve the problems we feel impending.[2]

In the favored terminology of Ch'an, our original mind is continuously and naturally (*tzu jan*) bright and clear, shining everywhere, leaving no shadow. Unlike Shen-hsiu's mirror-cleansing, realizing our original mind is understanding that as long as we keep responding as needed—as long, that is, as we maintain a completely improvisational relationship with all that occurs—'dust' is in fact no-'dust', form is already emptiness. It is only because we are in the habit of stopping at what 'we' can be aware of or know and taking 'that' to be reality that the essential brilliance of our own original body (*pen t'i* 本體) goes unperceived (T 2012.380b). It is then that we are blocked from seeing our lives *as* enlightened.

For this reason, Huang-po emphatically insists that, "If you would just have no-'mind'"—that is, drop all of your distinctions—"your original body would appear by itself" (T 2012.380b). When 'mind' no longer obtains, all divisions, all of our 'objective' differences and separations are undone. No longer capable of identifying ourselves as this or that individual who must act for anything to get done, no-'mind' means realizing that we are the entire world—a buddha-land which freely and creatively takes care of itself. In short, the bodhisattva life—the realization of unbound personhood—can be seen as unmitigated spontaneity. In it, all relations are improvised and all conduct social. What matters is just that things keep flowing together—that no interruptions occur which become fixed or habitual—and so no particular circumstances have to be maintained or aimed for. There is no need to judge anything—to divide what is seen, heard, made conscious, or known into things to be grasped or rejected—but only to remain open to the freely circulating joy of limitless concourse. Then, not approaching anything, not withdrawing, not dwelling or being attached, "from north to south and from east to west, all by itself there will be no place that is not the place of enlightenment" (ibid.).

Biasing Morality: Existence and Integrity

Granted the 'realist' dispositions prevailing in much of today's religious, philosophical, and political thinking, such an understanding of enlightening conduct cannot but appear suspect. In a world in which objective conditions and subjective needs and desires are often wildly at odds, even insuring basic human dignity—not to mention achieving happiness or the end of suffering—is often seen as a battle waged at high and irreversible cost. In such a world, the project of enlightenment is not infrequently thought of as a luxury—something that arises only when substantial headway has been made in alleviating the most dire attacks on our existence as both individuals and communities.

Where integrity—meaning here a bias toward individuality or atomic subjectivity and so a view of community as composition—is taken as a paramount value, talk of liberation as a kind of gestalt shift cannot but appear solipsistic. At the very least, such liberation seems tantamount to a devaluation—if not an outright ignorance—of the concreteness of our narration and so of the profoundly tragic elements of our suffering. Ch'an enlightenment may be social in the sense we have been using the term, but in the absence of a concern for real changes in the objective circumstances of our experience and hence our suffering, how can it avoid being something merely abstract or chimerical, a crassly private fantasy? In short, along with the "bathwater" of egoic effort and individual attainment, Ch'an would also seem to throw out morality and anything remotely resembling compassion. If enlightenment amounts to a gestalt shift, a reconfiguration leaving every particular of our prior lives intact, is it not inferior even to a placebo—a distracting narrative tangent that ultimately leaves our disease not only untreated but almost surely worsening?

Now, precisely because it focuses a profound differential in worldview, such a critique of Ch'an enlightenment as unconscionably quietist and even amoral cannot be summarily dismissed. And yet, it would seem that rational adjudication between the two is perhaps hopelessly complicated since it is in part the nature of reason itself that is at stake in evaluating disparate worldviews—in this case a rationality that zeroes in on 'what is' (whether defined relatively or absolutely) and a rationality that conceives its task as creation, as open-ended and indeed ever-blossoming improvisation. What, in other words, could serve as a common ground for even a "pragmatic" evaluation when we have on the one hand a world articulated on the basis of entitative existence and the possibility of ultimate definition, and on the other a world understood as fathomlessly ambiguous, as irreducibly neither 'this' nor 'that'?

But if it is beyond us to decide without prejudice whether Ch'an enlightenment must be admitted to be morally gratuitous or whether it eventuates the realization of a deeply foreign and yet undeniably 'better' moral cosmos, it is nevertheless possible to use the above critique as an impetus for exploring the relationship between the ontology of personhood and the meaning of morality. And this, if we are lucky, will enable us to better understand not just the sociality of Ch'an enlightenment, but who *we* are and might yet become.

To begin with, where entitative existence or being is presumed basic, personhood implies autonomous individuality and the task of morality is most easily taken to be one of insuring or safeguarding integrity—both our own and that of others. But since it is the nature of entities that they cannot occupy the same place at the same time, and since placement is of a piece with the question of advantage, morality will in this case tend to lean toward a calculation—more or less explicit—of relative goods and the negotiation of their necessarily unequal distribution. Indeed, this inequality is inexpungable as long as our uniqueness as well as that of each and every place is not drastically attenuated—one of the primary reasons why utopias are almost invariably rather boring places peopled by what we have to admit amount to frighteningly generic citizens. Taking existence—literally "standing apart"—as foundational, equality is either accepted as merely theoretical, an ideal, or is purchased by a difference and hence interest-deflating homogenization of the particular.

It is in fact just this implied tension between individuality and universality that lends a dramatic weight to integrity and existence-informed moral discourse. Therein, resolving a moral dilemma almost invariably pivots on the issue of justly identifying and allocating rights—for the unborn, the infirm, the poor, the young and so on. The task is not so much that of removing the disparities that obviously obtain among us, but of regulating them—discouraging any one of us turning to our own advantage the 'accident' of another's situation. Morality is in essence an inclination toward preserving each individual's rights without jeopardizing those of all others—a negotiation of claims for entitlement.

Underlying this commitment to preserving title and integrity and in fact underwriting the intelligibility of the above critique of Ch'an enlightenment is an acceptance of the inviolability of the disjunction or displacement of subject and object. While 'others' are ostensibly subjects from their own perspectives, they are for better or worse only objects for us. Related only externally—that is, after the fact of our autonomous individuality—we are not originally one, but many. We may guess at, but cannot directly apprehend, as we do for ourselves, what is right for others. Hence the development of moral law and principle—algorithms for rightly dealing with the impenetrability of the other.

In this sense, being moral is a willing negotiation of the gap between our direct awareness of our needs and desires and those we merely impute to others by analogy with ourselves, a kind of legislature or politics of experience. Because the individuality of the self is canonic and because that independence is ontologically grounded, such morality tends to appeal to universalism as a means of bridging our distinctness and ultimately our subjective incommensurability. Universally binding moral laws and standards and our obedience of them are thus not infrequently held to be all that stands between us and chaos. Without such a ligature, it is feared that our ineradicable and ontological separation will degenerate into wanton advantage-taking. In summation, where the bias of our world or narration is toward integrity and existence, morality is finally based upon and yet provides no practical alternative to our evident dislocation.

Since Ch'an is based on a system of practice which exposes existence as an artifice by means of which 'self' is held apart from and even identified in terms of 'other,' and since it further acts as a catalyst in the realization of a virtuosic ability to accord with our situation and respond as needed, such dislocation is radically undermined. Having no location, persons in the Ch'an sense cannot interfere with or displace others. Rather we interpenetrate—stories containing stories in endless intensity. And along with this realized absence of any real independence or individuation comes an equally powerful realization of the absence of all necessity—the absence of any implied, universally binding 'ought.'

A morality arising out of the practice of non-duality has no need to establish a universal medium for arbitrating our difference. Aiming at realizing harmony—at preserving meaningful difference—such a morality is deeply exceptional, irreducibly contextual. Because the individual existent is not taken as basic, the overarching concern of integrity-biased morality for insuring togetherness is simply absent—not because there is any lack of concern for community, but because community is not a composition, a thing put together and so liable to falling apart. To the contrary, where relationship—and not relata—is original, community is practiced directly in the preservation of our reciprocity, in the celebratory deference by means of which accord opens up in creative response. The necessity for mediating laws is precisely what the Ch'an practice of nonduality eliminates.

In the context of such practice, morality cannot consist of the project of integration, of bringing our circumstances and behavior into agreement with some necessary or even ideal, universal standard aimed at establishing a perfectly regulated state of affairs. Rather, morality must be understood as truing our narration, orienting it toward ever more extensive and hence more vulnerable harmony and intimacy. As such, Ch'an morality is not concerned with treating the symptoms of our dislocation, but with removing the conditions without which it fails to obtain.

Ch'an Enlightenment and the Intimate Disregard of What Is Right

A perfect example of how this morality works in practice can be found in the story of the Korean monk Won Hyo. Raised in a prominent, aristocratic family, Won Hyo was first trained in the Confucian classics. But when he encountered Buddhism, he retreated from the society of his peers, began practicing meditation and was soon ordained as a monk. He kept up his meditative training and Buddhist scholarship with remarkable zeal, but for all his understanding of the sutras and the *vinaya* (the monastic rules) enlightenment eluded him.

At one point, he decided that he would go to China and find a Ch'an master capable of leading him to a real breakthrough. He set off on foot, hiking until each day's light failed, and was soon deep in the mountains. One night, he was so tired that he went straight to sleep, without even so much as lighting a fire or looking for water. All through the night, he was tormented by fleeting, violent dreams and woke before dawn, aching and parched. Rolling over, he saw in the starlight what seemed to be a silver goblet filled with water. Lifting the goblet to his lips, he drank deeply. Never had he tasted water so fresh and sweet. His thirst quenched, he lay back and fell into a deep, empty sleep.

Waking with the sun rising from among the surrounding peaks, Won Hyo reached for the goblet only to discover that it was in fact a human skull filled with putrid, worm-infested water. He realized in that instant that it was only his mind that made 'pure' and 'impure,' 'good' and 'evil.' With this insight, he no longer felt there was a need to travel to China. He returned home and soon became one of the most sought-after lecturers on Buddhism.

But after twenty years of renown as a scholar-monk, he knew that something was still eluding him. Insight he had had, but en-lightenment was still only a concept. Hearing about a famous Ch'an master in Shilla, he decided to find him and ask for help. Some days later, he arrived at the old master's mountain retreat and found him weeping uncontrollably.

"What has happened that you're crying so?" he wondered aloud.

"Two days ago, I found a baby doe whose mother had died in giving birth. Wanting to feed her, I went to the village begging milk. But no one would give me, an old monk, anything but a handful of rice. Finally, I made up a story about getting a woman pregnant who had died giving birth to my son. This created a great scandal, but no offers of milk. In the end, I came back here and discovered the doe had already died."

"But why are you weeping? If all things have no self, what is there to mourn?"

"It's not that," the old master replied. "It's just that my mind and the mind of the doe had become one. I'm crying because I still want milk."

Hearing this, Won Hyo knew he was in the presence of a great master and asked for instruction. The old master asked Won Hyo if he was willing to sacrifice everything he had to realize his own true nature. Won Hyo agreed and the master invited him for a walk into town. They passed through many fine neighborhoods and eventu-ally arrived in the red-light district. The master led Won Hyo up the steps of a brothel where they were greeted by a prostitute.

"Look who I've brought you, the great monk Won Hyo," the master announced.

"Oh! Won Hyo!" the prostitute exclaimed. Smiling, she led the old master and a blushing Won Hyo upstairs where she began pre-paring food and wine.

The old master poked a stunned Won Hyo in the ribs. "For twenty years you've lived as a monk in the company of the rich and famous, but it's not good to dwell in heaven for too long. Sometimes you have to visit hell. Hell, too, is as clear as space."

Won Hyo objected. "But I never even broke a single precept. My life is so far unblemished!"

Turning to the prostitute, the master scolded her. "Don't you realize that this man is a monk? You'll go straight to hell if you take him in! Aren't you afraid?"

She smiled and reached out for Won Hyo's hand. "Not at all. I know Won Hyo will come down to save me!"

As the story goes, Won Hyo broke more than one precept that night, but by the time the sun rose, he had realized the true meaning of practice. Enlightened, he rushed out into the city streets beaming and singing like a morning bell, *De-an! De-an!* What had eluded Won Hyo during his years of strict and diligent training had burst upon him in the course of a single night of splendid impropriety.

There are many ways of understanding this story. In keeping with direction taken in working through Kisagotami's tale, we might say that in order to save all beings, we must be willing to live *with and as them*, not just in and among them. Their story and ours must be one. And so, if they are rushing to hell, we may well have to leave the safe and secure havens of our good karma and accompany them. And in this case, we will eventually find ourselves asking who is saving who? If Won Hyo had never taken the intimate risk of entering the brothel, is it only the prostitute's salvation that would have been sacrificed? Were it not for her willingness to go to hell for the purpose of serving Won Hyo and giving him pleasure, what would have become of our famous monk? Would he ever have understood what it meant to truly realize one-mind (*i-hsin*)?

By entering taking the prostitute's hand, Won Hyo willingly leaves the safety of the monastic life and reestablishes his unalloyed oneness with his community. Discarding his robes and his precepts, far from being a moral failure on his behalf, represent his determination to relinquish all his horizons for readiness, his boundless commitment to "accord with the situation, responding as needed." That is, by relinquishing his tightness, his close rein on experience, Won Hyo's *ch'i* is finally set free and his narration healed, made whole. Only then can he realize conduct that is truly without precedent. Only then does he blossom in exquisite demonstration of the bodhisattva life, his world become an incomparable buddha-land.

Stories like this one leave little alternative to seeing Ch'an morality is anarchic—not chaotic or gratuitous to be sure, but certainly free of any fixed principle. Quite simply, moral conduct is enlightening conduct—conduct that is thoroughly *wu-wei*. This means, of course, that the *vinaya* are ultimately of utility only for those who have yet to realize dramatic nonduality. As virtuosically improvised care, true anarchic morality depends on the realization of unlimited "skill-in-means" or *upāya*. And because of this, there can be no mistake that Ch'an morality is relatively rare. Arising only when there is a creative marriage of fluid vigilance and openly circulating *ch'i*, Ch'an morality cannot be a direct function of will—no matter how apparently unselfish. Nevertheless, insofar as *wu-wei* is possible only when our perceptual and responsive natures have been disentangled from impeding habits and energy-draining obsessions and aversions, morality also cannot in most cases be divorced from the energy-freeing techniques of what we have called indirection—meditation, bowing, chanting, repetitive manual labor, and so on. Won Hyo was not led to the prostitute at the beginning of his tenure as a monk, but only after years of diligent training.

Thus, while Ch'an morality is at root anarchic, it is not for that reason a matter of either chance or timely necessity. Popular associations of *wu-wei* and a kind of blissed-out going-with-the-flow are in fact deeply erroneous—a kind of "crackerjack-box zen" suggesting that indulgence precipitates liberation. In actuality, indulgence is no more characteristic of conduct that is *wu-wei* than is rigid adherence to some predetermined principles. It is just that the precedents for our impulse to indulgence are 'inside' and so 'ours' rather than 'outside' and so originating from 'others.' Like some musicians' unswerving predilection for playing in major keys, far from augmenting or stimulating sociality, such impulses are in fact impediments to free improvisation.

In summation, analogous to rendering the body supple and increasingly sensitive through a strict daily regimen of stretching exercises or hatha yoga, the anarchism of Ch'an morality is realizable only on the basis of a program that unblocks our *ch'i* and allows it to circulate freely. Only then will things spontaneously take care of themselves. This is practicing what the *Heart Sutra* directs us toward with the announcement that "form is emptiness, emptiness is form."[3]

It must be recalled, however, that ordered fluidity—the disciplined breaking down of habitual postures—is not itself able to give birth to virtuosity. For that, the unpredictable challenge of concourse is needed, the risks involved in open-ended sociality. In the absence of that fathomless uncertainty that dawns with our entry into limitlessly intimate relation, there can be correct behavior but not conduct that is truly moral. In Ch'an, no generic relation, no dwelling in the societal, in regulation, can be truly moral. That is, indeed, the true basis of the perceived antipathy of Ch'an and collective consciousness, of Ch'an and the preservation of the lineaments of any given society.

If ambiguity and not entitative existence is held basic, morality is most naturally not an orientation toward preserving integrity, but toward intensifying intimacy. Far from legislating the security of the 'self' by wrapping it in a protective, universal medium that at once binds us to and holds us apart from 'others,' such an orientation means a willing endangerment of the 'self.' And so, while as virtuosity, Ch'an morality is boundlessly caring, as anarchic, it is unavoidably critical—intent on breaking up the tendency toward rote agreement that is ever at odds with the harmony of realized nonduality. In short, Ch'an morality must be seen as inseparable from liberating intimacy.

Rejecting the Anonymity of Perfection

Part of what is involved in realizing the kind of internal relatedness characteristic of both intimacy and Ch'an morality is actively eschewing all forms of transcendence. As suggested above, an existence-informed morality prioritizing integrity and so personal dislocation attempts to soften our disparity by appeal to a transcendent, and yet mediating, universal standard. By contrast, in an emptiness-informed morality that valorizes intimacy and interdependence appeals are not made to something outside our situation to arbitrate our difference. Rather, it is our situation itself that directs us. Far from a diversion into rights discourse, resolving moral dilemmas entails here an intensification of our concourse, an embrace of our uniqueness, and so a recognition of what is already immanent in the sociality of our conduct. It is only when we create no barriers to our concourse with others that the possibility of realizing horizonless intimacy arises.

The implications of this for properly conceiving authentic personhood are manifold. For example, the prevailing understanding of perfection in the Indo-European traditions has been that of self-sufficiency and immutability. As represented in the visual and plastic arts, perfection has been associated with a loss of uniquely identifying features. A perfect beauty is thus "ageless," a perfect body is without blemish or offending bulges, a perfect mate is someone so sleekly ideal that they provide us with no purchase for complaint, a perfect understanding is one from which all perspectival and expressive biases have been eliminated. In a very important sense, such perfection implies a kind of exalted anonymity.

And so, where the West was once home to a pantheon of gods, each evidencing a special set of traits and foibles held in common with no others, the Christian God and the Muslim Allah are blatantly incomparable and so unidentifiable, impossible to regard. To the extent that we as humans draw ever nearer to such perfection, we shed the genealogical robes of our distinction, becoming ever more refined and at the same time more abstract or ideal. Our physical peculiarities are either lost or count for less and less; our personalities are gradually purified of all idiosyncrasy; the quality of our relationships with others depends less on who they are—family, friend, neighbor, enemy, or thief—than on who we have become. In short, our perfection implies both transcendence and universality. The perfect person—unlike the most endearing and engaging of our friends whether actual or imagined—is undeniably complete, having risen above any possible need of change. As an ideal, such a one has been weaned away from the vicissitudes of character, the unpredictable fallibility of the uniquely embodied.

In the Chinese world, the notion of perfection as characterless immutability has never been widely valued. While the words most commonly translated as "perfection" do imply completeness, the underlying connotations are of roundness or wholeness and suggest the dynamism of co-implication or mutual enfolding rather than the disjunctiveness of transcendence. For example, the supposition that the body and its peculiar traits are an impediment to perfection has no place in the Confucian project of self-cultivation. Indeed, for Mencius human perfection entails nothing short of the full realization of "bodily form" (see, for example, *Mencius* 6a.14, 7a.38). Our concreteness as unique members of our community is not to be sacrificed, but cultivated and eventually celebrated.

Not surprisingly, *jen* 仁—the signal characteristic of the fully realized, Confucian person—does not imply any kind of disjunctive superiority, but rather unhindered reciprocity. For the Confucian and for the Chinese in general, perfected human being shows in filiality, in the skilled choreography of living patterns of deference, in the unique quality with which the *li* 禮 are imbued in our enactment of them. Perfecting ourselves is thus not a matter of transcendence but skilled communion—a quality immanent in our conduct, our narration.

In reading through both Ch'an biographies and the collections of public cases or *kung-ans*, it seems obvious that the notion of human perfection as immanence—as something realized directly in conduct—is taken up with uncompromising zeal. But it is equally obvious that the fervor with which Ch'an understands community in terms of unmediated sociality leads to a valorization of our differences. The most loved masters of Ch'an—the ones appearing with the greatest frequency in the *kung-ans*—are those who display the wildest personas, whose teachings are the most iconoclastic. Lacking any traits that clearly identify them as a group or lineage, each one of them is what we might call "a real character," a kind of spiritual maverick. Some are outright rascals; prior to their realization, some are so diligently earnest that—like Won Hyo—they seem ready to sprout angelic wings; afterward they are as earthy and carefree as the village idiot.

In Ch'an, not only are idiosyncrasy and uniqueness not leveled down with the realization of enlightenment, they seem if anything to be accentuated. A Ch'an master is not an ideal human, but rather truly human—someone who weeps and sings, who laughs and curses, and who is undeniably one-of-a-kind. The ideal human is freed from desires and the karmic entanglements resulting from them, but such a one is also cut off from those around them, destined for relationships which are increasingly societal. Conduct that is truly human means being able *as we are* to improvise enlightenment in the context of whatever drama we find ourselves.

What this entails is not self-reform, but if anything a complete forgetfulness of the 'self'—an absence of that reflective turn by means of which we continually check ourselves in the mirror of our circumstance, constantly concerned with our own place and performance in the scheme of things. The person who is truly human is not concerned with 'bettering' him or herself, but with expressing their truth through whatever traits and abilities he or she has. Far from leading us in the direction of anonymity, Ch'an insists that we appreciate *who* we truly are and that we offer our character—our karma—fully and yet carefully to liberating this narration.

In *The Gateless Gate* (*Wu-men-kuan* 2), there is a story which makes it clear that not only is it unnecessary to transcend our character or karma, it is in fact dangerous to even affirm the possibility of such transcendence. While giving a series of lectures at a mountain temple, Pai-chang came to notice an old man who would only appear at the beginning of the lecture and leave immediately after it was over. But one day, the old man lingered and Pai-chang approached him, inquiring who he was.

The old man replied that he was in fact not a human being, but that he had long ago been a teacher of Buddhism in these same mountains. "At that time, one of my students asked me if a practicing person—an enlightened being—is subject to cause and effect. I answered that such a one was not subject to cause and effect and for this response have been born for five hundred lifetimes in the body of a fox. So, perhaps you can help me. How would you answer? Is a practicing person subject to cause and effect or not?"

Pai-chang replied, "*Pu-mei-yin-kuo* 不昧因果"—[she/he] is not blinded or suppressed by (*mei*) cause and effect. That is, a practicing person—someone who has realized Buddhist conduct—is not in the dark about the workings of his or her karma and so is not blocked by it. To the contrary, they are capable of according with and using their karma. Neither sentient beings nor buddhas are free from cause and effect, but unlike a sentient being, a buddha is not trapped or stymied by the unbroken web of our interdependence. Rather, such a one is able to improvise freely in and upon it. As Ch'an Buddhists, our job is not to 'perfect' ourselves or change our character, but simply to realize who we *truly* are.

Letting Go With Both Hands: Liberate One and 10,000 Follow

For the Ch'an Buddhist, being a bodhisattva means totally unprecedented and unforced freedom in improvising the mergence of previously disparate worlds. Not bound by any circumstances or societal norms or status, the Ch'an bodhisattva is free to enter either the ordained or lay life, to be a prince or a pauper, to frequent either the court or the brothel. And because of this—because the conduct or narrative movement that we refer to as "bodhisattva" is not *yu-wei*—no factual situation is inherently superior to or inferior to any other. For the true bodhisattva, any circumstance can serve as the *bodhimaṇḍala*, no disharmony is irresolvable.[4] In Lin-chi's famous phrase, s/he is a "true person of no rank" (*wu-wei-chen-jen*

無位真人)—a person who has no fixed place from which s/he acts, no set patterns of behavior or unchanging tasks and goals.

Asked once by a monk who exactly this person with no rank is, Lin-chi leapt down off his dais, began throttling the monk and demanded that he "Speak! Speak!" When the monk failed to respond immediately, Lin-chi thrust him away, exclaiming, "What kind of dry shit stick is this 'true person of no rank'!" (T 1985.496c). That is, Lin-chi's initial response is not to objectify the true person of no rank by saying something *about* him, but to unhesitatingly leap into action. Jumping down from his 'place' above the assembly, he adopts the posture of a highway bandit, takes the monk by the throat and demands that he speak—that he do what the circumstances would seem to make impossible. In order to successfully respond, the monk must drop his own 'role'—that of the 'one' being victimized—and enter true partnership with Lin-chi, directly resolving in conduct this unexpectedly confrontational turn in their relationship.

By relinquishing his own place or rank and opening himself to the complete unpredictability of unconstrained concourse, Lin-chi demonstrates how a true person of no rank replies to the objectifications of others. But by directly challenging the monk to give up his precious 'self' and respond in kind, Lin-chi also provides the monk an opportunity to become the host, to enlighten their shared narrative by entering into creative partnership. In this case, the monk hesitates, evidencing his own debilitating lack of confidence, his inability to meet Lin-chi's offer of immediate and unprecedented concourse. In short, he remains bound by the constraints of what is appropriate and inappropriate, what is 'me' and 'mine' and what is 'you' and 'yours.' Hemmed in on all sides by the distinctions through which we generate and identify our 'selves,' the monk fails to realize his nature as bodhisattva and the "essential brilliance" of his original nature remains obscured. 'Thief' and 'victim' remain bound together and yet undeniably held apart; in contact and yet incapable of concourse. In Lin-chi's graphic phrasing, the true person of no rank has gone into hiding, taking on the utterly useless form of an ass-wiping stick covered with dried shit.

Lin-chi makes it quite clear here and in other of his recorded conversations that the monk's mistake occurs the instant he hesitates—the instant the narrative movement already underway is interrupted in a silent query about where it should or can be taken. We may see ourselves in such situations as being held at bay, as thrown back on ourselves, but in fact it is the unpredictability of *wu-wei* that is being held at arm's length and it is ultimately our own doubt which is responsible. Not believing, that is not giving our hearts fully to who we are, we turn 'outward' in search of guidance or precedents. But Lin-chi insists that this is fruitless.

> Do you want to discern the Buddha and patriarchs? They are none other than the one who here listens to my teachings. Since you students haven't attained confidence in yourselves, you face outward and run around searching. If your seeking succeeds, you'll only obtain the winning forms of cultural precedents (*wen* 文) and written words (*tzu* 字). In the end, you won't attain the meaning of any living patriarch. (T 1985.497b)

That is, while we may manage to accurately imitate a Ch'an master or a buddha, the resemblance so engineered will be merely formal. In terms of their factual basis our words and actions may agree point for point with that of an enlightened person, but they will not have the same meaning, and the conduct in which they figure will continue to proceed *yu-wei*.

And yet turning inward is no more effective in bringing about the realization of our buddha-nature. Lin-chi is quite uncompromising in reviling

> the bald-headed yes-men who once they've eaten their fill of rice will sit down to meditate and practice contemplation. They fix their hearts, take hold of the stream of thought and don't allow it to arise. They abhor noise, seek quiet, attain samadhis and so on, but these are all beside the point.... [I]f you fix the mind to observe quietude, or if you arouse the mind to outwardly reflect (on things), or if you control the mind to be inwardly lucid, or if you concentrate the mind to enter samadhi, going on like this is just making (things, karma, etc.). *Who* is right now listening to my teaching? (T 1985.499b, emphasis added)

As long as we think that the Buddha—the one who is listening—is something objective or outside, we are wrong. If we take the Buddha to be something subjective or inside, we are still wrong. And retreating into the logical cul-de-sacs of 'both' or 'neither' is only to compound our error. Instead, we must drop every pretense of separation or difference and identity. Abandoning our 'selves' in the incomparable liveliness of unalloyed improvisation and "never faltering for even an instant, our pure and clear brilliance penetrates everywhere in the ten directions and the 10,000 things are one

Suchness" (T 1985.498b). This is what is meant in Ch'an by the so-called "awakening of faith" (*ch'i-hsin* 起信)—the realization of what Huang-po meant in saying both that "all the buddhas and sentient beings are just one-mind" (T 2012.379c) and that not obtaining a single thing is what we call "buddha" or "the transmission of mind" (T 2012.383a). No amount of skilled mimicry of the great masters and recitations of their infamous phrases can substitute for this—the realization of complete nonreliance (*wu-i* 無依) (T 1985.498c), the burgeoning of true Suchness (*chen ju* 真如). Conducting ourselves *wu-wei* depends on a horizonless and hence decentered confidence (*hsin*)—not a trust in someone or some doctrine or some miraculous experience, but a tirelessly creative virtuosity.

Throughout his recorded conversations, Lin-chi again and again returns to the image of the "true person without rank who goes in and out through the gates of your faces" (T 1985.496c), insisting that it is this "one functioning right before your eyes [who] is not different from the buddhas and patriarchs" (T 1985.500c). If for even an instant we can drop the pretense of being an individual, relinquishing all of the horizons we have projected in identifying ourselves as the center of experience, we realize that we are everything that is right now occurring. "What goes in and out of the gates of our faces" does not refer, then, to some spiritual substance or soul that enters and exits the body, but is simply a striking locution for the constant movement we refer to as our "lives"—a movement which implies both subject and object, perceiver and perceived, actor and acted upon, but which cannot be reduced to any of these. That, Lin-chi insists, is who we truly are. That is the Buddha.

But to say that this functioning (*yung* 用) is who we really are—a true person of no rank—is to say that we are just the movement of our narration. That is, who we really are is "how things are going." We are not ultimately the 'one' who experiences our life-story—whether as its principle character or its variously impersonated author—but its very ongoingness. If our world includes locally or globally intractable suffering and abysmal unhappiness, instances of physical or emotional abuse both calculated and random, families in which no one speaks to one another and cities in which homeless men, women, and children sleep on the sidewalks outside of museums housing the work of our greatest artists—that is who we are, even if we don't identify any of these situations or events as in any way our own, as our responsibility.

Conversely, if our world is like the buddha-lands described by Vimalakirti—lands in which even foul smells, wordy treatises, and the antics of the four Maras can do the work of a buddha (VS 11)—that, too, is who we are. At any moment, we can tell exactly who we are—whether a buddha or a sentient being or even a devil—by simply perceiving what is right before us. And yet because all things are in constant flux, what distinguishes a buddha and a sentient being is not what is *happening* in the sense of the momentary or present status of his/her narrative, but rather the direction of its occurrence—whether toward the regulative differences and identities implied in discourse or the realized nondualism of improvised concourse. In a word, the contrast is not one of fact, but meaning—never something contained in an event, utterance or intention, but played out as the unpredictable unfolding of our lives as communicative wholes.

Huang-po and Lin-chi both call this movement or functioning "mysterious" or "profound" (*miao* 妙) because it is ultimately ambiguous, having no fixed roots or ground, no set fruit or aim. That is, unlike 'selfish' activity which always implies a movement from-to—an incremental change definable in terms of the linear addition or subtraction of various elements of experience—the functioning referred to as "a true person with no rank" is not a vectoral or intentional translation of values into existence, but a "seamless essential clarity" (T 2012.382a).

As sentient beings attached to the centrality of our 'selves' we typically break this seamless whole up into the six senses and their objects, constituting a world of differences and divisions out of which we attempt to manufacture harmonious places of refuge—sometimes outer and sometimes inner—but always at the price of creating the unavoidable complexes of experiential disposition referred to as "karma." But as buddhas we are worlds in which there are no hindrances and in which there is at the same time no creation of 'a seamless, essential clarity' as something known and opposed to the world of distinctions (T 2012.382a). Thus, we can freely enter any situation without any of the differences and distinctions projected there being able to stymie or turn us back (T 1985.498b). Then, anything at all can accomplish the work of enlightenment. No limit can be found at which liberating virtuosity is cut off. In short, Lin-chi's true person of no rank is simply conduct that is wholly *wu-wei*—narrative movement in which all 'things' are continually emptied and so in which there are no obstructions and nothing which needs to be done.

Enlightenment should never be conceived, then, as something which we acquire through our actions and effort and which then enables us to help others alleviate their suffering. That way of seeing matters is—at least from the Ch'an perspective—entirely mistaken. Instead, enlightenment is given directly in the sociality of our conduct, in the creative movement of our entire narration. Thus Pai-chang quotes the scriptures as saying, "Liberate one and 10,000 follow. Confuse one and 10,000 are deluded. . . . This is the wonder of the path of awakening" (HTC 119.425b). If there ultimately are no individuals, but only the continual unfolding of the narration that we speak of as the one or whole-mind (i-hsin), there can be no solitary salvation—no private liberation which is attained at some special 'here' and then spread out to encompass 'others.'

Indeed, the constant references in the Mahayana texts favored by Ch'an (the *Flower Ornament*, *Lotus*, and *Vimalakirti* sutras, for example) to miraculous powers of interpenetration, of instantaneous travel, and of manifesting innumerable bodies are all just objective ways of describing the nonpropagational and hence nonintentional nature of enlightening conduct. Ultimately, the transmission of mind referred to by Huang-po is not a linear chain—an understanding of the process of enlightenment that was symbolically debunked with Hui-neng's refusal to pass on his robe and bowl—but communication in the sense of unprecedented concourse in which everything is always changing at once and in which it is thus impossible to say that anything is ever obtained. Being always whole and yet never unchanging, as an unbroken, radiant clarity through which nothing is attained or arrived at, the mind of enlightenment can only be seen as reservationless contribution or offering. It is that into which 'we' are taken up, and not something 'you' and 'I' cause or even discover.

And so it is said that we know we are at the point of attaining buddhahood when we "let go with both hands"—when we cease trying to take in or gather anything while remaining all the while uncompromisingly responsive to the needs of our present and constantly evolving situation. Ch'an enlightenment should never be seen as a result, but as that constantly renewed conduct by means of which an entire world is realized as thoroughly social, as a self-creating, free, and easy harmony about which we can only be mistaken the instant we try to point it out or exclaim, "This is it!"

Notes

Preface

1. The term *kang* has the primary sense of the drawstring or cord used to close a net. By extension, it came to mean a bond or tie, laws or principles, the social nexus holding a family or community together and making it a functional whole.

2. One of the historical considerations which casts some doubt on the veracity of either of these views is the fact Ch'an never idealized the life of a homeless wanderer but rather placed itself squarely at the vanguard of monastic Buddhism. That is, the daily life of a Ch'an practitioner—whether ordained or lay—was understood as basically communal in nature, as part of the overall architecture of society and not as a refutation or escape therefrom. Indeed, Pai-chang's monastic code strongly suggests that Ch'an understood itself not as living outside of and yet wholly dependent upon the marketplace, but as contributing directly to it.

Objecting that this emphasis on community was less a reflection of Ch'an orthodoxy than of the prevailing politico-economic conditions and the Confucian social fabric of which they were a part is effective only as long as Ch'an is presumed to be in some sense originally discontinuous with them—as long, that is, as Ch'an is taken to be Buddhist (and hence genetically Indian) first and only secondarily Chinese. Part of the thesis forwarded in the early chapters is that Ch'an is not a kind of transplanted Buddhism which took root in and was subsequently transformed by Chinese soil, but a hybrid way of life or spirituality which was first and foremost Chinese.

3. Thus, we entertain the possibility of telepathy as an ability to know the contents of other minds but not as the realization of an absence of the differences or distance on which 'otherness' is predicated. That is, 'I' may come to know 'your mind' in the absence of any messages being transmitted

in an objectively identifiable medium, but the distinction of these 'minds' remains unblemished.

4. As employed throughout our conversation, "conduct" is not an equivalent of behavior or action but is used instead to refer to the dynamic of our lived interpersonality. Conduct is that out of which we are able to identify individual thoughts, speech actions, and so on—what shall be termed narrative movement. Conduct is thus allied with the concepts of both karma (dramatic interdependence) and narration (personhood). On conduct, see chapter 3, especially the first two sections. For a discussion of person as narration, see chapters 1 and 3, or, for a more continuous exposition, "Person as Narration: The Dissolution of 'Self' and 'Other' in Ch'an Buddhism", *Philosophy East and West* 44.4: 685–710.

5. Thomas Kasulis' recent appeals to the intimacy-integrity polarity in discussing Japanese thought and culture have proven quite helpful in focusing the differences between Ch'an and its Indian/Central Asian ancestors. Interestingly, the polarity promises to be useful as well in distinguishing and appreciating the distinctive qualities of the Chinese and Japanese versions of Ch'an.

6. "Original" in this context does not necessarily connote absolute discontinuity with what preceded it or an inherently positive valuation. To the contrary, the present work is original in the sense of arising out of (L *oriri*) the tradition and not being merely about it.

1. Suffering

1. It should be pointed out, lest the above be misconstrued, that the toxicity of concepts is not a reason to reject them out of hand, any more than the toxic effect of drinking alcohol in excess is reason to never taste wine. Indeed, the relation of concepts and human being is much more symbiotic than that we enjoy with alcohol or any other substances of abuse. Instead, it is rather more like the relation we have with oxygen. Everyone knows that oxygen is necessary for our bodily survival. We can live for weeks without solid food, for days without drinking or having sense impressions. But we cannot survive without oxygen for more than a matter of minutes. Just so, we need concepts. Without them, we would wander in complete amazement, bereft of intention but filled with an open-mouthed appreciation of a peculiar, nondirectional sort. Those who have lived through a profound psychedelic experience often remark on the shock of losing their common stock of concepts about the world and how they could as a result stare at dirt for hours without either boredom or anxiety, simply attending to ever more subtle details and fluencies of connection to other

parts of experience. Without concepts, we should in all likelihood simply absorb what comes our way without discrimination of 'use,' 'nonuse,' 'harmful,' or 'helpful.' To search for—much less to grow or store—food would be impossible without a notion of what counts as food or nourishment. On this view, concepts are not a peculiarly human possession, but can be legitimately attributed to all organisms, perhaps to all self-organizing systems.

Nevertheless, too much conceptualization is just as harmful and dysfunctional as hyperventilating. At first, the excess makes us giddy. Later, we become anxious and think that perhaps the whole world is inhospitable and out of control. Finally, we begin to lose contact with reality altogether. We cease to be able to cope. Just as the oxygen- or alcohol-intoxicated person may behave in starkly inappropriate fashions, so the concept-drunken person is liable to commit the most unconscionable atrocities in the name of such highly refined abstractions as God, Truth, and Country. Such bizarre behavior never results from use of the relatively tame concepts we use in daily discourse—'rock,' 'tree,' 'sleep,' and 'sex'—but only from those we take to be of the highest importance and value. In still greater quantities or concentrations, concepts can, like oxygen, function quite literally as poison. In this light, the virtually unremitting invective directed at thinking by the Ch'an tradition and epitomized in the adoption of nonthinking (*wu-nien* 無念) as one of its guiding principles or methods should be seen less as an indictment of thinking or conceptualization altogether than as a criticism of the kind of repetitive, habitual thought (*nien*: to chant, intone, or recite as well as to think) which signals a liability to conceptual addiction and our subsequent disengagement from truly social endeavor.

The excessive vehemence with which so many of us are initially inclined to contest Ch'an's stance on thinking is itself rather suspicious, being reminiscent of the angry denials of an alcoholic that his or her drinking is any kind of problem. Just as alcohol solves one problem or complex of problems for the addicted drinker while spawning a host of others to which the drinker is effectively blinded, calculations and habitual thinking certainly prove their effectiveness in correcting certain ills. What is not so obvious are the "side-effects," the biasing of our conduct toward sociality and the consequent sequestering of our 'selves' behind a deceptively impervious network of 'facts,' 'principles,' and 'necessities.'

2. Such moves have, of course, come under considerable and highly critical scrutiny in the works of the hermeneutics tradition, a scrutiny given indirect but powerful warrant by the widely accepted conviction in the philosophy of science that all facts are theory-laden, including those supporting the universality of suffering.

3. A parallel, and for us particularly felicitous, examination of the nature of consciousness was undertaken by George Herbert Mead who concluded that consciousness is not a precondition of responsive behavior,

but rather a result thereof; that, "far from being a precondition of the social act, the social act is a precondition of [consciousness]" (1934, 18).

4. From this, it follows that if the Buddha is seen as the paradigm of personhood in Buddhism, our typical self-conception—relying as it does on marking ourselves off from others—cannot serve as a proper model for understanding Buddhist personhood. Rather, our idea/ideal of person and the egoic experience of existing are both functions of culturally and individually informed horizons for relevance—what in the notation that will be developed below we will refer to as 'persons.'

5. Seen in this light, Hegel's quite astute observation of the absolute ubiquity of the master-slave relationship reveals itself as a caricature rooted in one particular conception of consciousness, not in consciousness or spirit per se.

6. The reader may also want to consider Kalupahana's (1992) chapter on "Dignaga's Epistemology and Logic."

7. But the assertion that suffering is personal can be misleading, and misleading in a significant way. A prevalent tendency in the dominant Indo-European philosophical tradition has been to view the person in categorical terms, to downplay the importance of being located in a unique social space and to see our selves as rational agents embodied in this or that way and acting through this or that set of roles. In his paper, "Of Masks and Men" (1985), Martin Hollis trenchantly analyzes the underpinnings of contemporary individualism, noting that the various contemporary strands in social theory agree that the identity of a person is independent of roles and social positions (p. 226). If this is assumed, it is natural for suffering to be seen as either the generic distortion of equally generic agents or as the unique distortion of a self which is fundamentally autonomous. In either case, suffering is essentially abstract and irremediably private.

This interpretation of the nature of suffering, however, seems wholly inconsistent with the social and soteriological orientations not only of Buddhism, but of many of the world's cultural or religious traditions where the person is seen as a relational achievement which can only occur in a social matrix. In such cultures, the Hobbesian idea that societies are born out of the contractual agreement of pre-existing, autonomous persons or selves is simply unintelligible. Nor, at least from the Buddhist standpoint, is it any more intelligible to think of the a person as a sort of condensation out of a pre-existing, collective or group mind. From a Buddhist standpoint, this is simply another way of denying the interdependent origination of all things. What is germane at this point is not whether the Buddhist view is right or not, but that the way in which we conceive suffering depends on what we take persons to be, and what we believe such persons can reasonably expect in and from their lives.

Michael Carrithers (1985) has suggested that while according to the thinking of Durkheim and Mauss, the person is conceived as an individual human being who is a member of a significant and ordered collectivity (Carrithers' *personne*), Buddhism views the person as a psychophysical complex present within a natural or spiritual cosmos, interacting therein with other moral agents (the *moi*). The importance of this is that whereas the predominance of a view of persons as *personne* allows, as does the caste system in classical India, for the universalization of the experience of suffering, seeing persons from the perspective of the *moi* does not.

8. I would argue, in fact, that the Buddhist doctrine of the three marks is based on just such a realization. The three marks do not constitute a short catalogue of characteristics which are unrelated to one another in an intimate sense, but form a functional system. The emphasis within Buddhism on *anātman* suggests that the central problematic of suffering is related to our idea or ideal of personhood—in short, that it is a cultural construct erected within the unique frameworks of each of our individual life histories. To say that all things are impermanent (*anitya*) is to say that there is no free zone, no place of permanence to which we can retreat. Crises will continually occur and our only options are to either creatively incorporate them into our lives or to allow our lives to be destructively altered by their interruption. The mark of selflessness entails that there is no set identity to preserve or prohibit adaptive or creative change. We need have no fear of improvising. Impermanence entails that there is no shortage of energy for change. The process of existing is continuously operative. Suffering entails that there will always be irruptions of chaos, the occurrence of crises to stimulate evolution. Creativity is opened by realizing the ubiquity of the three marks. It might well be argued that the thrust of the teaching of the three marks it to lay the foundation for the creative transformation of culture (especially in its interpersonal/social dimension).

9. On the origination of persons in conversation, see for example the quite different analyses offered by Mead (1934) and Charles Taylor (1985), neither of whom, however, emphasize the narrative aspect of conversational encounter. It should also be noted at this point that the description just given of persons is somewhat at odds with that which will be developed in the succeeding chapters, where it will be argued that the implied objectification of our lives or selves necessarily runs contrary to that full and unmediated engagement with others upon which sociality and personal development ultimately depend.

2. Culture and the Limits of Personhood

1. That is, from the perspective of an outsider-stander. From such a perspective, cultures condition individual 'persons,' forming a context

for their emergence. But when persons are seen as worlds, such a point of view cannot be maintained. Then, person and culture are only arbitrarily distinguishable.

2. This objectification of actual suffering out of which we derive material for the egoic authoring of our life-stories provides, however, the possibility of thinking or talking about and not resolving the interruption—a phenomenon taken to a morbid extreme with certain obsessions or depressions and which is arguably becoming epidemic in our society. Like the man discovered by the Buddha with an arrow sunk deep in his chest, we want to discuss how it happened and who is to blame rather than pulling out the arrow and allowing the healing process to truly get underway.

3. It should be noted that it is exceedingly rare for any of us to have a single narrative thread connecting all of our experiences and activities. Even having a single main thread is quite uncommon. Rather, as persons we are more like threads made up of multiple strands, some of which are continuous over long periods of time, others of which, like the short bits of wool that are spun into yarn, achieve the appearance of continuity only when seen from a sufficient distance.

4. The social-societal distinction and the contrast of interpersonal and institutional orientations will be discussed at length in the following chapter.

5. One of the advantages of such a definition is that it is equally consistent with the both the most elaborate of the systems of thought on reincarnation (say the Tibetan) and with the most extreme hard-line materialism.

6. Recall here the direction in which Buddhism drives ontology (chapter 1). Death and birth are not originally things, but values.

7. I prefer the word "recursive" here to the more commonly used "reflexive." It is typical that one of the traits commonly ascribed to persons is self-reflexivity, their ability to think about or reflect on themselves. Yet this only forces us to beg the question: "Is a person something that can think about itself—that is something that is apart from its thinking—or are persons the very folding back itself?" The term self-reflexive seems to me to be a part of the vocabulary of substantialism, of the being of essences. In narrative terms, it implies that a person is someone who tells a story—the author of their tale—and not narration itself. It is imperative to note here that a recitation of facts is not a story. To begin with, facts are objective data which presume a subject who 'knows' or 'discovers' them. Seeing a narrative in terms of a list of facts or a series of events is only to invoke anew the idea of 'someone' that is very much like the substance Locke referred to as a "we know not what." The notion of recursion doesn't appeal to such an agent or author, implying only a flowing back, a dynamic incompleteness that is at every moment paradoxically resolving.

8. Viewing both persons and death in narrative terms involves allowing that no one is completely dead so long as they are remembered, so long as they continue to figure in some story. However, this also suggests that the person—like suffering—is located in narrative, not in the 'natural' world. The body, then, is not a physical thing which we have or are associated with. Rather, the body is the complex, the folding together, of the modalities of our conduct and relations with others. In Buddhist terms, it is fundamentally karmic. The body provides the basic 'grammar' of the improvised and always co-evolving narratives that constitute our persons.

9. The discussion below of Indian ideas on birth might be seen as a contradiction of this claim. The confusion arises because while the Indian may anticipate rebirth, it is not, in the sense used here, in fact their *personal* recurrence, the recurrence of the narrative of which they wholly consist. Rather, a new narrative occurs with which there is a karmic relation that is nearly always unexperienced—that is, untold. Meditative adepts may be able to "recall" their past lives, but that is really a matter of adopting a set of nonrecursive narratives as a uniquely well-suited context for one's ongoing story. Karma sets the overall topography of experience, but it is not itself a narration.

10. What counts as "normal" in any given culture varies, of course, and infanticide has been widely practiced as a corrective to births which are either not "normal"—children born physically deformed—or not "ideal." That it has been more often than not been the case that the births of girl children have not been considered ideal—especially when there have been no prior male children born to a particular set of parents—tragically underscores the fact that it is the communal, culturally directed story which is responsible for any given birth being seen as an unmitigated cause of celebration or not.

11. Shastri (1963) gives a very detailed account of both the ritual and metaphysical dimensions of Hindu ancestral rites in his *Origin and Development of the Rituals of Ancestor Worship in India*.

12. See, for example, *Chāndogya Upaniṣad* V.10.5.

13. More confusing still is the existence in the *Purāṇas* of assertions that some *pitṛs* are born directly from Brahman and were *never* humanly incarnated (Shastri 1963, 290, 298).

14. See the *Maitri Upaniṣad* IV.1.3–4, and especially the *Bṛhadāraṇyaka Upaniṣad* II.iv.5–14.

15. The disastrous nature of this fate is evidenced in the extent to which banishment was considered a capital sentence in classical Chinese culture. To be sent away from one's family and village was to be rendered inhuman, to be stripped of one's personhood.

16. And if Hansen's arguments succeed, this is true for Chinese culture generally.

17. As shall be argued later, this same ideal became incorporated as part of the fundamental practices of Ch'an.

18. For a contemporary working out of the consequences of seeing man in terms of between-ness, see especially the first chapter of Watsuji Tetsuro's *Ethics*. Watsuji's work is based on his analysis of the Japanese language, but many of his conclusions—seeing the problem of ethics as lying in the "betweenness between men," for example—apply equally well for Chinese culture.
It might be thought that a conflict exists between stressing the improvisational nature of learning and the spontaneity of personhood on one hand and the indispensability of ritual or *li* on the other. In fact, no conflict exists at all. The *li* provide the ordered context without which action can never be improvisational, but only chaotic. The *li* do not dictate or determine behavior, but, to press a musical analogy, provide a mode or key within which each person's improvisations can be seen as meaningful.

19. Of course, insofar as a person is a recursively structured narrative—and not an "author" who freely fabricates this or that tale—the loss of personhood can only signify the final interruption of a life-story. In other words, suffering ends only with death. This seemed to have been the view of even some Indian Buddhists who maintained that full enlightenment came only with the death of the body.

3. Dramatic Interdependence and Improvisation

1. Joanna Macy has explored the compatibility of the Buddhist and systems-theoretical views of personhood in her recent book *Mutual Causality in Buddhism and General Systems Theory* (1991). Other texts of some interest are Laszlo's *Introduction to Systems Philosophy* (1972) and *System, Structure and Experience* (1969), Bateson's *Steps to an Ecology of Mind* (1972), and Maturana and Varela's *The Tree of Knowledge* (1987). While the systems view provides us with a useful theoretical framework for discussing the Buddhist approach to both personality and sociality, it is not fully satisfactory. Especially on practical or methodological grounds, its adoption of a descriptive regard is highly problematic since it presupposes an objectification of the system/subsystem relationship which effectively allows the latter to be seen as elements used in the composition of the former. The narrative view of personhood suggested in chapter 1 and developed in more detail below is intended as a corrective for this shortcoming by disallowing an ontologically valid gap to be opened up between any of the

various characters whose relations constitute who we, as persons, are in the process of becoming. That is, narrativity provides an opportunity to see the narrator or observer as in no way superordinate to the narrative as a whole and acts as an insurance against projecting into what we are study-ing—personhood—the principles of our 'self'-made relation to it.

2. It has become a psychological commonplace that we do not live in a point-like present, but are spread out over a range of times—see, for exam-ple, Bergson's (1960) discussion of the heterogeneous time of concrete dura-tion. But such a recognition that our mode of temporality is regional fails to exhaust the sense in which I would claim Buddhists necessarily regard the self as temporally indeterminate. At the very least, it is the case that who we are crucially depends on the constant revisioning not only of our current awareness and projects, but of all our past and future. Far from being inaccessible, our personal past and future are continually being told and retold, revised and amended. Narrative time is not linear, but recursive—a fact not to be confused with either the theoretical reversibility of Newtonian time or Nietzsche's eternal recurrence—and because of this, development or evolution always involves changing not just the 'present' and 'future,' but the 'past' as well.

3. On the view that who we are depends on psychological and/or physiological continuity with the right kind of cause, see part 3 of Derek Parfit's *Reasons and Persons* (1984).

4. Some systems-theorists, like Ervin Laszlo (1972), explicitly avow a monistic metaphysics, assuming that what is basic is not a world of matter or mind, but a universal "matrix" out of which all systems emerge. That this is undisguised foundationalism should be apparent, even if the matrix is left undefined. Laszlo remains dedicated to the existence of some appar-ently objective (that is, identifiable) reality prior to and independent of us as knowers. The foundation here—the originating matrix—may not be defined in any strict sense, but its existence is taken as inarguable: elsewise, how could any system have begun? Every system is built on some *precursor* and this defies the Buddha's insistence on a thorough eschewal of all imputed independence. If everything is dependently arisen, there can be no ultimate precursor or matrix. That this matrix is not 'matter' or 'spirit' no more excuses it from the charge of being a foundation than the ubiquity of land does of recognizing that it serves as the foundation for all our building. Laszlo's supposition of an originating matrix comes about as a result of adopting a descriptive regard with respect to the world/narration of which he is a unique characterization. In looking *at* and talking *about* the world it assumes the appearance of finitude and entitativeness and hence of being able to both act as a precursor and be itself surrounded by a void—that is, independent.

5. It should be noted that just as it is a technological advance which allows us to directly counter the dictates of the ordinary experience of dawn

and dusk, experiencing the nonseparation of self and other is not accomplished by simple intellectual fiat, but only by developing and making systematic use of a particular technology. The fact that not all of us can manage this should no more count against the claims of mystics, shamans, and Ch'an masters than does the fact that only a handful of humans have traveled far enough away from the earth to see it in its entirety.

6. Two points should be made here. First, it is crucial that we recognize that what we can control directly is, in the context of a karmically ordered world, less a function of power or capacity as of perception. That is, like it or not, our intentions transform the topography of our future experience. The fact that we typically don't see any direct connection between what we think about and yearn for and what actually comes about is a function of our imperceptiveness—ultimately of our identification with the temporally determinate nexus of the six senses. With the Buddha's acquisition of "paranormal" sense faculties, what is directly under control appears rather differently. We should also note that while the suggested "Copernican revolution of the self" entails that persons cannot ultimately be identified with any particular stream of consciousness or suitably connected series of bodily states, it does not deny that our experience is typically private. What is claimed is simply that this privacy has the same value as any other common experience which admits of exceptions. The Buddha and many others have claimed to have brought about through meditative discipline a loss of the usual boundaries to the ego or self and the usually concomitant identification with the stream of consciousness or the body. Those of us who have experienced "telepathic" communication, who have had our thoughts "read" by others or who have had a stranger ask us only for the date and time of our birth and then tell us in minute detail what happened on a particular day now five years in the past, can have no doubt that it is possible for the privacy of the inward aspects of the self to be opened up to access by 'others.' A de-centered view of the person allows these exceptions to be seen as rational, even if exceedingly rare—something the standard view cannot admit.

7. Thus, no one we meet is our partner in mere accident. The people or encounters may surprise us, may seem unexpected, but we belong together. Maturity is knowing exactly what this belonging to one another means.

8. That is, if we had intended things differently, we would have been born at some other time or place than we have been, on some other planet perhaps, in some other form. That we are in *this* world, with *this* 'objective' history, *these* heroes and villains is a function of our own story-in-telling. To turn Heidegger's terminology around, it is not that our historicity evidences our thrownness—our having been thrown into a fundamentally foreign existence—but rather that we have caught ourselves in *this* narrative net and not some other.

9. It should be noted that Mead's analysis of the emergence of the self and of mind as a function of social acts entails our responding to an other seen as being like ourselves. Thus, the social act itself apparently presumes a prior distinction of self and other and Mead's derivation of the self from the social act appears to be inescapably and perhaps viciously circular. This, I believe, is a consequence of his using conversation—and not narration—as the primary social act giving rise to persons since such a choice amounts to carrying out an unjustified abstraction by means of which it is possible to posit the presence of a listener and speaker as not only necessary for the occurrence of sociality, but sufficient as well. As will be indirectly argued in the following chapter, this sort of reduction is inconsistent with a fully narrative mode of inquiry. The appeal to the family, not the dyad, as the basic social unit *à la* Durkheim fares no better. It is still an abstraction which never occurs naturally.

10. In order to forestall any supposition that this will land us in some form of crude, Watsonian behaviorism, I should remark that as defined, conduct comprises not only those activities carried out by what could be referred to as the "motor system," but activities which are cognitive and affective as well. That is, thinking, feeling, emoting, wishing, and intending are all dimensions of conduct in the sense of being dynamic orientations of an ongoing narrative.

11. This is especially clear for Durkheim, who defines social facts as ways of thinking and acting external to the individual and endowed with a power of coercion by means of which they control him. To be social for Durkheim is to be rational as opposed to personal/egotistical, to be universal as opposed to individual, to develop institutions which regulate our behavior at least in part by having us see one another not as unique persons but as members of a given collective. In all these senses, Durkheim's use of the term "social" more closely approximates what I have here referred to as the societal.

12. Granted the distinction of these two orientations, a society can be seen as the site of the (variable) interpenetration of the social and the societal, and its overall character or flavor as a function of the relative balance of these orientations among those dwelling in its midst.

13. In systems-theoretical terms, this increased vulnerability is a function of attaining progressively improbable and hence complex and difficult to maintain forms of order. Simple systems are less open to challenge, requiring much greater influxes of energy to be threatened with disruption, but at the same time are less capable of responding to crises that do arise because their internal organization is too rigidly limited. Thus, for any viable system, vulnerability and flexibility must increase in direct proportion. See Prigogine (1980).

14. In this light, the problem with Bourdieu's solution is perhaps thrown into greater focus. Insofar as he defines improvisation in terms of our strategic employment of "durably installed generative principle(s)"— the habitus—which derive from "the structures constitutive of a particular type of environment," our practices tend to reproduce the regularities immanent within the objective conditions currently prevailing. That is, necessity is made a virtue and improvisation is in fact a societal and not fully social act. Thus, Bourdieu insists that our practices amount to neither the "creation of unpredictable novelty [nor] a simple mechanical reproduction of the initial conditionings." (See Bourdieu 1977, 72–78, 95.)

This relationship between societality and suffering also raises interesting questions about the diverse merits of various moral systems. Arguably, a moral system based on fixed principles (Kantian deontology) or on a calculation of universally construed goods and ills (classical utilitarianism) will tend to bring about an inability for responding creatively to novel crises and so incline us toward perpetuating suffering. A moral system which eschews all rules and principles will then maximally prepare us to resolve crises and end suffering, but will also leave us increasingly vulnerable to new challenges. In Ch'an, this is not seen as particularly problematic since suffering is the necessary impetus for the integrative practices of emptiness, responsibility, and readiness. More on this in part II, especially chapter 6.

15. The term "same" is not wholly satisfactory as it implies the possibility of a surrounding difference. The logic of narration is not based on the reality or objectivity of identity and difference. As characters in a shared narrative, we are neither identical (after all we have apparently disparate bodies) nor different (being inconceivable apart from our concrete narration). The narrative *as a whole* is who we are and it is into this *we* that our characters are taken up. Here it is that 'you' and 'I' first appear.

4. Communicative Conduct

1. As noted earlier, in his discussion of the hermeneutical conundrums presented by early Taoist texts, Hansen (1981) comes to a very similar conclusion regarding the conventionality of language. Taking as his starting point Lao-tzu's iconoclastic injunction to "discard knowledge, abandon the self" (*ch'i chih ch'u chi* 棄知除己), Hansen notes that no progress in understanding this phrase and its place in the text as a whole can be made without first coming to grips with what is entailed by the term "knowledge." On largely philological grounds, he makes the case that while the prevailing Indo-European conception of knowledge is related to states of belief propositionally represented by sentences of the general form "I know that . . . ," the Chinese conception of knowledge involves no appeal to

beliefs and takes the form of "knowing to. . . ." In the Chinese context, and (I would posit) within the Buddhist tradition, "knowledge of things is the ability to conform to the community's practices of discriminating things" (1981, 325), and epistemic activities are best seen as "conventionally generated and shaped responses of persons" (1981, 326). The Taoist injunction to "discard knowledge" and Pai-chang's injunction to "cut off words" both amount to a call for relinquishing those conventionally constituted horizons for responsive conduct embodied in the linguistic medium supporting the vast majority of our social interactions and cultural endeavors.

2. At least since the demise of rhetoric as a legitimate epistemic activity in classical Greece, it is a bias largely shared by our own European intellectual traditions where the linguistification of understanding has been carried to such a radical extreme that it has become commonplace to reduce everything to a kind of text and to accept as canonic the inviolability of the so-called hermeneutic circle—the claim that everything is ultimately linguistic.

3. All translations of the *Mūlamadhyamaka-Kārikā* are taken from David Kalupahana's (1986) excellent translation of and commentary on Nagarjuna's text.

4. Since the presupposition of discourse is that language is basically propositional and not inventive, these distinctions and the way of life resulting from them are typically assumed to in some sense represent the way things really are. That is, we presume that our language reflects *the* real world and that even if our conduct is regulated in conformity with the invention of new (and what we almost invariably take to be better) mirrors, this is all for the best. We are simply getting closer to being able to adequately and accurately describe what is. That this is unacceptable in a world where value precedes being and where permanence is always horizonal in nature should by this point be clear. And yet, such new inventions are not inherently "bad" as long as we remain aware of the fact that they do not represent reality but rather help to define it, establishing what we *can* do and what we *cannot* in the face of any given crisis or suffering.

5. A reasonably close analog in Western philosophy for this manner of conceiving meaning, understanding, and knowledge can be found in the work of G. H. Mead. For instance, in his *Philosophy of the Present*, Mead claims that "knowledge is not . . . to be identified with the presence of content in experience. There is no conscious attitude that is as such cognitive. Knowledge is a process in conduct" (1932, 68). In *Mind, Self and Society*, he directly addresses the problem of meaning and like Ma-tzu insists that, "Meaning is . . . a development of something objectively there as a relation between certain phases of the social act; it is not a psychical addition to that act and it is not an 'idea' as traditionally conceived" (1934,

76). Meaning is, for Mead, an "adjustive response" fully present in social conduct.

6. For a more extensive argumentation along these lines, see my "Structure of Change in the *I Ching*," *Journal of Chinese Philosophy* 18.3 (September 1991).

7. It must be mentioned that in actual and not merely ideal conversations, there is typically a great deal of overlapping and interruption. Sentences go unfinished—that is remain without any clear semantic content—are completed by others, or change direction in mid-stream forming a grammatical bastard which nevertheless may figure brilliantly in the conversational context. Not infrequently at least in certain cultures, many people talk at once and often with an increase in the feeling that things are being better understood by everyone involved. What this suggests is that discourse can be deconstructed and used narratively to bring about concourse. This is obvious in poetry, for instance, but everyday conversations are often poetic in the relevant sense of being polythetic structures the meaning of which cannot be reduced to a monothetically apprehended atom. As might have been expected, then, discourse is an ideal—a value— and not some thing or being independently existing in communal space.

8. Hence the Buddha's oft repeated warning that even though a bodhisattva saves innumerable beings, he or she must not direct their attention at any such beings. Doing so not only objectifies others, but creates a virtual center or 'self' from which help is then thought to proceed. Enlightenment remains a mere goal.

9. For an extended treatment of intimacy as used herein, see chapter 5.

10. It is imperative that it be stressed, however, that ending suffering is not the extinction of change or challenge, but rather their creative incorporation into the ongoing improvisation of our life-narrative. Given this, enlightenment cannot be an achieved state—hence the *Heart Sutra's* insistence that there is "no attainment and nothing to attain"—but must be seen as the way we respond, the quality of our improvised concourse with 'others.'

5. Intimacy and Virtuosity

1. This is a reference, of course, to the account of Ma-tzu's enlightenment. One day, Master Jang called through the window of Ma-tzu's hut and asked what he planned on with sitting in meditation. Ma-tzu replied that he intended to become a Buddha. Jang retorted by picking up a clay roofing tile and scraping it against the stone walk in front of Ma-tzu's hermitage.

Irritated by the sound, Ma-tzu came out and asked what he was doing. "Polishing this tile to make a mirror," he replied. Objecting that this would never work, Ma-tzu was about to return to his meditation when Jang agreed and suggested the same held for his student's ambitious intentions, informing him that Ch'an is not a matter of sitting or reclining and that becoming a Buddha has nothing to do with any fixed form. In fact, sitting as a Buddha is killing Buddha and holding on to the form of sitting Ch'an is to entirely forfeit its profound principle.

2. The philosophical problem of 'other minds' thus came to prominence only with the skepticism that goes along with a distrust of the senses based on the independence of mind and its natural objects. That is, 'other minds' are taken to be of doubtful ontological status only when they are taken to exist in a world which is itself understood to exist apart from us as its knowers and which we can only access through the intervening media of experience—this latter being neither part of us or the world, but something different from and yet uncertainly linking them.

3. From which it should be concluded that Buddhists simply don't buy into the Cartesian inference of "I am" from the mere presence of thinking/experience. Rather, they would insist that the only inference to be drawn from Descartes' doubtful reflections is that there is doubting going on. Now, as understood by Buddhists, this is not to say that all that remains is behavior—the stance taken by certain European philosophical traditions. Instead of this "nihilist" position, the Buddha recommended that we turn our attention to the cause of experience (whether doubt or anything else). That is, we are referred away from experience itself to the value coordinated development of relationships known as karma. What remains basic is again the narrative level of human interaction and not a purely objective behavioral tableau.

4. It is in such a light that the Buddhist must find fault with Habermas' depiction of communication as involving one person who makes claims and another who must say either "yes" or "no" in response.

5. Importantly, while the Buddha's claim that he does not take a stand on either 'is' or 'is-not' (*sat* or *asat*) can be seen as a purely objective matter of choice leaving him the chooser unaffected in any direct way, the Chinese term typically translated as "is" or "being" (*yu*) has the primary connotation of "having." To eschew 'is' and 'is-not' for the Chinese Buddhist is also to eschew 'having' and 'not-having,' even when these refer to the experience of enlightenment.

6. Hence the numerous references in the literature of Ch'an to the danger of meditation sickness (*ting ping* 定病).

7. It must be stressed that "self-consciousness" implies here both the awkward sense of being "on stage" as well as the so-called "normal"

awareness of ourselves as individuals occupying a particular place in some "social" situation. The former mode of self-consciousness clearly limits effective relationship with others while it may be that the latter is a kind of prerequisite of successful societal interaction. For the Buddhist, however, the adoption of a place in the scheme of things is indicative of identifying one's self as a subject which could be here or there. Not only does this lead to a tendency to get caught in thinking about where 'I' ought to be or want to be instead of being wholly involved in responding with others, it reinforces the self-ish propensity to act calculatively since someone else could as well be in my shoes as I could in theirs. Becoming interchangeable, 'we' become generic.

8. Thus, in speaking English it is quite permissible to say that my hands know how to type, it goes without saying that this doesn't mean that my hands know that they are now typing the word "enlightenment." Knowing how doesn't imply a subject of knowledge. At the same time, if we catch the tail end of a remark the last words of which are "knows that," we fully expect there to be someone—even anyone—who has undergone the relevant experience. Interestingly, in the same way that the Chinese did not explicitly distinguish knowing how and knowing that, their question words are notoriously open from our perspective. The single word *ho* 何, for instance, covers the same ground as our questions "what?," "how?," "why?," and "which?" (but, significantly, not "who?"), indicating a tendency not to discriminate between what is happening, its meaning, and the manner in which it is appropriately engaged. Whereas we break apart present fact (what), the causal and telic bases of fact, and the way in which facts are either arrived at or handled, the Chinese made no such hard distinctions—all of which suggests a blurring of what we refer to as the difference between subject and object, knower and known.

9. Indeed, the relationship between *li* and the person as body (*t'i* 體) was considered close enough by Chinese lexicographers for them to use *t'i* to define *li*. Notably, of all the common characters in the Chinese language, only two share the *li* 豊 phonetic, "ritual vase"—ritual action (*li*) and bodily self (*t'i*). The interested reader is referred to Boodberg (*Philosophy East and West* 2: 317–32) and Hall and Ames (1987, 87ff.).

10. Pai-chang goes on to define offering (*pu shih* 布施, literally expansive giving, a giving which brings about connection or relationship) as eschewing duality—refraining from the projection of any horizons (see HTC 119.422a).

11. The ease with which the Chinese appropriated this notion is perhaps due to the overwhelming predominance of so-called "mass nouns" in the Chinese language. Unlike the nouns with which the speakers of the Indo-European languages are most familiar, Chinese nouns do not typically signify individual things or even abstract entities, but instead refer to common patterns in the configuration of natural energy—that is, recurring

constellations of dispositions to behave in certain ways. Thus, *erh* 日 and *yueh* 月 ("sun" and "moon") do not refer to things as much as they do to regular patterns of activity—including our own. Moon is indistinguishable not only from seeing at night, but from the predatorial habits of nocturnal animals and the confession of new love. And so, where we and the speaker of Sanskrit take "person" to be a singular object of inquiry and "persons" as a plural object, the Chinese word *jen* 人 acts much more like our words "water" or "flour." Pluralizing—the enforcement of a distinction of one and many—seems awkward if not outright inappropriate.

12. *Shou* 收, rendered here as "select," involves both what we refer to as receptive and active modes of conduct, embracing both sensation and the rudimentary judgment of what is sensed in terms of like, dislike, and neutrality. Suggesting that we not select what comes our way is on the one hand to recommend that we not fight our karma, but it is also to insist that we not limit what comes in any sense—that is, that we eschew the projection of any horizons marking off what 'is' and what 'is-not.' Attaining this point is cutting off the 84,000 conditions, realizing our original nature.

13. Hence the astute remark of the spiritual maverick G. I. Gurjieff, who insisted that the last thing any of us are willing to give up is our suffering.

14. This claim may leave the reader feeling most uncomfortable, if not on the verge of rational outrage. The notion that our problems will be ultimately dissolved only when we leave off trying to solve them is an affront to the kind of self-reliance that has been the canon of freedom and responsibility at least since the European Renaissance. The claim is not meant to deny that we can intentionally reap the 'goods' we seek, at least some of the time. But it is meant to deny that this will lead to liberation in the Ch'an Buddhist sense of the word. Ch'an masters are quite willing to admit that it is possible to cultivate merit—to make 'good karma'—and to thus insure at least initially happy circumstances for our selves in the future. They insist, however, that such merit-oriented action binds us no less securely than do the sufferings we undergo. Hence the injunction to cut off the very distinction of 'good' and 'evil.'

15. In fact, the graph for *ting* entails *p'i* 疋 (foot) and has the sense of walking, of embodied movement—a movement which for the Chinese is seen as a social/relational event and not a fundamentally private undertaking. It is always done in context, in community.

16. In this light it is interesting that one of the classics of the later Ch'an tradition is the (apocryphal) text attributed to Asvaghosha entitled *Ta-ch'eng-ch'i-hsin-lun* or *The Mahayana Raising of Faith* since the Chinese term for faith (*hsin*) does not entail a belief in some doctrine, person, or deity, but what we would refer to as confidence. *Hsin* 信 is being not just true to one's word (as implied in the character's union of *jen* [person] and

yan 言 [word]), but unswerving in one's conduct. Being confident is acting without hesitation and, when that confidence is well founded, with absolute assurance of the sort that comes only with excellence.

17. The most notable and commonly referred to use of mirrors in Chinese Buddhism is arguably Hua-yen Master Fa-tsang's metaphor of the net of Indra, where each crossing point of the threads of the net is a mirror reflecting all the other mirrors. That is, each thing, no matter how small or humble, contains and is contained by all other things and the differentiations we create reflect not the true nature of the world, but our own values, our own biases.

18. Recall here the above remarks about the co-implication of having and being in the Chinese term *yu*. Once we cease taking ourselves to be self-identical individuals and realize that we are without either set location or substantial ground, we can no longer think of having things, even personality traits. We come to enjoy the particulars of our life-story—of our character and the dispositions according to which we typically respond to challenge—in much the same way as we do the green of springtime grass and the opalescent quality of an autumnal sunrise.

19. And perhaps as well for the Japanese, regarding which, see Tom Kasulis on intimacy (*Philosophy East and West* 40. 4 [October 1990]).

20. To allay the concern that Ch'an recommends a kind of free-for-all existence, it should be mentioned that the teachings of the Mahayana all involve not making a value judgment which separates samsara (bondage) and nirvana (liberation). That is, there is not only no 'one' to be bound, but no 'thing' which can bind us. The 'facts' of our situation are never as important as how we respond in it. Once we cease identifying ourselves as things apart from the rest of our worlds, calling a situation 'good' or 'bad' is beside the point. All things are part of who we are, part of our great body, and as such are no more in need of being dealt with or replaced or cut off than are the shapes of our noses. Beautiful and ugly noses both serve the same purpose of connecting us with parts of ourselves—flowers, foods, the scent of our lover—that would be absent otherwise. The kind of nose we have—the kind of self or karma we have—is less important than how we use it.

21. Hence Nagarjuna's explicit warning to not take emptiness as something to rely on, a kind of transcendent reality opposed to the mundane sphere of worldly existence.

22. This way of thinking reached its apogee in the Hua-yen School—a school which did for Chinese Buddhist theory what Ch'an did for practice.

23. See, for example, T 2012.380b, 381a, 381c.

24. In Confucian thought, the impropriety of standing out is only partly a function of it offending our sense of humility. More importantly, it

would seem to conflict with the natural flow of virtue, a flow which effects harmony without any apparent medium or application of force. Thus, "the rule of virtue can be compared to the Pole Star which commands the homage of the multitude of stars without leaving its place" (A II.1), and the best ruler is one whose works are unnoticed or invisible and whose virtues are so boundless as to be unnamable (A VIII.19).

25. Karma is discursive in that it occurs as a result of actions intended, of the separation of self and object (*neng-suo* 能所). In a word, karma implies selfishness, even when it is 'good' and not 'bad' karma that is in question. Karma can, of course, bring two people together, and in this sense would seem not to serve a solely discursive function. But a karmic bond is effective only to the extent that there is some 'one' to be bound, some identity to serve as a kind of gravitational center attracting what it has already projected. However, as long as we conduct ourselves *wu-wei*, there is no 'one' to be liberated or bound. This is the bodhisattva's great challenge.

26. It might be objected that a tension exists between the exhortations made here in promotion of concourse (as opposed to discourse) and Ch'an's open encouragement of refraining from chasing after any 'good' or avoiding any 'ill.' It has, however, been my contention that concourse can arise only when there is no decision of 'right' and 'wrong,' 'good' or 'ill'—when nothing blocks the free movement of our narration or the realization of conduct which is eminently (although perhaps not exclusively) social. Yet it is true that having conceived the realization of furthering and yet integrative relationships as concursive leaves us in the position of asserting some foundational aim or 'good.' What Ch'an would say, of course, is that seeking 'concourse' is to guarantee its continuing absence, just as seeking 'enlightenment' or 'buddhahood' is at root their forfeiture. Any 'this' can only be conceived in opposition to some 'that.' It would seem, then, that 'this' (say, concourse) is really (both 'this' and 'that'). But since our 'both' implies duality—a definite shortcoming from the Buddhist standpoint—the higher 'truth' is perhaps (neither 'this' nor 'that'). Unfortunately, this begs further appeal to (both 'both this and that' and 'neither this nor that') which regresses yet again to (neither [both 'both this and that' and 'neither this nor that'] nor [not both 'both this and that' and 'neither this nor that']) and so on ad infinitum. Conception is necessarily discursive and, once begun in earnest, there can be no hair too fine to split. Ch'an advises restraint early on.

27. For more on this, see the story of Pai-chang and the fox-monk from the *Wu-men-kuan* discussed below in chapter 8.

28. Doctrinally, Ch'an produced very few treatises or commentaries of the sort that held the day in Hua-yen for instance. Instead, the primary texts of Ch'an are the *kung-an* (J *koan*) or "public case" collections and the biographies of eminent sages, both of which consist almost entirely of anecdotes of personal, conversational encounters which end in the attainment of the concourse of enlightened master and the ripe practitioner. The

centrality of *kung-ans* to later Ch'an and Zen practice is, of course, well known—a way of placing master and student in a communicative crisis which if successfully dealt with will lead to the realization that their mind is no different from the minds of buddhas as numerous as the sands of the Ganges.

29. A much shorter version of this story can be found in the thirteenth-century Japanese text, the *Shaseki-shu* (*Collection of Stone and Sand*). See Paul Reps' *Zen Flesh Zen Bones* (p. 24) for a translation.

6. Opening the Field of Virtuosity

1. Again, truthful here denotes a dynamic quality of self-correction, not an abstract agreement of principle and fact. Truthful relationships are those that wean us of the tendency to isolate ourselves as distinct egos, bringing about more extensive and profound intimacy and virtuosity.

2. It should be added that even when we have created enough good karma to not experience the sort of material or emotional suffering that we know others sometimes do, this is not an indication that we have reached the end of practicing Ch'an. As long as the world in which we live is fraught with anger, hatred, violence, and greed, as persons we are not yet living in a "pure buddha-land" and there is much left to do.

3. It should be borne in mind that this offering is not done on the basis of an altruistic feeling and does not amount to a commitment to doing good deeds. If it were, our offering would still be a form of pollution, of spreading disparity and distinction. The bodhisattva life is in a sense lived "unconsciously" and the benefit enjoyed by others is simply a "matter of course," apparently arising all by itself (*tzu jan*).

4. In other words, all the polemic regarding the split of the Northern and Southern schools is an obfuscation of the true intent of Hui-neng's teaching of readiness. The long-standing preoccupation of Chinese, Japanese, Korean, and now Western Buddhists with the sudden/gradual dichotomy and its resolution are thus indicative of the extent to which the Ch'an and Hua-yen traditions became detached from their own meaning.

5. The character for *li* 利 is composed of the graph for a growing grain (*ho* 禾) and the graph for knife (*tao* 刀) and implies not only advantage or gain (the result), but the knowledge that is embodied in using a knife to reap the grain we have previously sown and make good use of it. To be *li* means understanding timing and causation—that is, knowing how to use our karma.

6. Because persons are seen as narration or a world and not as individuals, this phrasing indicates not only that we orient ourselves toward the furthering of the drama in which 'we' as egoic beings are mere players, it emphasizes the fact that serving 'others' is already serving ourselves. It is not that we will get some benefit later as a result of their "returning the favor," but that the very gesture of serving 'others' augments our narration—fruitfully deepens the relationships constituting it.

7. The term *i-hsin* 一心 might also be rendered "whole mind" or "continuous mind" in order to de-emphasize the individualistic connotations of "one" and the suggestion that Huang-po may still be buying into the one-many distinction. I have, however, elected to translate the term as "one-mind" partly in order to stress the singularity of the narration out of which 'you' and 'I' have been abstracted. More to the point, however, given the prioritization of value carried out by Buddhist ontology and the recurrent theme of orientation that has recurred throughout our conversation, the term "one-mind" seems to capture the realization of a clear direction in our narration. Since mind is understood as dispositional, the term "one-mind" does not signify an independent or monolithic entity, but an unbreached compatibility of orientation in conduct. Understanding this is, in fact, crucial to understanding the significance behind the importance of vows in East Asian and especially Chinese Buddhism.

8. The fact that we often doubt what is best for ourselves or what we are capable of is no different, indicating the kind of bifurcation without which we would find it impossible to ask "What shall I do with my life?"— a question which can appear only when life is objectified as 'life,' when living is divorced from the always communal we who live.

9. It is not possible in the space of an endnote to give a full accounting of the significance of *dṛṣṭi* in Buddhist thought, but the following observations can be made. Paralleling the English use of terms like standpoint, theory and opinion, *dṛṣṭi* connote a conceptual or verbal expression of a perspective on the way things are or have come to be, whether individually or collectively. All views have the unifying characteristic of taking something as their object, of being "about" something distinct from them, and can be effectively contrasted with *darśana*—a "direct seeing" in which the cognitive or conceptual component in experience is maximally attenuated it not altogether absent. Whereas *darśana* is an immediate perception of what has come to be, views are conceptually mediated, mental constructs *about* the perceived. In short, views are the abstract results of a calculative relationship with our own experience. As such, and no matter what their content, they serve to maintain the root distinction of subject and object that underlies both our fascination with being and our craving for closure.

10. The use of the same character/word for practice and what is antithetical to it strikes speakers of Indo-European languages as highly confusing. But, there are many terms in Chinese that represent a kind of marriage

of opposites. Much as the English length entails both shortness and longness, many Chinese qualifiers cover both sides of what we would see as an opposition and which the Chinese respond to as relative aspects of a continuum. Thus, habitual behavior and Buddhist practice are equally expressions of conduct and what distinguishes them is not a difference in being, but of value. Thus, *yin* and *yang* are not beings that arise out of the primordial *t'ai chi* 太極, but are differently and complementarily oriented expressions of it. The same can be said of Huang-po's declaration of the teaching of one-mind and his unswerving exhortations for us to have no-'mind'. One-mind and no-'mind' are again expressions of something for which we have no word or concept.

11. Thus, in deciding how to stop the tidal wave of inner-city drug abuse and violence, the Reagan administration shifted the horizons of its concern to the "supplier" countries in an attempt to stop the flow of drugs into the United States. While this represents a correction to seeing the inner-city dealer as the source of the problem, it hardly represents an open-ended appraisal of the situation. For instance, the Reagan program effectively regarded drug abuse as a criminal problem traceable to the physical addictiveness of the substances being abused. In terms of policy, the social and spiritual roots of abuse were entirely ignored. Never once, for example, did the administration question the role that television advertising plays in undermining the sense of personal worth and potential in inner-city youth. If anything, the materialist biases of the administration would likely have seen the lives portrayed in television advertising and programming as attractive goals which would give these young men and women the desire to "better" themselves.

12. As an example of the direction a *paramārtha* approach to the drug problem would head, we can imagine policy makers questioning the role of media in altering the nature of the feedback relationship between action and perception and the possibility that this would create a propensity for what feels like frustration and what looks like laziness. Parallels to the psychology of slaves might be noted. Questions would then be raised as to whether a truly democratic society can survive when its economic base fosters the use of substance abuse to obliterate what otherwise appears to be an intractable disparity between what is desired and what is happening. The values underlying the term "abuse" would be called to account, leading perhaps to a recognition that if sociality is held in highest regard, the coping strategies of substance abuse and working two jobs to maintain a "close to ideal" suburban life-style may seem different and yet equally unsavory— both being characterized by a marked absence of spontaneity, individual creativity and communal intimacy.

13. Some of the patterns generated may, depending on the level of energy present in the disrupting crisis, strike us as mutant forms of "personality"—egos that have been severely deformed by either a single or a series

of traumatic events. The resulting 'self' may be relatively stable—that is, self-maintaining—but completely cut off from others as is the case in certain autistic, catatonic, or schizophrenic individuals. Here, stability is won at the cost of severing the lines of communication or relationship without which our world becomes socially perverse—full of variations on the themes of our imagination, but completely bereft of truly creative improvisation.

14. The importance of the vow in Ch'an pivots on just this need for a self-less cultivation of a horizonless mind. While 'we' decide to take a vow—the four great vows discussed by Hui-neng, for example (PS 21)—once taken, it is the vow and not the ego which decides what course of action is appropriate. Vows undermine the very 'selves' responsible for taking them and establish a unanimity in our disposition or direction—the realization of *i-hsin*.

15. Once again, according to the classical Chinese conception of the cosmos, the interdependence of all things and the realization of a world order cannot be divorced from the unexpected. For the authors of the *I Ching*, in the absence of the unexpected, order will always be riddled with lacunae.

7. Techniques of Unmaking

1. Seen as a system of distinctions or value projections which exists only through the deflection and retention of energy, the 'self' is not at all illusory, but marks the presence of a relatively stable ordering of relationships which is itself neither good nor bad but which is maintained precisely on the basis of determining what is desirable, what is undesirable, and what makes no 'real' difference. For a discussion of the relationship between such a conditional existence of 'self' and judgments, see the account of perception given in the Madhupindika Sutta where it is made clear that when feeling (*vedanā*)—or the judgment of pleasant, unpleasant or neutral—arises on the basis of contact (*phassa*) between the appropriate sense consciousness, its organ, and its object, so does the experience of one who perceives. "Because of contact arises feeling; what *one* feels, *one* perceives; what *one* perceives, *one* reasons about; what *one* reasons about, *one* proliferates conceptually; what *one* proliferates conceptually, due to that concepts characterized by such obsessed perceptions assail him" (MN I 111, emphasis added).

2. A myriad psychological and ego-historical reasons for this difficulty exist, of course, and delineating them is the typical student's most effective and clandestine method of insuring the uninterrupted existence of both his

or her difficulties and the 'selves' they protect. Digging into the reasons why we find it so hard to let go of our 'selves' is a diversion from doing so—a way of forestalling the advent of true practice. Recall in this regard the story of the Buddha meeting a man who has been shot in the chest with an arrow and who insists on knowing who shot him and why before pulling it out and stitching the wound. Since the roots of our present situation extend back into beginningless time, we will never have a full accounting of how and why we have come to be where and as we are. Better to begin in earnest the task of relinquishing our 'selves' than analyzing the causes for our difficulty in doing so.

3. It should be allowed that since the process of relinquishing our 'selves' is synonymous with realizing our true natures—with realizing who we are as persons and not merely as individuals—this partner or partners with whom we enter into concourse can manifest in or as any part of our narration. In short, they need not be human. Thus, while most of the enlightenment stories collected in the records of Ch'an involve a student-master interaction, there are cases where the help needed in relinquishing the 'self' is afforded by, for example, a stone striking a stalk of bamboo, by the honking of flock of geese, or by the moonlight shining through a tracery of autumn branches.

4. For a convenient table listing the symbolic attributes of the trigrams, see Govinda 1981, 46–47.

5. Huang-po's remarks here may be a Buddhist gloss on a renowned passage in the *Analects* where Confucius remarks that, "The virtue of an exemplary person is wind while that of the small person is grass. As the wind blows, the grass bends" (A XII.19). It is the quality of our personal energy (*te*) which determines the actions of those around us.

6. There is a story in the oral tradition of Korean Son (Ch'an) which takes up precisely this theme. The master at one of the larger training monasteries in Korea was often given to sitting in his rooms reading, taking long walks, and napping during the designated training periods. The head monk at one point reproached him for his laziness and accused him of doing nothing at all in his role as master. The master shrugged off the remark, but a week later he called the head monk in to inform him that he would be taking over the monastery for a month or two while the master journeyed south. From the day the master departed, things at the monastery began to go wrong. The monks began feeling out of sorts and edgy. Factions developed and soon a bitter controversy split the community. Hundreds of monks simply left. Others remained for a month, hoping the master would return and sort things out, but most of them eventually moved elsewhere. When the master did finally return after some three months absence, the head monk was in a state of total dismay. The master listened as the monk chronicled the downfall of the monastery and then nodded. "And here I thought I wasn't doing a thing!"

7. Of course, what makes us "human" is also a shared complex of distinctions—a shared karma that has us born in similar bodies and behaving in much the same way. Our distinctions—our values—are thus what identifies and differentiates us as members of the human race, from which it follows that we can completely divorce ourselves from making distinctions only at the expense of no longer maintaining an existence.

8. What is crucially at stake here is a shift in attitude from conceiving of ourselves first and foremost as doers and makers to seeing ourselves principally in terms of responding and allowing. That is, instead of positing ourselves as points of origin, we see ourselves as unique and yet ultimately inseparable phases in the articulation of an always communal narration. To be sure, part of our uniqueness is the character of what Heidegger included under the rubric of our thrownness—our concrete limitations due to when and where we were born—and which Buddhists see as one aspect of our individual and individuating karma. When a person is conceived primarily as responding, however, these limits have nowhere near the kind of negative connotation proper to an outlook determined by a drive to produce. Instead, and much as a trumpet player not only accepts but appreciates the difference between the responses she can offer a rhythm section and those possible for a pianist, each of us not only accepts but deeply appreciates the formal constraints proper to our particular karma. We play with and not against our limitations. Only in this way is the world capable of being seen as our partner and not a ubiquitous source of resistance—something the 'maker' must always feel.

9. While the attainment of *shou-i* was in the later Taoist tradition almost invariably thought of as part of an alchemical transformation by means of which the body came to be endowed with what would normally be thought of as supernatural powers, at least in the early Buddhist era of China the preoccupation with attaining powers and immortality had not entirely overshadowed the essential 'self'-lessness implicit to the attainment of *wu-wei*. That Ch'an did not, and in spite of plenty of miraculous powers being attributed to bodhisattvas and buddhas in the later Mahayana sutras, follow in the Taoist footsteps here is clear in Ma-tzu's claim that "even if you were to get as far as splitting the body, emanating light and manifesting the eighteen transformations"—all powers associated with the alchemical transformation of the body—"they would be like unsevered barbs and chains. If you awaken sagely mind, everything without remainder is served" (TTC 45.406b).

10. For a discussion of the relationship between beneficence or being expert (*shan* 善) and suppuration (*lou*), see HTC 119.423b. *Lou* is difficult to directly translate, but it typically refers to a negative discharge through the sense organs—an effluent which contaminates what is sensed. In a literal sense, it is having a "jaundicing eye" and is the counterpart of being stained

by things in the environment. In short, being stained and staining is a 'self'-perpetuating cycle of negative energy.

11. The use of the term "*chakra*" is here largely a matter of convenience. For example, the Freudian terms "id," "ego," and "superego" could be mapped over the same energy continuum as the system of seven chakras. The point stands that self-consciousness is not the sole criterion for some act being 'self'-generated. The 'self' includes all of our inclinations and dispositions—all of our karma—and so involves what is usually below as well as above conscious awareness.

12. Of course, 'we' will only be willing to do so to the extent that we are convinced there is something to attain by doing so. That is, we are promised what might be called "dharma candy"—a nice prize for unrelentingly carrying out our discipline. This 'candy' may be called "equanimity" or "better concentration" or "relaxation" or "a better future birth" or even "enlightenment," but these are all just verbal lures. As mentioned before, even the Buddha himself attained nothing when he realized complete and perfect enlightenment (*anuttara samyak sambodhi*). Neither shall 'we.'

13. The term "*chien*" carries a very wide range of connotations including "to see," "to perceive," "to meet," "to interview," "to introduce," and "to manifest." I would submit that Hui-neng did not discount any of these. To the contrary, all of these seem implied in a personal understanding of *chien fo*.

14. The association of artistic genius, intuition, and madness in our culture is indicative of the extent to which creativity and improvisation are mistrusted and resisted as anarchic in the most negative sense of the term. That is, we typically think of artistic genius as being cultivated—if at all—only by breaking societal norms, by forcing ourselves into situations where no habit will allow us to survive. We must flirt with psychic and spiritual disaster to produce great art—often without any approval or encouragement from our contemporaries. By contrast, artistic genius and hence creativity in China were seen as models for all social relation and the standard education in ritual, music, calligraphy, archery, charioteering, and calculation was heavily biased toward activities where improvisation and intuition were highly valued.

15. In the final case, what Lin-chi steals nothing because the student is at the point where he or she need only be challenged with the roar of a keen-eyed master to leap to the occasion and respond as a bodhisattva. See T 1985.501b, where he discusses these four kinds of students and their various needs.

16. This is especially notable in cases where the shocks are either accidental or 'self'-induced through fasting, isolation, extreme physical exertion, or the use of psychedelic or other consciousness-altering plants or substances. There is a substantial body of religious and anthropological

literature on mystic experience which bears out the same fact—initial insights or revelations are not only typically the most profound, any successive experiences often serve only to so isolate the experiencer that they no longer find it possible to enter into full community with others. In this sense, mystic experience has at times been rightfully regarded as dysfunctional. Ch'an tries to forestall this disjunction by seeing the moment of enlightenment as irreducibly social—a matter of responding with others as needed and not achieving some transcendence of or freedom from concrete, daily relationship with them.

8. The Mastery of Ch'an

1. This does not mean, of course, that a bodhisattva or buddha will never work to bring about factual change or that such changes will not eventually attend the gestalt shift by means of which the work of enlightenment is actually enacted. What a buddha does not do is to get involved with trying to *cause* factual changes—say in the standard of living, of health, of education, and so on—with the intent of that precipitating liberation. Not only would such activity be karmic or binding in the long run, it is simply ineffective. In the same way that no circumstance is not enlightening for the true bodhisattva, every circumstance is binding for a sentient being.

2. It is often at this point, of course, that a conversion occurs. Driven to completely giving up the attempt to make things better, there is often experienced a 'spontaneous' transformation of our lives which mimics the sort of sustainable release set up through the Ch'an techniques of indirection and partnership. Depending on our situation, we may chalk this transformation up to luck and simply take up where we left off in trying to control our experience, or we may attribute it to some form of divine intervention and do our best to humble our 'selves' in the face of superior forces. In virtually all such cases, however, this transformation is understood as a power-mediated alteration of the ontic dimension of our lives and the sense we have of ourselves tends to remain that of isolated individuals who can enter into relationship with others and not as pure and unprecedented conduct having no fixed location.

Tanabe Hajime's (1986) account of such metanoetic experiences makes a good case for their religious and societal efficacy—at least when they are most intensely realized—and by drawing on both the Christian and Pure Land Buddhist traditions serves as an intriguing bridge between what have hitherto been typically disparate worldviews. But as his analysis makes clear, such transformations—especially when preceded by the 'practice' of repentance—tend to reinforce the 'self'/'other' dichotomy and hence inhibit the realization of who we are in the fullest Ch'an sense. Instead of realizing that we are an entire world the meaning of which can be changed without the least application of factual power, we tend to see ourselves as dependent parts of a world in which we have what are "all too obvious" limits to what we can do. For Ch'an, the advent of the bodhisattva life marks the dissolution of the 'self-power'/'other-power' distinction itself and with it the conviction that matters never get any better unless someone does (*tso*) something about them. In short, change ceases to be seen as necessarily brought about through any kind of force, and is realized instead as self-presencing or free and easy (*tzu-tsai* 自在).

3. Importantly, the relationship between energy and morality sheds considerable light on the otherwise paradoxical commitment in Ch'an to continuing meditation, chanting, bowing and so on even after realizing our true nature. Conduct that is *wu-wei* is not attained once and for all, but depends on the continual relinquishing of form, of our horizons for readiness, responsibility, and relevance. As such, it is an continuing endeavor—a responsive *tao* by means of which our *te*, our virtuosity, openly manifests and grows.

4. Made into an ideal, of course, this kind of freedom from circumstance can make for lives of wanton 'self' and 'other' abuse. Again, 'you' and 'I' cannot act like buddhas and the desire to do so is indication of our inability to pull it off. Anyone who tries to live the free and easy life is doing no more than indulging the 'self' and binding both her or himself and others.

References

Aṅguttara Nikāya, trans. by F. L. Woodward and E. M. Hare, 5 volumes. London: Pali Text Society, 1932–36.

Bateson, Gregory. *Steps to an Ecology of Mind*. San Francisco: Chandler Pub. Co., 1972.

Bergson, Henri. *Time and Free Will*. New York: Harper Torchbooks, 1960.

Bhagavat-Gītā, trans. S. Radhakrishnan. New York: Harper Torchbooks, 1973.

Bourdieu, Pierre. *Outline of a Theory of Practice*, trans. Richard Nice. Cambridge: Cambridge University Press, 1977.

Bṛhadāraṇyaka Upaniṣad, trans. P. Lal. Calcutta: Writer's Workshop, 1979.

Carrithers, Michael. "An Alternative Social History of the Self." In *The Category of the Person*, ed. Carrithers et al. Cambridge: Cambridge University Press, 1985.

Chāndogya Upaniṣad, trans. Raja Rajendralal Mitra and E. B. Cowell. Delhi: Nag Publishers, 1979.

Chappell, David. *The Teachings of the Fourth Ch'an Patriarch Tao-hsin*. Berkeley: University of California Press, 1983.

Chen-chou Lin-chi Hui-chao Chan-shih Yu-lu. Taisho shinshu daizokyo 1985.

Chin-k'ang Pan-jo Po-lo-mi Ching. Taisho shinshu daizokyo 235.

Chuang-tzu. The Complete Works of Chuang Tzu, trans. Burton Watson. New York: Columbia University Press, 1968.

Confucius. *The Analects*, trans. D. C. Lau. New York: Penguin, 1973.

Derrida, Jacques. *Margins of Philosophy*, trans. Alan Bass. Chicago: University of Chicago Press, 1982.

Ebrey, Patricia. *Confucianism and Family Rituals in Imperial China.* Princeton: Princeton University Press, 1991.

Gadamer, Hans-Georg. *Philosophical Hermeneutics*, trans. David Linge. Berkeley: University of California Press, 1976.

Geertz, Clifford. *The Interpretation of Cultures.* New York: Basic Books, 1973.

Govinda, Lama Anagarika. *The Inner Structure of the I Ching.* New York: Weatherhill Press, 1981.

Graham, A. C. *Disputers of the Tao.* La Salle, Ill.: Open Court, 1989.

Habermas, Jürgen. *The Theory of Communicative Action*, 2 vols., trans. Thomas McCarthy. Boston: Beacon Press, 1984, 1987.

Hall, David and Roger T. Ames. *Thinking through Confucius.* Albany: SUNY Press, 1987.

Hansen, Chad. "Linguistic Skepticism in *Lao-Tzu*." In *Philosophy East and West* 31.3 (July 1981).

Heidegger, Martin. *Introduction to Metaphysics*, trans. Ralph Manheim. New Haven: Yale University Press, 1959.

Hershock, Peter. "The Structure of Change in the *I Ching*." *Journal of Chinese Philosophy* 18.3 (September 1991).

Hidemi, Ishida. "Body and Mind: The Chinese Perspective." In Kohn (1989), pp. 41–73.

Hollis, Martin. "Of Masks and Men." In *The Category of the Person*, ed. Carrithers et al. Cambridge: Cambridge University Press, 1985.

Hoover, Thomas. *The Zen Experience.* New York: New American Library, 1980.

Huang-po-shan Tuan-chi Chan-shih Hsin-fa-yao. Taisho shinshu daizokyo 2012a.

I Ching, trans. Wilhelm/Baynes. Princeton: Princeton University Press, 1971.

Illich, Ivan. *Tools for Conviviality.* New York: Pantheon Press, 1973.

———. *Deschooling Society.* New York: Pantheon Press, 1970.

Kasulis, Thomas. "Intimacy: A General Orientation in Japanese Religious Values." *Philosophy East and West* 40.4 (October 1990), 433ff.

Kalupahana, David. *A History of Buddhist Philosophy*. Honolulu: University of Hawaii Press, 1992.

Kiang-si Ma-tsu Tao-i Chan-shih Yu-lu. In *Ta Tsang Ching*, vol. 45.

Kohn, Livia. *Taoist Meditation and Longevity Techniques*. Ann Arbor: University of Michigan Press, 1989.

Kuan-tzu, trans. by W. Allyn Rickett. Hong Kong: Hong Kong University Press, 1965.

Kuhn, Thomas. *The Structure of Scientific Revolution*. Chicago: University of Chicago Press, 1970.

Lao-tzu, *Tao Te Ching*.

Lamotte, Etienne. "Assessment of Textual Interpretation in Buddhism." In *Buddhist Hermeneutics*, ed. Donald Lopez. Honolulu: University of Hawaii Press, 1988.

Laszlo, Ervin. *Introduction to Systems Philosophy*. New York: Gordon & Breach, 1972.

———. *System, Structure and Experience*. New York: Gordon & Breach, 1969.

Leng-chia A-po-to-lo-pao Ching. *Taisho shinshu daizokyo* 670.

MacIntyre, Alisdair. *After Virtue*. Notre Dame, Ind: University of Notre Dame Press, 1981.

Macy, Joanna. *Mutual Causality in Buddhism and General Systems Theory*. Albany: SUNY Press, 1991.

Mahābhārata, Critical Edition. Pune: Bhadarkar Oriental Research Institute, 1984.

Maitri Upaniṣad, trans. Raja Rajendralal Mitra and E. B. Cowell. Delhi: Nag Publishers, 1979.

Majjhima Nikāya, trans. I. B. Horner, 4 volumes. London: Pali Text Society, 1954–59.

Maturana, H. and F. Varela. *The Tree of Knowledge*. Boston: New Science Library, 1987.

———. *Autopoiesis and Cognition*. Derdrecht, Netherlands: Reidel, 1980.

Mead, G. H. *Mind, Self, and Society*. Chicago: University of Chicago Press, 1934.

———. *The Philosophy of the Present*. Chicago: University of Chicago Press, 1932.

Mencius. *Mencius,* trans. D. C. Lau. New York: Penguin, 1976.

Milindapañha, trans. T. W. Rhys. *Sacred Books of the East,* vol. 35. New York: Dover, 1963.

Mūlamadhyamakakārikā, trans. by David Kalupahana. In *Nagarjuna: The Philosophy of the Middle Way.* Albany: SUNY Press, 1986.

Munro, Donald. *The Concept of Man in Early China.* Stanford: Stanford University Press, 1969.

Nagel, Thomas. *The View from Nowhere.* New York: Oxford University Press, 1987.

Nan-tsung tun-chiao tsui-shang ta-ch'eng Mo-ho-pan-jo po-lo-mi ching: Liu-tsu Hui-neng ta-shih yu Shao-Chou Ta-fan ssu shih-fa t'an ching. Edited by Philip Yampolsky from the Tun-huang MS. *Taisho shinshu daizokyo* 2007.

Parfit, Derek. *Reasons and Persons.* Oxford: Clarendon Press, 1984.

Prigogine, Ilya. *Order out of Chaos.* Boulder: New Science Library, 1980.

Reps, Paul. *Zen Flesh, Zen Bones.* Rutland, Vt.: Tuttle, 1957.

Ricoeur, Paul. *Hermeneutics and the Human Sciences,* trans. John Thompson. Cambridge: Cambridge University Press, 1982.

Ricouer, Paul. *Oneself as Another.* Chicago: University of Chicago, 1993.

Saṁyutta Nikāya, trans. by Caroline A. F. Rhys Davids, 6 volumes. London: Pali Text Society, 1942.

Schutz, Alfred. *Collected Papers,* vols. 1–3, ed. Maurice Natanson. The Hague: M. Nijhoff, 1967.

Shastri, D. R. *Origin and Development of the Ritual of Ancestor Worship in India.* Calcutta: Bookland, 1963.

Sutta-nipata, trans. H. Sadhatissa. London: Curzon Press, 1985.

Tanabe, Hajime. *Philosophy as Metanoetics,* trans. V. Viglielmo et al. Berkeley: University of California Press, 1986.

Therigatta, ed. H. Oldenberg and R. Pischer. London: Pali Text Society, 1883.

Tu, Wei-ming. *Confucian Thought: Selfhood as Creative Transformation.* Albany: SUNY Press, 1985.

Tun-wu Ju-tao-yao-wen Lun. In *Hsu Tsang Ching,* vol. 119.

Wei-mo-ch'i So-Shuo Ching. Taisho shinshu daizokyo 475.

Index

231